BRAVE BATTALION

Other Military History by Mark Zuehlke

*For Honour's Sake: The War of 1812 and the Brokering of an
    Uneasy Peace*

*Terrible Victory: First Canadian Army and the Scheldt Estuary
    Campaign: September 13–November 6, 1944*

*Holding Juno: Canada's Heroic Defence of the D-Day Beaches:
    June 7–12, 1944*

Juno Beach: Canada's D-Day Victory: June 6, 1944

The Gothic Line: Canada's Month of Hell in World War II Italy

The Liri Valley: Canada's World War II Breakthrough to Rome

Ortona: Canada's Epic World War II Battle

*The Canadian Military Atlas: Four Centuries of Conflict from
    New France to Kosovo* (with C. Stuart Daniel)

The Gallant Cause: Canadians in the Spanish Civil War, 1936–1939

Maps

Table of Contents

Order of Battle for the Canadian Infantry

- 1 9 1 4 – 1 9 1 8 -

Section: 12 men, commanded by a corporal. Also a small unit performing special duties (signals, machine-gun detachments, bombers) alongside or within companies.

Platoon: Four sections, 48 men, commanded by a lieutenant or second lieutenant.

Company: Four platoons, 200 men, including company HQ, commanded by a major or captain.

Battalion: Four companies, 1,000 men, including battalion HQ and specialists, commanded by a lieutenant colonel.

Brigade: Four battalions, 4,000 men, commanded by a brigadier general.

Division: Three brigades, 12,000 men plus 6,000 artillery, commanded by a major general.

Corps: Two or more divisions, 60,000–100,000 men, commanded by a lieutenant general. Also a large body of troops devoted to a specific purpose (e.g., Royal Canadian Ordnance Corps).

Army: Two or more corps, 200,000 or more men, commanded by a general.

Order of Ranks in
the Canadian Infantry

- 1914–1918 -

Generals

General (Gen.)
Lieutenant General (Lt.-Gen.)
Major General (Maj.-Gen.)
Brigadier General (Brig.-Gen., or Brig.)

Officers

Colonel (Col.)
Lieutenant Colonel (Lt.-Col.)
Major
Captain
Lieutenant (Lt.)
Second Lieutenant (2nd Lt.)

Non-Commissioned Ranks

Regimental Sergeant Major (RSM)
Company Sergeant Major (CSM)
Staff Sergeant (S/Sgt.)
Sergeant (Sgt.)
Lance Sergeant (L/Sgt.)
Corporal (Cpl.)
Lance Corporal (L/Cpl.)
Private (Pte.)

Acknowledgements

The genesis for *Brave Battalion* arose out of a conversation with Don Loney, executive editor at John Wiley & Sons Canada, Ltd. Don was thinking about the fact that 2008 marked the 90th anniversary of the armistice that ended World War I on November 11, 1918. His paternal grandfather, William Loney, had been a World War I veteran, emigrating to Canada from his native Perth, Scotland, in 1908. A sergeant, he had suffered a shrapnel wound to the leg while serving in the 42nd Battalion Royal Highlanders of Canada (perpetuated as 2nd Battalion, Royal Highlanders of Canada). One of Don's prized possessions is *42nd Battalion Royal Highlanders of Canada, 1914–1919*, a history of the battalion by Lt.-Col. C. Beresford Topp published in 1931 by the 42nd's regimental association. Such histories were common in the years that followed the end of World War I and the outbreak of World War II. As was normally the case, this one was written by an officer who had served in the battalion—Topp having risen to the rank of major while with the 42nd Battalion.

Most recent Canadian works on World War I, Don noted, either provided a general overview of the course of the war or chronicled one specific landmark battle, such as Vimy Ridge or the 2nd Battle of Ypres. While such approaches had their obvious merits, the former generally lacked the personal experiences of soldiers, such as William Loney, while the latter was limited to a tightly confined timeframe. Don's idea was to follow the war's course from beginning to conclusion through the lens of a single Canadian battalion. Was I interested in writing such a book?

I had a personal link to World War I as well. Two great-uncles, Fred and Frank Zuehlke, had served in Canadian battalions. Great-Uncle Fred had lost an arm at Vimy Ridge. Great-Uncle Frank spent much of the war as a prisoner in Germany. Deeply scarred psychologically by his prison experiences, Frank took his life in the 1920s. As a boy, I had known Great-Uncle Fred well. But, like most veterans, he seldom spoke of his wartime experiences. A battalion history would present a good opportunity to explore what my two relatives had lived through.

Don's idea was not, of course, entirely original. A few similar books had appeared in the 1980s and 1990s, but I was intrigued by the idea and thought a new work in this mould warranted if the battalion selected was present from outbreak to end of hostilities. That limited the selection to the 1st Canadian Infantry Division battalions or the Princess Patricia's Canadian Light Infantry. This latter battalion was distinct in that it had been privately funded and raised, so I eliminated it from consideration. As I homed in on the 1st Division battalions it was the 16th Battalion (The Canadian Scottish) that kept drawing my eye. One reason for this was that the Canadian Scottish was formed of young men drawn from four communities that in large measure typified the national character in 1914. The other was that the battalion was present at virtually every major battle Canada fought during the war. It was also a Highland regiment and had arguably been the Canadian battalion most attached to the tradition of going into battle led by pipers, which yielded some fine anecdotal material.

I am grateful that Don left the decision of the battalion to be chronicled in my hands and for approaching me with the idea. His faith in my ability to deliver a compelling book never wavered.

Of immeasurable assistance in creating a compelling recounting of the Canadian Scottish battalion's World War I experience was its official history: *The History of the 16th Battalion (The Canadian Scottish), Canadian Expeditionary Force* published in 1932 and written by Hugh MacIntyre Urquhart. This former Canadian Scottish officer was able to draw on many letters from those who served with him during the war. Having kept a personal diary, Urquhart was able to enrich the battalion history with many intimate details and observations about daily life in the trenches and within the battalion.

Urquhart's diary was one of many documents I was able to consult at the University of Victoria's Special Collections where the Canadian Scottish Regiment has deposited its archival collection. Staff at Special Collections were endlessly helpful in making these documents available for study. Bob Darnell and others at the Canadian Scottish Regiment's museum in the Bay Street Armoury were also forthcoming with advice and much support for this project.

Thanks also to Carol Reid and Jane Naisbitt at the Canadian War Museum and to staff at Library and Archives Canada.

Once again my agent, Carolyn Swayze, stickhandled the contractual negotiations and details with her usual consummate skill.

Yet again Frances Backhouse provided endless support as I stepped once more into the breach to write another military history.

prologue

Make Every Sacrifice

- AUGUST 1914 -

From the Atlantic to the Pacific the nation simmered under a heat wave that first August weekend of 1914. The Bank Holiday—a time when families traditionally gathered on beaches and picnicked in parks, when lovers strolled arm in arm, when crowds thronged downtown city streets to watch parades of marching bands and club floats and cheered the local teenaged queen. In Victoria, Vancouver, and far to the east in Hamilton, cooling breezes eased the heat while Winnipeg and the rest of the prairies sweltered under temperatures ranging between thirty-four and forty degrees Celsius. A few blamed the heat for the air of distraction that noticeably diminished the appetite for the festivities, but most recognized a far graver reason was responsible. For this was the first August weekend of 1914. Canada and the world teetered on the edge of a precipice.

War. That was what waited in the void beyond. A war that, no matter how many European diplomats and rulers professed a desire to prevent its outbreak, had drawn inexorably closer through this long summer of disquietude. "One day the great European War will come out of some damned foolish thing in the Balkans," Chancellor Otto von Bismarck had predicted toward the end of the nineteenth century.

That foolish thing had come on June 28 in the Bosnian capital of Sarajevo—the troublesome Balkan province occupied for thirty years before its formal and forced annexation by Austria in 1908. Bosnia was the *cause célèbre* of Serbian nationalists, whose expansionist ambitions the annexation frustrated. On June 28, a Serb terror organization called the Black Hand struck during a royal procession through the streets of Sarajevo by Archduke Franz Ferdinand and his wife, Sophie. In a matter of seconds a young man named Gavrilo Princip jumped on the running board of their limousine and fired two shots from a small pistol. Ferdinand and Sophie each took a bullet. "Don't die, Sophie," Ferdinand sobbed. But their collective lifeblood drained away in minutes. With breathtaking rapidity, two hurriedly fired bullets unravelled the intricate spider's web of treaties and agreements between European nations that had been intended to ensure decades of peace.

Having long considered Serbia an irritating source of the instability that plagued its Balkan provinces, the Austrians decided the assassination provided the pretext to expunge the problem entirely. On July 23, the Austro-Hungarian Empire issued an ultimatum that effectively demanded an end to Serbia's independence and reduced it to a vassal state. Granted forty-eight hours to accede or face invasion, Serb diplomats frantically tried to negotiate a conciliatory compromise. Austria responded by breaking off diplomatic relations on July 28 and declaring war.

The Dual Monarchy had hoped against all reason to localize the war, but the web of treaties ensured its rapid escalation to engulf the entire continent. Russia was allied with Serbia. Germany, Austria-Hungary, and Italy were bound together by the Triple Alliance to stand as one. Russia was linked to France in a defensive pact intended to bookend Germany and frustrate its imperial ambitions. When Russia began general mobilization on July 30, Germany responded by declaring war on her two days later and against France the day following. Austria weighed in against Russia and France on August 7, while Italy demurred and abandoned its former allies by claiming neutrality.

During the days between Princip's shots and these declarations, Great Britain—which had no alliances with any of these European powers—had vainly tried to broker a peace deal. But on July 30, a German diplomat warned a British counterpart that his country best remain neutral if Germany opted to invade France by a route that took its armies through Belgium. Britain was now snared by a point of honour, for in 1839 the British, French, and German governments had mutually pledged not to violate Belgium's neutrality in the event of a war. When Germany formally demanded on August 2 the right of unopposed passage through the lowland country to France, Britain supported Belgian King Albert's refusal and demanded the old pledge be respected. Two days later, the Germans having offered no response, Britain declared war on Germany.

That was Tuesday. The Bank Holiday in Canada had ended by then. In fact, the festivities had simply fizzled out with each passing hour as the attention of most Canadians turned to watching the advance to war. On Friday, the *Winnipeg Free Press* had thought peace would prevail. "Great Britain, it is to be confidently expected as certain, will do anything to avert the danger of a general European war, and unless her commitments are very definite will consider herself an outsider, unless and until she is compelled by the necessities of the situation, to take a different view." By Monday, the Winnipeg editor had undergone a sea change. "Here in Canada, we must wait upon events. The need of the moment is for Canadians to keep their heads cool ... If Great Britain is involved in war, either by her own decision ... or through the aggression of an outside party, it is quite certain that Canada will come to her assistance with all the fervour at her disposal."

Vancouver's *Daily Province* added its affirmation of Canadian support: "It is said that the British Cabinet at its meeting yesterday was divided on the question of War or Peace ... It is a relief to turn to Canada at such an hour and find the whole nation speaking with one voice. All Canada in the past may not have believed in the emergency which has become a catastrophe, but now when we are dealing with realities, Canada offers 50,000 men for service. There is no talk of neutrality any more. Canada speaks with no uncertain voice—'We are united, we are ready, strike before it is too late.'"

On the Tuesday, anticipating the inevitability of war, Montreal's *Daily Star* proclaimed: "If we are beaten in this struggle against two of the greatest armies ever seen in the world we will pass finally from the roster of great Nations, and our Empire will become one of the defaced mileposts which mark the tragic road by which the human race has journeyed."[1] The paper's editor was not speaking here as a citizen of Canada, but as a British subject, and in this he mirrored the feelings of most Canadians.

At eleven that evening a cable from London was delivered to Prince Arthur William Patrick Albert, 1st Duke of Connaught and Strathearn, Canada's Governor General at Rideau Hall (the newly renovated mansion that had been formally declared his official residence only the previous year). It was by this cable, delivered to the King's representative who quickly passed its contents on to Prime Minister Robert Borden, that the Canadian government learned it was at war.

There was no question of the country refusing the clarion call to arms. In 1914 Canada remained inextricably a part of the great British

Empire. A dominion, the government had no say in matters of foreign policy. Its only right was to decide the extent and nature of Canada's participation. In the recent South African War its commitment had been much limited, with only a little more than 7,000 troops deployed to a war that had failed to stir the martial ardour of most Canadians. But this time the response would be clearly different, something the Governor General had recognized as he read one newspaper editorial after another and was able to happily report back to his masters in London. Canadians, he signalled, "will be united in a common resolve to put forth every effort and to make every sacrifice necessary to ensure the integrity and maintain the honour of our Empire."[2]

His confidence was well placed. Across the country the planned celebrations of the Bank Holiday had been overshadowed by impromptu parades of thousands of flag-waving citizens. Even in Montreal the crowds demonstrated their patriotism by repetitiously singing first "La Marseillaise" and then "Rule Britannia." Throughout the country, militia headquarters had quietly opened, and the regiments' officers had taken to their desks to receive a steady stream of men reporting for duty.

The Duke of Connaught was, however, not entirely beguiled by this outpouring of patriotism. The third son of Queen Victoria, he was a man with a long soldiering career behind him and well knew that the strong emotions of the day would weaken as the complexity of mustering and financing an army for service abroad became apparent. To keep enthusiasm running high, he counselled his British superiors to ensure Canadian troops were sent to the front, wherever that might eventually be, as soon as they were trained to even the most minimal standards of proficiency. Having men fighting and bleeding on European soil for the Empire would ensure the commitment of Canadians to the cause.[3]

On August 10, the Canadian government issued an Order-in-Council for the immediate raising of a contingent 25,000 strong. Mobilization had already begun in some parts of Canada, but it was the day after the Order-in-Council that the 72nd Seaforth Highlanders of Canada assembled at the Arena Rink in Vancouver. At the same time, the 50th Gordon Highlanders of Canada gathered on the Exhibition Ground in Victoria. Two days later, Hamilton's 91st Canadian Highlanders (informally known as the Argyll and Sutherland Highlanders but not yet formally possessing this designation) mobilized at their James Street Armoury, while, in

Winnipeg, the 79th Cameron Highlanders of Canada reported to Minto Armoury.[4] In four separate cities men mustered, as yet unaware that soon they would be training side by side as members of a single infantry battalion—the 16th Battalion, Canadian Expeditionary Force (C.E.F.). Nor did they know that this battalion would come to be known as the legendary Canadian Scottish. This is the story of that battalion's epic odyssey through the grim crucible of the Great War.

chapter one

"Ready, Aye, Ready!"

- A U G U S T   1 9 1 4 – F E B R U A R Y   1 9 1 5 -

As Canada's Parliament had been prorogued on June 12 it took until August 18 for the nation's parliamentarians to journey from their constituencies to assemble in the House of Commons. Their mood was sober, faces set with grim resolve. In years to come a myth would arise that Canada went to war with no sense of the horrors ahead and a belief victory could be had by Christmas. But Sir Robert Borden's speech, although typically ponderous, was coldly prescient. "In the awful dawn of the greatest war the world has ever known," he began, "in the hour when peril confronts us such as this Empire has not faced for a hundred years, every vain or unnecessary word seems a discord. As to our duty, we are all agreed; we stand shoulder to shoulder with Britain and the other Dominions in this quarrel, and that duty we shall not fail to fulfil as the honour of Canada demands. Not for love of battle, not for lust of conquest, not for greed of possessions, but for the cause of honour, to maintain solemn pledges, to uphold the principles of liberty, to withstand forces that would convert the world into an armed camp; yes, in the very name of the peace that we sought at any cost save that of dishonour, we have entered into this war; and while gravely conscious of the tremendous issues involved and of all the sacrifices that they may entail, we do not shrink from them but with firm hearts we abide the event."[1]

A more skillful orator than the prime minister, opposition leader Sir Wilfrid Laurier, kept his remarks brief and to the point. In 1910, Laurier declared, he had stated that if "Britain is at war, Canada is at war, there is no distinction." Nothing had changed since then. "When the call comes, our answer goes at once, and it goes in the classical language of the British answer to the call of duty, 'Ready, aye, ready!'" Thereafter, the enlistment order for a 25,000-man contingent was readily confirmed without a single dissenting vote. To finance the effort a $50-million war appropriation was approved and the Canadian Patriotic Fund created to raise money to support the families of men sent overseas.

Despite habitual parsimonious military funding, Canada was relatively prepared for mobilization because in recent years the army had developed a plan for fielding an overseas expeditionary force by quickly assembling composite units from existing militia units at the large Petawawa military camp north of Ottawa. This approach would enable local militia commanders to select men for immediate service from a pool of militiamen, trained to various degrees, whose strengths and weaknesses were known to those commanders.

Unfortunately the army's planners were unable to account for the actions of an erratic and eccentric boss—Minister of Militia and Defence Sam Hughes. On August 6, Hughes swept aside their plan in favour of his own. In a lettergram to all 226 Canadian Militia unit commanders, he ordered development of a roll of volunteers drawn from men aged between eighteen and forty-five who met prescribed physical requirements and were skilled in musketry and general soldiering proficiency. These rolls were to be submitted to Hughes's office in Ottawa no later than August 12 for examination—presumably personally by Hughes and his staff. The unit commanders would be informed as to which men listed on their specific rolls would be accepted. With typical pomposity, Hughes described his plan as "really a call to arms, like the fiery cross passing through the Highlands of Scotland or the mountains of Ireland in former days."[2]

The scheme's cumbersomeness was quickly recognized in Ottawa and modified to allow allotments to be determined locally based on the number of immediate volunteers. Yet Hughes refused to be sidelined. Daily he issued more instructions that often contradicted those of the day previous. Most damnable of all for the militia commanders, Hughes—who distrusted professional soldiers and the traditional military system—ordered each infantry militia regiment to immediately provide either a two-company-strong contingent of 250 men or one company numbering 125 men. While this hastened the assembly of the expeditionary force, it shredded the traditional fabric of the army whereby battalions comprised men drawn from a specific geographical area and its local militia regiment who knew each other. Years spent inculcating a

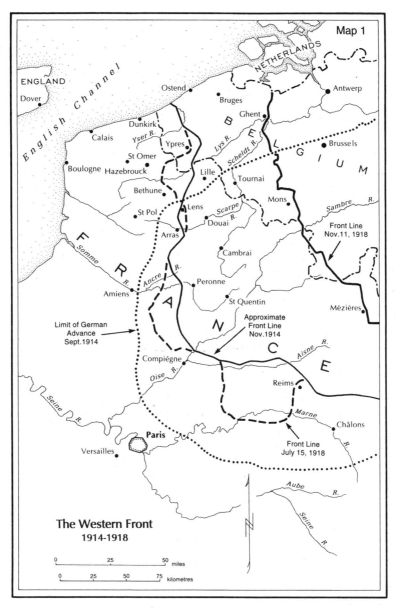

Map 1

The Western Front
1914-1918

ENGLAND
Dover
English Channel
NETHERLANDS
Antwerp
Ostend
Bruges
Ghent
Brussels
Dunkirk
Calais
Yser R.
Ypres
Lys R.
Scheldt R.
BELGIUM
Boulogne
St Omer
Hazebrouck
Lille
Tournai
Bethune
Lens
Mons
Sambre R.
St Pol
Scarpe R.
Douai
Front Line
Nov. 11, 1918
Arras
Somme R.
Cambrai
FRANCE
Ancre R.
Peronne
St Quentin
Mézières
Amiens
Limit of German
Advance
Sept.1914
Approximate
Front Line
Nov.1914
Aisne R.
Compiégne
Oise R.
Reims
Seine R.
Marne
Châlons
Paris
Front Line
July 15, 1918
Versailles
Aube R.
Seine R.

0   25   50 miles
0   25   50   75 kilometres

sense of regimental spirit and affiliation were swept aside by Hughes's scribbling pen.[3]

Hughes further disassembled the army's mobilization plan by ordering that the expeditionary force be concentrated at Valcartier rather than Petawawa. Whereas the latter was an established military base, the former consisted of 12,428 acres of mixed woodland broken by farms, patches of swamp, and sandy stream flats that bordered the east bank of Jacques Cartier River 16 miles northwest of Quebec City. Given control of the land only ten days before the first recruits were scheduled to arrive on August 18, the military began a mad scramble to have a camp readied for the recruits' arrival.

They could not do so, of course, without Hughes's personal intervention. This time, however, the defence minister's boundless energy came usefully to the fore and his constant haranguing helped bring about the rapid transformation of rural countryside into a sprawling military camp. Hordes of lumberjacks descended to fell trees while contractors deployed bulldozers and hundreds of workers to cut roads and erect buildings. When the first recruits arrived they were assigned to barracks in a functional military base. In a report to the government, Hughes trumpeted the results of just ten days of intensive construction: three and a half miles of firing ranges completed with 1,500 targets positioned on them, 12 miles of water mains laid, 15 miles of drains, Army Service Corps and Ordnance buildings constructed, railway sidings laid, "fences removed, crops harvested, ground cleared, streets made, upwards of 200 baths for the men put in, water chlorinated, electric light and telephones installed…and 35,000 men got under canvas." Hughes credited himself for making this achievement possible.[4]

* * *

Neither Hughes nor the militia commanders professed surprise that the initial mobilization far surpassed the 25,000 volunteers the government had mandated. At almost every militia armoury the numbers of volunteer recruits had greatly exceeded the one- or two-company strengths Hughes had sought. In Winnipeg, a recruitment parade on the afternoon of August 6 through the downtown streets and into St. Boniface netted almost 1,400 volunteers. Most of those reporting to the armouries were city dwellers, townsmen, or farmers working land close to population centres. This was simply a result of proximity to the only local source of information—newspapers. As the news filtered out into the hinterland by telegraph or local mail, men there packed bags and headed for the nearest regimental headquarters. In British Columbia, for example, word reached the Okanagan Valley through a ham radio operator named George Dunn in Kelowna. He told a British remittance man lolling in front of a nearby hotel. Jumping astride his horse, the man galloped off to spread the word to his colleagues living in shacks scattered through the nearby hills. Soon several hundred volunteers rode to Vancouver to enlist.

Farther afield, a surveyor working in the province's Cascade Range more than 150 miles from the nearest telegraph office only learned in late September that a war had broken out somewhere. Trying to get more details was a challenge, for the man who told him could only communicate via the Chinook trade language. "Who was fighting?" the surveyor asked.

"Everybody," the Indian replied. In Victoria and in Vancouver they fought, but not in Seattle.

None of this made sense to the surveyor, whose questions only elicited more images of street battles in front of the Empress or Georgia hotels. Finally the Indian paused and shouted triumphantly, "King George, he fight." Knowing that King George in Chinook meant Great Britain and that Englishmen were called King George's Men, the surveyor suddenly understood. "I knew this meant that England and Germany were at it, and it took no time for me to decide as to what I should do."[5]

By the time the surveyor understood Canada was at war, the first contingent of volunteers from Victoria and Vancouver were well on the way to Valcartier. The Seaforth Highlanders boarded a troop train on August 22. In Winnipeg, the Camerons entrained the following day. The day thereafter the 91st Canadian Highlanders left Hamilton with the 50th Gordon Highlanders departing Victoria on August 28. The last of these four groups had disembarked at Valcartier by September 3.

The commanders of each contingent had no idea how it would be incorporated into the expeditionary force, for Hughes had not yet announced how battalions were to be formed. Some officers had tried unsuccessfully to take matters into their own hands. While still in Vancouver, the Seaforth's Lt.-Col. Robert S. Leckie had attempted to communicate directly with other Highland regiments across the nation in an attempt to amalgamate their respective forces under the banner of a single Highland battalion. But Hughes had quickly dismissed this notion.

The first of the four contingents off the train at Valcartier had been five officers and 132 other ranks of the 91st under command of Major

Henry Lucas Roberts. They arrived later the same day as they had departed from Hamilton. Already in place was a contingent of 48th Highlanders from Toronto who allowed the Hamiltonians to join their mess. Two days later, seven officers and 250 Camerons marched into the camp. Their commander, Captain John Geddes, rebuffed the 48th Highlander invitation to join their mess, which was under canvas. Instead he drew the Camerons off to a location on the northerly fringe of the camp facing the Jacques Cartier River. Here officers and men alike took their meals out of mess tins on a grassy football pitch. Active service conditions, Geddes declared, required living in the open with only such comforts as one could carry in a pack. Prematurely greying, the thirty-six-year-old Geddes was an unsparing man with a prickly and obsessive personality. Having turned to soldiering, he applied the same unwavering fullness of attention that he had previously accorded to his days as a student at Rugby, or as a Winnipeg businessman after that.[6] As the Argylls of the 91st had situated their camp next to the Camerons and the two shared a common parade ground, the men from each were soon getting to know each other in an amicable fashion.[7]

On August 27, the Seaforths arrived and paraded before the Camerons and Argylls on the football pitch. The Winnipeg and Hamilton troops were impressed by the newcomers' parading skills, but noted disdainfully that instead of Scottish headgear those men wearing full military kit were equipped with "stove pipe" helmets. There was also a noticeable lack of Scottish brogue to be heard, the Vancouverites' accents being distinctly English and noticeably upper class in tone. This generated a justified suspicion that despite the kilts few Seaforths had Scottish blood running in their veins. In fact, and this was also true of the 70th Gordon Highlanders from Victoria, most Seaforths were either English public school men or young cadets born and bred on the west coast who adhered to the prevailing English values of that region. For their part the Camerons and Argylls were of a rougher hue, labourers and farmers of Scottish descent.

For the next five days, although the men of these three contingents marched and trained together, they had no idea whether they would be officially affiliated or not. Then, on September 2, the headquarters of 1st Canadian Infantry Division delivered orders that, when the 70th Gordon Highlanders arrived the next day, all four contingents would be amalgamated into a single battalion numbered the 16th and would serve in the newly minted 3rd Canadian Infantry Brigade. Lt.-Col. Leckie, who had brought the Seaforths from Vancouver, was named the battalion commander while brigade command fell to Lt.-Col. Richard E. W. Turner. The senior battalion major and Leckie's second-in-command was his younger brother, Major John E. ("Jack") Leckie.

All three were Boer War veterans. Indeed, the slight, bespectacled Turner, who tended to meet cameras with a crooked grin, had been awarded a Victoria Cross for bravery during the British withdrawal from Leliefontein on November 7, 1900. A Royal Canadian Dragoons lieutenant, Turner had led twelve men in a hasty ambush that broke an attack of more than two hundred Boers threatening to overrun an artillery train. Prior to returning to uniform, Turner had been a Quebec merchant with strong Conservative Party ties. Close political links to the government, particularly to Sam Hughes, largely determined which officers received senior divisional postings.

While political affiliation was crucially important, so too was past military experience. A considerable number of the division's officers had fought in South Africa. Indeed, a small percentage of the division's other ranks—about three percent—had also either served in South Africa or India as a British regular. This quickly proved a blessing for an army being cobbled hastily together, for these (usually older) regulars provided a ready pool of experienced men to serve as the non-commissioned officers who, at the company, platoon, and section level, formed a battalion's backbone.[8]

Of the 36,267 men comprising the first contingent, sixty-three percent had been born in Britain or had immigrated to Canada from other parts of the Empire. In no other battalion was this more the case than in the 16th where fully half its officers and eighty percent of the other ranks were British-born. The majority of the 10,880 Canadian-born troops who formed 1st Division traced their lineage back to Britain. Only 1,245 of them were French-Canadian.[9] Asians and Blacks were barred from enlisting at all, while First Nations were much encouraged because Hughes and most army officers believed they made particularly ferocious soldiers.

* * *

Opting for subordinates familiar to him, Lt.-Col. Robert Leckie put a distinctly Seaforth stamp on 16th Battalion headquarters. In addition to his brother, the adjutant, signalling officer, transport officer, quartermaster, medical officer, machine-gun officer, pipe major, drum major, all wore the Seaforth tartan. Leckie's command style defused any discontent that might have arisen among the officers of the other three regiments. Having commanded "A" Squadron, 2nd Canadian Mounted Rifles in South Africa—a unit comprised not only entirely of westerners but largely ex-North West Mounted Police officers—Leckie had developed a deft hand for imposing discipline without stifling individual initiative. The forty-five-year-old battalion commander regularly reminded those under his command that they were an integral part of a team and the four disparate contingents rallied to his example.

But when the 1,162 men comprising the 16th Battalion paraded on the football pitch, it looked as if four Scottish clans had decided to gather together. Only the Camerons were equipped for the field with web equipment, sun helmets, and the like that had been dictated as active service uniform. Often they forsook this gear in favour of their kilts so as not to be outdone by the others. The Gordons were decked out in full uniforms identical to those worn by Britain's Gordon Highlanders with whom they were affiliated, while the 91st Canadian Highlanders all sported the Argyll tartan. By comparison the Seaforths were a ragtag lot with only half wearing full Seaforth uniforms while the rest "wore civilian clothes of most known varieties, with Glengarries, cowboy hats or sun helmets."[10]

Robert Leckie and the battalion's other officers puzzled over how to fuse together these four militia units, each fiercely proud of their particular Highland traditions. Adopting one of the tartans invited controversy, so they initially decided on another altogether—the MacKenzie. But Leckie feared that even this compromise would incite bad feelings. Instead, he decided regimental spirit would best be preserved if each regiment privately funded kitting its men out in their respective uniforms.

In addition to its profusion of tartans, the 16th Battalion was noticeably distinct from other units in 1st Division due to the presence in its ranks of a greater number of men who had seen more than just regimental service. Fully 850 of its officers and men were found to have served in one of ninety-five different corps. While most had been British regiments, there were also men who had gained military experience in the "Australian Navy and Militia, the New Zealand Forces, various South African units, the Barbados Regiment, British Guiana Militia, Punjab Infantry, the American Navy, Holland Volunteers, Norwegian Corps, the Danish Army, the French Foreign Legion, the Belgian Cadets, Shanghai Volunteers, the Mexican Army, and the Chinese Imperial Army." Gazing upon these men in their mismatched tartans and hearing of the diversity of past service, one senior officer turned to Leckie and barked: "Good God, Leckie, where does this battalion come from?"[11]

Where the battalion came from was less a concern to Leckie and his headquarters staff than ensuring that when it arrived in England its men were fully equipped with uniforms and weapons. With his usual fervour, Hughes was frantically working to properly equip his army against a self-imposed deadline. On August 10, he had let a series of contracts aimed at providing uniforms for 50,000 men by September 21. In factories throughout the country, workers wove wool into cloth while leather makers produced boots and harnesses for horses. The deadline was to be met, Hughes told the suppliers, "even though you have to work night and day until then."[12]

After failing to lure a British armament company to set up in Canada to manufacture Lee-Enfield rifles for the army in 1896, the government contracted Sir Charles Ross to produce his self-designed .303 rifle. When the first rifles were delivered from his Quebec City factory in 1905, problems were immediately noted, most ominously its tendency to jam whenever exposed to rain or mud—all-too-common conditions in battle. But Hughes, who saw standing by the Ross rifle as akin to preserving the nation's honour, remained its staunchest proponent and placed an order for 30,000 of the Mark III pattern Ross rifle, which had supposedly been modified to eliminate the previous deficiencies. The modifications chiefly entailed lengthening the barrel from 28 inches to 30.5 and increasing its weight from 7.5 pounds to 9.5.

In the midst of this vast purchasing frenzy, which also included acquiring motor vehicles, horse-drawn vehicles, and more than 7,000 horses, Hughes pursued another fancy by ordering the manufacture of 25,000 MacAdam shovels. Although designed personally by Hughes, he had sought to avoid any perception of a conflict of interest by patenting it under the name of his personal secretary. Drawing from a Swiss invention, the shovel was intended to serve as both shield and entrenching tool. It had an 8½-inch by 9¾-inch blade constructed of three-sixteenths-inch steel that reportedly could stop a bullet at 300 yards. A soldier could jab its four-inch handle into the ground and lie behind the shield for protection. In the shield's centre were two holes, one above the other. One was large enough to accommodate a rifle barrel while the other was to be used for sighting. Awkward to dig with and heavy to carry, the shovels were immediately unpopular. But Hughes was undaunted. The 1st Division would go overseas lugging 25,000 MacAdam shields.

With all the attention given to equipping the contingent, there was little time for coherent training. But Leckie and his subordinate officers were little concerned because most of the men had been trained by the militias to active service standards. They were also highly motivated and possessed a strong sense of duty.

Before breakfast each morning, the men raced by squads up the slopes to a plateau east of the camp. Here they carried out physical drills before sprinting back to camp. The remainder of the day was spent alternatively marching, conducting close formation drills, and skirmishing at platoon and company level. Much time was spent on the two-and-a-half-mile-wide range equipped with 1,700 targets. Each man was required to qualify with the Ross rifle by firing fifty rounds at targets ranging out to distances of 300 yards. While far from being, as Hughes declared, "trained to handle a rifle as no men had ever handled it before," the troops did become relatively proficient.[13] Route marching up and down one side of the river after another was also a daily activity. But only on two occasions was there opportunity for 3rd Brigade to actually conduct a tactical exercise.

Worse, there being more men and units at Valcartier than intended for the first overseas contingent, Hughes deliberately kept to himself which would be sent in the belief that this would encourage all to give their utmost effort. Soon after the contingent assembled, Hughes had gathered all the officers together. Standing on a little rise of ground with the officers seated on the grass before him, Hughes sternly warned them that none "would be permitted to go overseas in command of men until he had proved himself entirely fit for his responsibilities." He said each officer holding a command in the division would be brought before a board of examiners, and if he did not meet the required standard of efficiency, he would at once be replaced by one of the surplus officers, "dozens" of whom, he explained, were waiting for each vacancy. The examination never took place … but the suggestion of it … created a most unsettling effect.[14]

Not only were officers anxious about facing an examination board, but upon marching into the camp at the head of a full-strength battalion of 1,400 men, some were dumbfounded to see this unit broken up and sent to the reinforcement pool only to subsequently be assigned to a battalion with as few as eleven officers and fourteen ranks from its founding militia regiment. So capricious was Hughes's hand on the tiller of one battalion, there were three commanding lieutenant colonels simultaneously seesawing for overall authority, while another battalion had four majors vying for second-in-command and the right to ride the single horse provided for that position.

Although the 16th was largely spared such chaos, its adjutant, Major Gilbert Godson-Godson, arrived at the orderly room one day to find all his clerks suborned to other duties. With orders for the day waiting to be issued, the major began typing only to discover that he had reversed the carbon paper and consequently the impression on the copies was a mirror image. Hurriedly he scribbled along the top of each copy, "To read these orders hold them up to the looking glass."

Despite all the hiccups and disorder, the contingent gained a little more readiness with each passing September day. On Sunday, September 20, in "brilliant sunshine" the Canadian Expeditionary Force paraded before the Governor General, Prime Minister Borden, Hughes, and most of the federal cabinet. Thirty-three thousand men formed in lines of double companies across a frontage of 130 yards and moved toward the reviewing stand in a semi-circular movement that required two left wheels to carry off. All nearly collapsed into confusion as the men out on the edge of the wheel had to sprint to keep pace with those at its axis, but panting and gasping they managed to maintain formation throughout the parade.

With the parade concluded word filtered down that the 1st Division would immediately leave for England. And true enough, within a week, the 16th Battalion marched out of Valcartier. The movement of troops toward the ships had begun on September 26, so when the 16th marched out two days later through snow flurries the divisional area of the camp was a veritable ghost town. To the skirl of bagpipes the battalion marched to the docks and boarded H.M.T.S. *Andania*, a 13,400-ton Cunard liner capable of 15 knots. After spending twenty-four hours with the troops aboard, *Andania* cast off from the wharf at noon the following day and anchored midstream to await the rest of the convoy's formation. Also aboard *Andania* was the 14th Battalion (Royal Montreal Regiment).

In a farewell message read to the troops aboard the ships Hughes declared: "The world regards you as a marvel." On October 3 the convoy, consisting of thirty-two transports escorted by six cruisers, departed Canadian shores at Gaspé Bay in three lines in echelon formation with an interval of one mile between each line. *Andania* was the fifth ship in the right-flanking line. The "great adventure," as many of the 16th's officers referred to the overseas deployment, had begun.

* * *

After the frenetic pace of Valcartier there was little for either men or officers to do during the two-week voyage, but the enforced leisure time served to provide time for socializing that helped bond the battalion. At Valcartier each regiment had mostly kept to itself, except when duty dictated otherwise. This was partially the result of a decision that the companies would each comprise men from a single regiment. "A" and "B" companies were made up of Gordons; "C", "D", and "E" of Seaforths; "G" and "H" of Camerons. Only "F" Company was a mix, because the 91st Canadian Highlanders had needed leavening by Seaforths to attain company strength.

Aboard ship, however, individuals from different companies were thrown together and soon acquaintances between men from different units became common. Cloistered below decks in crowded, stuffy quarters, and fed "indifferent food," save the occasional platoon tug-of-war competition or boxing bout, there was little to do but play cards and engage in desultory conversation.

On the upper decks the officers enjoyed a fine cruise. The mess food was first rate and the lounge comfortable. Highland dancing and French classes were held. Over cigars and drinks discussion returned endlessly to speculation about the likely duration and intensity of the war toward which they sailed. Captain Cecil M. Merritt thought "it would be a war to the death; the Germans would use any and every means to attain victory." Major Henry Roberts was more optimistic. Once "the wheels of the German war machine were turned backward," he opined, "the machine would break up." The Germans, Roberts added, had not considered that they could and would be beaten on the battlefield. That would prove their downfall.

Captain Hamilton Maxwell Fleming forecasted "appalling" casualties to achieve victory. Infantrymen, the thirty-nine-year-old Vancouverite declared, would have about "one chance in a thousand" of surviving unscathed. Displaying a confident "bearing, always well groomed, with the glow of health on his cheeks … Fleming was Fleming and nobody else." Despite his confident demeanour, he was also fatalistic, stating without the slightest concern that he would die "early in the game." Such a fate was inevitable, he said, for "all platoon or company officers, if they did not shirk duty, were bound sooner or later to get 'smashed or killed.'" The first real test of Canada's resolve to fight this war, Captain John Geddes offered, would come when the casualty lists were posted at home. Currently the horrendous reports of losses suffered by British and other Allied troops, he said, made scant impression on Canadians. It would take the blood of their own to harden their resolve to make the sacrifices that would be required of the nation. Forty-one-year-old Captain George Ross of Winnipeg, a lawyer in civilian life, predicted a world-wide religious revival after the war if the struggle proved severe enough.[15]

Discussion also turned to the matter of cementing the battalion's identity as a homogenous unit despite its mongrel roots. A battalion badge was agreed—a St. Andrew's Cross set on a scroll and surmounted by the Coronet of a Royal Princess. That princess the officers decided should be seventeen-year-old Princess Mary, whose father was King George V. Accordingly they drafted a petition to the authorities requesting that the battalion be given the title "The Princess Mary's 16th Canadian Highlanders." While these decisions were being made by the officers, two privates, Alexander MacLennan and Norman Cameron, came forward with a proposal for the battalion motto and it was quickly adopted. "Deas Gu Gath," which translated from Gaelic to English as "Ready for the Fray." With the badge designed so that the coronet of Princess

Mary adorned it, the 16th bet all its markers on its petition being successful. These decisions were all finalized on October 9.

Meanwhile, below decks tensions were rising between the men of the 16th and the 14th battalions. Although part of the 3rd Brigade, the 14th was the only one of its four battalions not to have Highland origins. When some of its troops disrupted nineteen-year-old piper Jimmie Richardson's pipe practice, the news of this assault on their Highland pride raced through the companies. The slender five-foot-seven Richardson had joined the battalion on September 22 at Valcartier. His only linkage to one of the four units was a six-month stint with the Seaforth Cadets unit in Chilliwack where his parents had settled after emigrating from Bell's Hill, Scotland, so that his father could take the position of the town's police chief. An amiable lad, Richardson was popular with all the men regardless of which tartan they wore, and everyone vowed that this slight must not go unavenged. A plan of action was quickly agreed; the complete pipe band hurriedly assembled and was escorted by the entire battalion through the ship to where the 14th's men were quartered. As the 16th stood guard, the "pipers played to their hearts' contents" with the 14th warily and wisely choosing to offer no complaint.[16] Esprit de corps was indeed being born!

Mid-morning of October 15, the *Andania* passed the breakwater and entered Devonport harbour near Plymouth, England. Thousands of civilians thronged the foreshore and a message of welcome from Lord Kitchener, the British Secretary of State for War, was read. Kitchener expressed his confidence that the Canadians would "play their part with gallantry and show by their soldier-like bearing that they worthily represent the great Dominion from which they come." Then, perhaps out of concern about the "soldier-like bearing" they might demonstrate if set loose in Devonport, the men learned they were to be confined shipboard until the transports arrived to take them to their military camp. That transport took two days to organize whereupon the 16th left the ship and marched "through the grimy streets of the dockyard town" past cheering crowds that seemed bent on taking the packs off the men in what might have been a gesture of assistance but struck them more as attempted thievery. The troops pushed on, defending their packs, and soon boarded a train for the Salisbury Plain. Arriving in the early hours of the next morning, the 16th marched through a cold mist and at dawn stood on a bluff overlooking a broad, undulating plain that stretched off across almost 90 square miles of what was one huge military training ground.[17]

The Canadians were soon setting up bell tents grouped into four separate camps that extended over a five-mile-wide area in the western corner of the military grounds. Lt.-Gen. E. A. H. "Edwin" Alderson, the division's first commander, had his headquarters in Ye Olde Bustard, a small country inn about three miles northwest of Stonehenge.

Alderson was a fifty-five-year-old British officer who, as a brigadier general, had commanded Canadian troops in South Africa. He had a long history of active service in various Empire hotspots and had recently commanded a division in India. Alderson quickly established a good rapport with the officers and men. If not charismatic, he exuded a reassuring air of confidence and competence. But his relation with Sam Hughes, who had hoped the division could be commanded by a Canadian, was accordingly strained.

Although Canadians at home often parroted Laurier's call that they were "Ready, Aye, Ready," Alderson quickly realized that the division was anything but prepared for combat. Much essential equipment had still not been supplied and there were many shortages of what was in place.

Making matters worse and greatly hampering training schemes, the weather broke just after the division had arrived on Salisbury Plain. On October 21, a quarter-inch of rain bucketed down and, over the next five days, another inch fell. The Canadians would remain here for 123 days of which 89 brought rainfall that totalled 23.9 inches—double the 32-year average.

Living in tents that lacked flooring and around which no foot boards had been installed meant that it was impossible for the men to escape the eternal dampness. With each passing day the camp became, increasingly, a flooded quagmire of mud as it was discovered that a few inches below a layer of clay was an impermeable layer of chalk that prevented the water being soaked up. Abnormally low temperatures only added to the general misery. Strong winds buffeted the tents, ripping holes in the canvas that were reopened almost as fast as they could be repaired. Even those that remained intact were unheated and the fabric proved no barrier to the icy winds. During one three-week period, strong gales flattened almost all the tents.

In the 16th Battalion's area the mud ebbed and flowed as if pushed by the rise and fall of a tide, now oozing into the tents, now sliming back out again. Boots were caked with clots of the muck and were quickly soaked through. Men desperately dug into their own pocketbooks to shell out for high-cut rubber boots hawked throughout the camp by private profiteers selling them at exorbitant prices. An attempt to use a snowplow to push the mud away and create paths only exposed the chalk, which proved treacherously slippery, and the mud inexorably reclaimed the paths soon after the plow passed through.

Things went from bad to worse when a gale that had abated during the night of December 3 returned with renewed fury late the next morning. One side of the battalion's large, seven-poled, mess tent was smashed in while the orderly room tent and many of the bell tents were overturned. As the entire battalion was on divisional duty the men were scattered throughout the camp performing one maintenance chore or another. Only a party of about fifty men and two officers was close enough to try to avert disaster. "They rushed," the battalion historian wrote later, "through the slough of mud and held on to the ropes of the large mess tent hoping to save it from complete destruction, but in this effort the ropes came off the poles and the majority of the party were precipitated backward into the mud banks. The camp as a whole was in a sorry plight—smashed tables, broken crockery, sodden canvas flat on the ground, personal kit and orderly room papers flying in all directions and soaked, bedraggled men holding on to the tents left standing, or running around in an endeavour to salvage part of the wreckage."[18]

Lord Kitchener had promised that the Canadians would be able to move to permanent barracks in huts by the end of November, but the contractors had fallen hopelessly behind schedule. Christmas found more than 11,000 men still living in tents.[19] Fortunately for the 16th, the disaster of the December 4 gale prompted its move to a new camp area called Larkhill, where they were able to occupy some recently finished huts. The battalion war diarist noted with satisfaction that these "are more comfortable than tents."[20] They were still, however, "draughty," which did little for the men's health.[21]

But the cold only worsened, and on one particularly bitter night a 16th Battalion sentry died from exposure. Sickness was rampant through the division's ranks with the war diarist reporting on December 22: "Many of the men have bad colds." By January 15, an outbreak of spinal meningitis had infected about forty men, and killed several. With the entire divisional camp increasingly resembling a natural disaster zone, the men spent more days than not digging drainage ditches or in other ways trying to keep the mud at bay.[22] This meant little time could be found for combat training. One 16th Battalion soldier noted in his diary that only forty of the days spent on the plain entailed any training.[23]

Even when training days were allotted, all too often they were disrupted by weather. Two out of the four days the battalion mustered on the firing ranges they were met by a heavy snowstorm and dense mist that made it impossible to see any targets.

Adding to the difficulties throughout the last months of 1914 was an inability on the part of the War Office to decide how the division's battalions should be organized. At Valcartier each had been composed according to Colonial regulations of eight companies designated by the first letters of the alphabet. But the War Office now wondered if the division should conform to Imperial regulations with each battalion reduced to four companies numbered one to four, for this was the normal establishment adopted by the regular divisions of the British Expeditionary Force in Flanders. Unable to reach a decision, orders were issued that saw the battalions "see-sawing from single to double companies and the frequent transfer of officers from one command to another, instruction during the days entirely given over to it was subject to confusion, unnecessary repetition of effort in some directions and neglect in others."[24]

While decisions such as this remained in the air, the War Office came down with a definitive verdict on the battalion's petition to call itself the Princess Mary's Canadian Highlanders by refusing it. On the evening of December 14, the officers gathered to discuss what title to seek next and decided to petition for designation as the 16th Battalion Canadian Scottish. Two days later the War Office approved this request. Informally the battalion members were nicknamed Can Scots.

Another issue that the battalion's officers had been wrestling with was whether they should march into combat wearing their respective tartan kilts or adopt something a little less colourful but likely more practical for field duty—khaki kilts. On the 21st they settled on acquiring ones made of khaki.[25]

* * *

With the New Year, the War Office finally ruled that the Imperial battalion model would be adopted. The decision sent a shockwave through the battalions as each had to forfeit three officers from its headquarters and eight subalterns deemed superfluous due to the streamlining of command. Lt.-Gen. Alderson was not particularly happy with the decision as he was left with a hefty number of surplus officers. In mid-January a further shrinkage occurred as the entire 4th Brigade was disbanded and its battalions—save the 4th, which had been transferred to 2nd Brigade when its 6th Battalion (Fort Garry Horse) was transformed into a reserve cavalry regiment—were designated as reinforcing units that would remain in England to form the Canadian Training Depot.[26]

While all this reorganizing was going on, the unrelenting weather and mud had served to reveal many deficiencies in the Canadian-made equipment. In November a shipment of 48,000 overshoes arrived from Canada to great welcome, but within ten days most had come apart and the boots with which the men had been outfitted in Valcartier were proving equally worthless. Alderson ordered British regulation boots distributed and required every unit commander to return a certificate attesting "that every man is in possession of a service pair of Imperial pattern Army boots."

Alderson would have liked to be rid of the unreliable, overly heavy, and unwieldy Ross rifle as well. Even without the bolt being exposed to mud or rain it jammed frequently and was difficult to properly clean in the field. But Hughes would hear none of it and the British had insufficient Lee-Enfields to entirely equip the Canadians. So there was no alternative but to take the rifle with them to France.

A lot of other Canadian equipment would not be going. Despite Hughes's efforts to prevent it, the MacAdam shovel was declared ineffective as a shield, ridiculously heavy to carry, and a poor implement for the most essential soldier's task of digging a slit trench. British shovels were secured and the MacAdam shovel would remain in Britain. Eventually, 2nd Canadian Infantry Division conducted extensive field trials with it in France only to prove its unworthiness. Withdrawn from use, the shovels were sold for $1,400 as scrap metal.

Of 1st Division's battalions, seven—including the 16th—had arrived mostly equipped with the obsolete Oliver pattern of webbing.

Capable of carrying only 50 to 80 rounds rather than the regulation 150, it also lacked a pack or any means to lash an entrenching tool to it. The British War Office provided replacement webbing.[27] Like most of the British Expeditionary Force (B.E.F.), the Canadians had been issued peaked caps for headgear—which provided no protection. (Steel helmets would not be introduced until just before the Battle of St. Eloi in the spring of 1916.[28])

Both motor and horse-drawn vehicles manufactured in Canada were plagued with parts shortages and the division had far too many different models of each. Two types of the motor trucks were proven to suffer from serious defects, and fifty-one British lorries were substituted. Most of the horse-drawn wagons were replaced by British wagons, and the Canadian harnesses were scrapped in favour of British designs.

As these substitutions were put into effect, Hughes railed against every decision. "Our transport, our rifles, our trucks, our harness, our saddles, our equipment, our shovels, our boots, our clothing, our wagons," he declared, "were all set aside and in many cases ... supplanted by inferior articles."[29] But the troops on the sodden Salisbury Plain applauded each change.

On February 6, the battalion sent all unnecessary kit to stores and everyone knew the deployment was imminent as an advance party commanded by Captain Fleming departed for France that evening. As the replacing of equipment was still underway, the pace of getting ready became frantic. When Lt.-Col. Leckie discovered that the stamping of particulars on each soldier's identity disc had not yet been done, shifts of men were required to work round the clock hurriedly carrying out this task.

Sickness and other calamities had also rendered the battalion under strength and efforts to draw reinforcements from the Canadian Training Depot based at Tidworth Barracks on Salisbury Plain came to naught. One officer sent to Tidworth to get reinforcements thought the depot's commander either suffered "from nervous shock or sunstroke." He could make no headway with the man and came away empty-handed, but also painfully aware of the disappointment "and irritation everywhere amongst the battalions left behind or being broken up."

Finally, a second visit yielded an allotment of men but, upon arriving at the battalion, they refused en masse to don kilts and so had to be sent back to Tidworth only to be turned away at the gates. After much back and forth negotiation the men were returned to the 16th and told they had no choice but to wear kilts.

On February 10, with the battalion to sail for France the next day, an outbreak of measles among the Gordons, who made up No. 1 Company, was reported and the entire 16th Battalion found itself facing the spectre of being quarantined. The relief was palpable when it was discovered that only the forty men of No. 1 Company's third platoon, all sharing two huts, had actually been exposed. This group was immediately isolated and would not rejoin the battalion until determined to be free of the disease.

Early on the morning of February 11, the rest of the battalion formed up and "a happy and proud bunch of boys bid farewell to our mud-hole." Their last glimpse of the deserted camp where the men had endured such misery revealed a swarm of civilians descending on it "like vultures, making ready to cart away … everything they could lay their hands on."[30]

In the late afternoon the battalion reached Avonmouth and boarded the 8,500-ton transport *Maidan*—one of the many ships forming a convoy that would carry the Canadian contingent to France as the first step toward the trenches of Flanders.

chapter two

Learning War

- FEBRUARY–APRIL 1915 -

At 0400 hours on February 12, *Maidan* weighed anchor and sailed from Avonmouth at the rear of the convoy. As senior officer, Lt.-Col. Robert Leckie commanded all the troops aboard, which included not only the Canadian Scottish but also 3rd Canadian Infantry Brigade's artillery headquarters section and three Canadian Field Artillery batteries. Close to 2,000 men were jammed into "bare holds, into which they were so closely packed that it was impossible to lie down." Hatches were left open and permission was granted for the men to go up on deck, but as this was crammed bow to stern with horses, vehicles, and artillery pieces, only a handful could leave the holds at any given time. In addition to the battalion's 79 horses, 14 four-wheeled wagons, 21 two-wheeled wagons, 9 bicycles, and 5 motorcycles, the artillerymen had loaded 214 horses, 6 field guns, 4 four-wheeled wagons, 28 two-wheeled wagons, 2 bicycles, and one motorcycle.[1]

The predicted quick and straightforward crossing proved anything but when a sudden storm struck in the evening as the convoy entered the Bay of Biscay. *Maidan* pitched and rolled alarmingly in the growing swells prompting the ship's captain to order the hatches rammed home as waves crashed onto the deck and threatened to flood the holds. All night long the storm only worsened and by first light had transformed itself into a fierce gale "with incessant violent squalls." The convoy had been scattered, each ship fighting alone to make way at whatever best speed it could manage. At 1600 hours, *Maidan*'s captain scribbled in the ship's log that "a strong gale and squalls of hurricane force were experienced with high dangerous seas."[2] Shortly thereafter, about 70 miles west of Ushant, he ordered the ship turned southwestward to meet the winds head on. The "gale could not be worse," the ship's captain warned Leckie as waves surged over *Maidan*'s bow and it wallowed forward at a mere two knots per hour.

Several hatch covers were punched in by waves that cascaded down to drench the helpless troops below. Icy saltwater mixed with the ever-increasing volumes of vomit sloshed around their ankles. The stench in the holds became almost unbearable. When the quartermaster doled out rations, most of the men who had not yet been sick became so. The battalion's medical officer, Captain G. E. Gillies, warned Leckie that seventy-five percent of the troops aboard were seasick, some critically so.

On deck, a massive wave smashed the starboard horse shelter to pieces. Two animals were swept overboard only to be hurled back onto the deck by the following wave so forcefully that each suffered multiple bone fractures and had to be shot on the spot. An artillery officer and four of his gunners who had rushed to the ruined shelter in a vain attempt to prevent the loss of the untethered horses there were injured under the animals' milling hooves. A Can Scot momentarily grasped the reins of one horse only to be plucked up by a wave and cast through an open hatch cover. Freefalling 15 feet, the man came down hard on his rear and cried, "By God, if I had landed on my other end, I'd have broken my neck."[3]

That evening the storm eased slightly and *Maidan* turned back on course for St. Nazaire. Finally able to take stock, transport officer Lt. Colin Marshall was happily surprised to discover that only four horses had been killed. Although the storm still blew at dawn, it was clearly weakening. Late on the afternoon of February 14, *Maidan*, which had been at the convoy's tail, was the first to drop anchor off St. Nazaire. To lift the spirits of his battered troops, Leckie assembled the Canadian Scottish's seventeen pipers and ten drummers on the forecastle and bridge to play a long medley of marches and reels that greatly entertained the hundreds of French civilians gathered dockside in their Sunday best.[4]

The following morning, the troops started disembarking from *Maidan* and all men, animals, equipment, and stores were ashore by noon. Determined that 16th Battalion's arrival at the head of the Canadian contingent should be appropriately recognized, Leckie obtained the base commander's permission to parade his men in a long circuit through the city's streets that would return them to the docks. With the pipe band at the fore, the thousand soldiers marched proudly past throngs of cheering civilians and French *poilus*, who were in St. Nazaire on leave from several nearby army camps. Along the way the Canadians were regularly besieged by children who insisted on carrying off their water bottles and bringing them back brimming with hearty red wine.

When the parade broke up at the dock, the men found stacks of "hairy, smelly goatskin coats" had been set out for them. After shrugging into these winter-issue coats, the battalion personnel quick-marched to a railroad wayside where a freight train waited. Thirty-eight men and nine junior officers were crowded into each boxcar while the senior officers settled into several first-class passenger carriages. Darkness was falling as the train chuffed out of St. Nazaire bound for Hazebrouck in France, just south of the Belgian border. A major railway centre connected by a spiderweb of lines to all points of the British front lines, Hazebrouck served as the British Expeditionary Force's major supply and reinforcement distribution depot.

The rail trip took two days, the train shunting into Hazebrouck at 1230 on February 17. While the men began marching on foot the seven miles to the village of Caestre, where 3rd Canadian Infantry Brigade was to be billeted, Leckie raced ahead on horseback to report to the commander of the advance headquarters there. He arrived only to find all the officers were absent, and learned that nobody had anticipated the battalion's arriving so soon. Consequently, no preparations for housing the men were in place. An icy rain fell while Leckie frantically got the headquarters staff to have billets readied before his cold and soaked soldiers arrived. Yet when the battalion marched into Caestre, billets still had to be finalized. Despite the bitter rainfall, Lt. Hugh MacIntyre Urquhart later recorded in his personal diary that the battalion was forced "to stand in the street for a full hour before anything [was] done." Finally the battalion was broken into groups by platoons or even sections and directed to houses in town or marched out into the countryside to occupy farmhouses or barns. Urquhart's platoon trudged up a muddy road to a farmhouse only to be kept waiting outside for a half hour before being marched back to town and then out into the countryside again to another farmhouse that turned out to already be full of soldiers. Returning to Caestre, Urquhart finally managed to divide his platoon between a small schoolroom, a nearby hayloft, and a couple of cottages shortly before midnight.[5]

While the men were long in getting settled, the battalion's senior officers had been assigned "most comfortable" billets in the village. The battalion's official war diarist, however, noted with slight concern that the sound of "gun fire [was] quite audible" in the distance.[6] A mere sub-altern, Urquhart did not rate a comfortable billet. He bedded down at brigade headquarters. There were "no blankets, so slept on mattress with my wet coat above me. It was cold and very uncomfortable but being terribly tired I slept a little."[7]

* * *

Caestre lay about 15 miles south of a front line that had remained large-ly unchanged since German and Allied forces had battered each other to a standstill in mid-October of the previous year. Initially the German invasion in the summer of 1914 had carried through to the village it-self, but a British counterattack had regained Caestre and driven the en-emy back about 10 miles before running out of steam a little less than three miles north of the Belgian textile town of Ypres. Both sides had begun digging in and, by year's end, the two lines of facing entrench-ments snaked for 500 miles from the North Sea across Belgium and France to the Swiss border. The two British armies, Gen. Sir Douglas Haig's First and Gen. Horace Smith-Dorrien's Second, held a 28-mile section of this front. First Army's 11 miles centred on Neuve Chapelle while Second Army, to the immediate north, manned 17 miles running through the Lys and Douve valleys north from Bois Grenier to just be-yond the Ypres-Comines railway immediately south of Ypres. Second Army's left flank was guarded by the French Eighth Army, while First Army had the French Tenth Army to its right.

As Commander-in-Chief of the B.E.F., Field Marshal Sir John French's initial intention for 1st Canadian Infantry Division was that it would form a reserve for Smith-Dorrien's III Corps (each British Army being com-posed of three corps) after receiving a short indoctrination in trench warfare methodology.[8] On February 19, however, the 16th Battalion's training exercise consisted of the routine bayonet practice that saw the men in company formation "charging and thrusting at Sacks filled with Straw, strung on Rope between Trees," the war diarist recorded. While the men vigorously tore straw enemies apart, Lt.-Col. Leckie and the oth-er three battalion commanders of 3rd Canadian Infantry Brigade accom-panied Brig. Richard Turner in an examination of ground selected for a

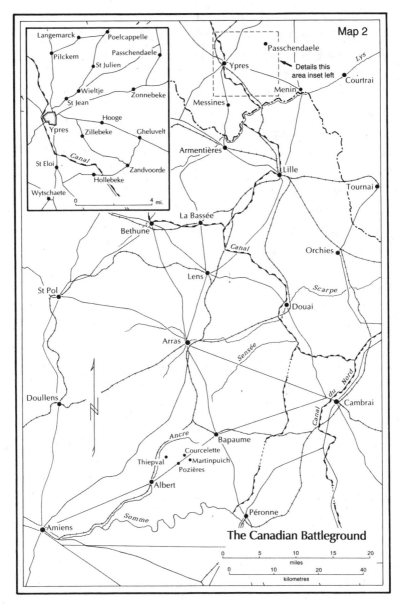

Map 2

Langemarck
Poelcappelle
Pilckem
Passchendaele
St Julien
Wieltje
Zonnebeke
St Jean
Hooge
Ypres
Zillebeke
Gheluvelt
St Eloi
Canal
Zandvoorde
Hollebeke
Wytschaete
0   4 mi.

Passchendaele
Ypres
Lys
Details this
area inset left
Courtrai
Menin
Messines
Armentières
Lille
Tournai
La Bassée
Bethune
Canal
Orchies
Lens
Scarpe
St Pol
Douai
Arras
Sensée
Canal du Nord
Doullens
Cambrai
Ancre
Bapaume
Courcelette
Thiepval
Martinpuich
Pozières
Albert
Péronne
Somme
Amiens

The Canadian Battleground

0   5   10   15   20
miles
0   10   20   40
kilometres

brigade parade before Field Marshal French. At one point Turner drew
Leckie aside and warned him that, in just four days, the 16th Battalion
would enter a section of trench for an on-the-ground orientation.

The front north of their village remained mysterious and unknown to
the Canadians, a source of boundless rumour and speculation that substituted for the gap in factual knowledge. During the day, camp sounds

close at hand dominated, but after nightfall the distant, rumbling thunder of artillery and the crackling sound of rifle and machine-gun fire came to the fore. On the night of February 18, the war diarist noted: "Lights of firing line show up brilliantly tonight."⁹

At 1130 hours on February 20, a Saturday, 3ʳᵈ Brigade paraded through heavy rain before Field Marshal French, Gen. Horace Smith-Dorrien, and 1ˢᵗ Canadian Infantry Division commander, Lt.-Gen. Edwin Alderson. After, French confided to Turner his opinion that "if the Canadians fight as well as they look, they will prove a formidable enemy." He was particularly impressed by Leckie's men complimenting him for having "a very smart Battalion."¹⁰

Many Can Scot officers would have disagreed. Lt. Urquhart, serving with the Winnipeg Camerons of No. 4 Company thought it "extraordinary how inefficient the Canadians are and yet how they think they know everything." Scots born and raised, the thirty-four-year-old Urquhart was concerned about how his company commander, Captain John Geddes, "fusses a great deal because of over anxiety as to [the] men," while the company's second-in-command, Captain George Jameson, seemed "quite undisturbed" by anything, "absolutely disinterested" even. Urquhart felt that Lt.-Col. Leckie went "after Geddes quite a lot," but for little apparent reason. As for Major John Leckie, Urquhart was amused at his views that there were "too many Imperial officers in Canada. If they had a few more Imperial officers," Urquhart noted in his personal diary, "things would not be so horribly mixed up in [the] Canadian contingent."¹¹

The older Leckie had been born in Halifax, the younger in Acton-Vale, Quebec. Each had followed a remarkably similar track by first attending Bishop's College School in Lennoxville, Quebec, then Royal Military College, and finally King's College in Windsor. Robert Leckie had become a civil engineer and his brother a mining engineer. Both had spent the early part of the 1890s deeply involved in respective local militias before volunteering for South African service and, once back in Canada, renewed their militia ties. The two men were close friends and there was no trace of rivalry between them despite John Leckie's being subordinate to his elder brother. Robert Leckie was a short whippet of a man with a lean, aesthetic face that appeared all the more so due to a deep scar on his right cheek inflicted by a leopard attack while hunting big game in Somaliland. Leckie often compensated for his natural shyness by affecting an aloof and superior air, which he then countered by over-playing the role of "courteous gentleman." He treated subordinate officers with studied respect, praising them when deserved and rarely rebuking those in error. In combat, he remained perpetually calm and keenly observant, delivering orders in a soft, conversational voice. Seemingly unflappable, his battle demeanour would serve to steady the battalion from the top down.[12]

Leckie's unflappability was steadily put to the test during these first days of overseas service. On the Sunday after its arrival in France, the battalion paraded for Church services, but despite the fact most of the men were Protestants, religious differences resulted in a "sad mix-up over Presbyterian and [Church] of [England] service." Captain George Ross, a Cameron who was second-in-command of No. 1 Company's primarily Gordon troops, loudly "objected to the Church of England clergyman, so left with some of his men." In an attempt at mollification Leckie passed word down "that any Presbyterian who did not wish to attend service might fall out," Urquhart wrote after, "and when I looked around only 4 of my Platoon were left, likewise large part of 16 [platoon].... [It] seems a pity more consideration should not be shown to Scottish National religion and Presbyterian chaplains."[13]

After the Church parade sputtered to conclusion, Major John Leckie stumped off at the head of a group of officers and men for a short, five-mile march to the summit of Mont des Cats in hopes of catching a glimpse of the mystical front lines. Climbing a windmill that surmounted the summit, Leckie and the other officers "looked down on a panorama of field, wood and village stretching to the horizon line—thrilling experiences which in due time would be related in detail to their fellows; but there was not a sight of the trenches or a sound of battle, nothing but the quietness of a sunny, spring-like, Sunday afternoon."[14]

* * *

Two days after the church-fealty fiasco, the 3rd Brigade marched 10 miles east from Caestre to Erquinghem for a period of front-line training in the Bois Grenier Trench system. Over five days all 1st Division battalions were to send small groups of officers and men to spend time in the line with British troops stationed there. Everyone from company commanders to private soldiers were assigned to individuals of equal rank for a forty-eight-hour period. Thereafter platoons of Canadians assumed responsibility of a trench section for twenty-four hours in association with a British infantry company. While this process went on, battalion commanders and their staff studied alongside their immediate opposite numbers "the many details of battalion administration in trench warfare." Artillery officers and brigade and divisional staff meanwhile did the same with their British counterparts.[15]

When No. 15 Platoon marched toward the trenches, Lt. Urquhart noted that his "men presented a weird appearance clad in their goatskin coats and laden down with heavy packs, surmounted by firewood and the long French loaves sticking well out to both sides, for in early 1915 the troops went into the line with all their worldly goods on their backs." As they closed on the front in the gathering dusk "the distant rolling sound-waves of the machine-gun and rifle fire" intensified. Suddenly the farms were nothing but ruins, buildings reduced to burned-out shells with rotting corpses of animals strewn about. Bois Grenier village was a ruin. A British Argyll & Sutherland Highlander guide ticked off the names that had been given to various farms now used as marking points for passage into the trenches: Ruined Farm, Burnt Farm, and Dead Cow Farm. When one man lit a smoke a voice snapped out of the darkness, "Put out that damned cigarette!" Suddenly the Canadians discerned about them "small groups of British soldiers standing … with slung rifles, talking in low tones or passing silently to and fro with burdens of sandbags, shovels and rations, the nearer bang of musketry or rat-tat of the machine gun and the more frequent whine and crack of the bullet." One patch of ground was cluttered with crude wooden crosses that marked the graves of men recently killed and hurriedly interred.[16]

Rather than the entire battalion being sent directly into the trenches, the men were quartered in several farms and then fed forward by platoons. Urquhart's platoon billeted at Joseph Delecourt's farm. "I have my horses no longer," he told the lieutenant in French. "They are working for Germans." About 300 yards away, a battery of large naval guns fired at irregular intervals with massive thundering roars that shook the house to its core.

On February 24, Urquhart joined several other officers in meeting their Argyll & Sutherland counterparts for a trench visit. He thought the trenches here were unreasonably wide and therefore "rather unsuitable for shell fire." The following night, Urquhart and Captain Sydney Goodall took their No. 4 Company platoons into the trenches for forty-eight hours' orientation. Soon the Canadians were warned they had entered a "fire zone" and seconds later heard "shots whizzing over our heads. Went forward with instructions to fall flat if flare went up. However, beyond bullets whizzing nothing happened."[17]

The officers were guided to a dugout housing the company headquarters while the sergeants got their platoons situated. After dining with their British counterparts, Urquhart and Goodall joined the troops in the trenches and were surprised to find the defences here were not trenches at all but rather raised earthen banks called breastworks that had periodic overhead protection provided by sandbagged roofs. A thin line of barbed wire and some scattered forward listening posts that were also above-ground provided the only advanced defensive works. Urquhart again fretted over how exposed the men behind the earthen wall were to shellfire. Just 300 yards across the way the Germans had erected a similar embankment from which rifle and machine-gun fire emitted regularly at a desultory rate that ensured men new to this life remained anxious. The Canadians soon learned that neither side had erected above-ground defensive works out of choice. A system of trenches had been dug in the late fall but "in that flat country all of them, including communication trenches, had become completely water-logged."[18]

The Canadians' introduction to the trenches was alternately frightening and tedious, something they would soon realize was common fare for soldiers whose trench sectors were subject only to holding actions rather than full-scale battles. Snipers posed a constant danger, a bullet invited if one risked a glance over the parapet during daytime hours or lit a match at night. Seemingly at random, artillery fire would bracket one section of line, so there was never warning of its arrival. Noise, particularly gunfire, continued around the clock and made sleep difficult. Dugouts were draughty, usually muddy, and generally uncomfortable. During its orientation period, the Canadian Scottish were fortunate to suffer only one man wounded. But another of its men was injured by flying glass while he lay sick in hospital after a concentration of high-velocity shells fell on the battalion's rear area.[19]

On February 28 the division's orientation was abruptly cancelled and the Canadians rushed to relieve 7th British Division, which was part of IV Corps in Gen. Douglas Haig's First Army, instead of going to Gen. Horace Smith-Dorrien's Second Army as originally planned. It took two days for the division to be quietly extracted from the front and on March 3 take full control of a 6,400-yard frontage in the area of Fleurbaix. Here 16th Battalion relieved the 2nd Battalion of the Border Regiment and looked out at Aubers Ridge, which rose toweringly in this flat plain to heights of 70 feet.

As had been the case in their orientation area, the ground here was so waterlogged that trenches had been abandoned in favour of breast-works constructed with sod and sandbags. Rather than being linked continuously together, however, this defensive system consisted of in-dividual outposts that, by day, were cut off from each other and the rear areas because the intervening ground was exposed to enemy fire. These "forts," as the British designated them were soon discovered to be only "just bullet-proof." They were also small, with the largest of them capa-ble of housing only two platoons while most could accommodate only one. Behind these frontline fortifications ran a network of more sub-stantial breastworks termed "defended localities." Having some overhead shelter, these afforded a degree of protection from weather but were still completely vulnerable to any artillery fire.

All around the Canadians lay "complete desolation. Broken farm implements lay around, the carcasses of dead animals tainted the air; no sign of life was visible in it beyond the occasional signaller charily test-ing lines. At night the scene was very different. The desolation of the day was hidden; its silence replaced by the sounds of the activity of many men engaged in the improvement of the defences, or on carrying and ration parties, and by the crack of rifle fire and bursts of machine-gun fire which went on from dusk to dawn. As dusk closed in the odd shot would be fired here and there, the fire gradually increasing in volume as it became darker until it reached a crescendo of sound up and down the whole front, gradually dying down as dawn approached, until, when daylight came, it ceased, as it began, with the occasional shot."[20]

On March 4 the hazards presented to anyone trying to duck from one isolated fort to another became clear when Sgt. George Arthur Biddlecombe of No. 2 Company was hit in the chest by a sniper's bul-let that lodged in his body. Despite the severity of the wound he could not be evacuated from one of the forts until after nightfall. Even then the carrying party "had a hot time from snipers," as it carried the man to the rear. Biddlecombe survived.[21]

At regular intervals the Can Scots swapped front-line duty with the 13th Battalion (the Royal Highlanders of Canada). Each transition reinforced the surreal nature of their war zone. Whereas, at the front, the risk to life was constant, in the rear area, only a short distance away, "there was no interference from the enemy. There was little hostile artillery fire and no aerial bombing. The houses as far forward as brigade reserve, say one thousand to 1,200 yards behind the line, were intact and occupied by the French people, old men and women who worked in fields within sight of the enemy.

"And there was a greater freshness and cheerfulness amongst the troops generally. The siege warfare outlook had not seized upon the imagination. The trenches were looked upon as temporary barriers only."[22] But the Canadians had yet to be exposed to a real battle—something that changed on March 10 when the Allies launched a major offensive at Neuve Chapelle, immediately to the right of the division's frontage.

The Can Scots had just re-entered the fortification line under cover of darkness in the early morning hours of March 9 amid rumours that a major battle was shaping up. What should have proved an orderly changeover proved chaotic from the outset and took four-and-a-half hours to effect, as the Royal Highlanders guided their replacements into their positions in a "very haphazard" way while appearing "anxious to get out."

Lt. Urquhart lost half his section in the inky blackness, and his sergeants—Murdo Ridge and John Steele—also lost contact with some of their sections leaving the platoon "at sixes and sevens." When Urquhart visited Ridge's designated fort, he found the sergeant "much flustered and [that Cpl. James Gordon] Craig also did not seem quite on the job and exceedingly nervous about position. [Sgt.] Steele was at Fort 10 and they also were in a most anxious, even dazed, position."

Eventually the lieutenant got his platoon settled into its two forts and set them to filling sandbags to strengthen the positions. Captain Geddes warned Urquhart "there might be a general advance tomorrow and that at 8 a.m. we were to start bursts of rapid fire and machine-gun fire so as to give the idea to the Germans that an attack might be contemplated from this front."[23] This Canadian deception was intended to prevent the Germans shifting men to reinforce the line where the offensive was to fall. Only if the British to the right achieved a major breakthrough would 1ˢᵗ Canadian Infantry Division advance in earnest.

* * *

Originally the offensive had been conceived as an Anglo-French joint assault. But on March 7, Gen. J. J. Joffre apologetically advised Gen. Sir Douglas Haig that, as the French army was already conducting an offensive in the Champagne area, it lacked sufficient reserves for an offensive alongside the British. Rather than cancelling the operation, Haig decided to go it alone with an assault aimed at piercing the German front and advancing out of First Army's centre a half mile to secure the gaggle of buildings that made up Neuve Chapelle. The attack was to begin on March 10 with a massive artillery barrage shattering the German breastworks and shredding their wire defences to open the way for two corps—the IV and Indian—to strike like a "battering ram" and "carry the Germans off their legs." Once through Neuve Chapelle the combined Indian-British force would advance a further three miles to gain Aubers Ridge. Haig and Field Marshal French confidently predicted the preponderance of men they were committing to such a narrow-frontage assault assured success.[24] Against an estimated three German battalions manning the defensive works with four more standing in immediate reserve, First Army was committing forty-eight. The British also had, as described in Haig's Order of the Day, artillery "both more numerous than the enemy's and also larger than any hitherto used by any army in the field. Our Flying Corps has driven the Germans from the air." With the Germans so weak on the ground, Haig hoped to overwhelm and send them reeling backward without losing his momentum. "Quickness of movement is therefore of first importance to enable us to forestall the enemy and thereby gain success without severe loss. "At no time in this war has there been a more favourable moment for us, and I feel confident of success. The extent of that success must depend on the rapidity and determination with which we advance."[25]

In the grey light of dawn, on a welcome and rare clear morning, the Canadians looked to their flank as the massive barrage began thundering at 0730 hours. Half an hour later British troops could be seen advancing on Neuve Chapelle. Within twenty minutes a 1,600-yard gap had been punched through the German front lines. An hour later Neuve Chapelle was declared clear, the leading British battalions meeting virtually no resistance as they paused on the first phase halt line to await orders from corps headquarters to resume the advance.[26]

Meanwhile, Canadian riflemen and machine gunners had opened up as scheduled with rapid bursts of fire they continued to lay down at fifteen-minute intervals throughout the day. At about 1000 hours, forty-two-year-old L/Cpl. Duncan Patterson was blazing away when a German sniper's bullet struck his rifle "between stock and barrel, glanced off into Patterson's cheek and then into his body." Lt. Urquhart and a couple other men "tried to staunch [his] blood but it was impossible." Stretcher-bearer William Mowat quietly cautioned that it was no use. "Jugular," he whispered. Patterson quickly bled to death. "We could see him die and, as he was the first man killed and we were covered with his blood, we got quite a turn."[27]

The Canadians kept up their fire while wondering how the attack on their flank was developing. There seemed little indication now that a major offensive was underway, the gunfire from that area desultory and seemingly coming from static positions. In fact, the rigid dictates that higher command must control the pace of the offensive had brought it to a grinding halt when enemy counter-artillery fire destroyed telephone and telegraph lines. Forced to rely on runners, orders from corps headquarters and reports from the front were taking more than an hour to travel to and fro. Trying to keep the battalions aligned across the breadth of their frontages, the corps commanders waited on their lagging outer flanks to catch up to those in the centre, which had broken deep into the German lines. Farther ahead than the Indian Corps, IV Corps halted to allow the other to come abreast.

At 1530 hours, French realized the attack was losing all momentum and ordered each corps to advance from where they were without regard to the position of the other. But as the order trailed from corps to each division and then down to each brigade and subsequently to the battalions, time trailed away. Not until 1730 hours, with dusk falling, did the offensive get moving again. With five hours to reorganize, the Germans had doubled their forces by this time, and as the British infantry moved in broad lines across flat fields, German machine guns opened up from well-sited positions and the slaughter began.

For the next two days the British tried to renew the offensive but were repeatedly brought to a bloody halt by heavy defensive fire. At 2240 hours on March 12, Haig cancelled the operation. Neuve Chapelle cost First Army 12,892 casualties. This included about one hundred men from the Canadian division, which was deemed to be "no more than the normal wastage period for that [length of] period in the line."[28]

While the offensive had raged on, rumours and constantly changing orders had whirled through the ranks of the Canadians so that everyone was constantly on edge. Expecting the battle to spill over into its area, divisional headquarters ordered night patrols sent across No Man's Land to the German wire to explore how it might be breached. The 16th Battalion, like the rest of the division, had no previous experience in such patrols. But soon men by twos and threes were creeping about in the darkness of a No Man's Land rife with slimy mud and crisscrossed by waterlogged trenches. One patrol from Urquhart's platoon consisting of privates Jack Ross and Alick MacLennan came upon a seven-foot-wide trench "and to cross it MacLennan had to get down into the water well over the waist line, carry Ross over on his shoulders and in turn be pulled out by the latter when they reached the further side."[29]

Back at the forts, Urquhart grew more anxious with each passing hour that the night patrols remained out—not because of concern that the patrols would be ambushed by Germans, but rather because the men around him "were exceedingly nervous and might fire on our own patrol." He was much relieved when the men returned after three hours of scouting.[30] The news they brought was far from encouraging. Rather than suffering from low morale as higher command insisted was the case, the Germans had been busily repairing gaps created in the wire by artillery. And on returning to their lines the patrols had discovered two lanes, each about 30 feet wide, cut through the battalion's defensive wire by German patrols—hardly the behaviour of an enemy considering retreat.

The night of March 13 brought more of the same, with the battalion sending out patrols and the Germans doing likewise. At one point Pte. Walter Ahier, standing sentry duty in Fort 10, spotted some shadows prowling down one of the lanes cut in the wire that had not yet been closed and fired on them. When a flare went up a German patrol was spotted quickly beating a retreat. In the morning the corpses of two Germans were found hanging on the wire in the area where Ahier had directed his rifle fire.

For the next two weeks the division remained in place on what was now considered an inactive front. Yet this did not mean that the 16th was spared casualties. The day-to-day sniping and random artillery fire ensured some men were either killed or wounded. On the evening of March 27, the Can Scots along with the rest of the Canadian division were relieved by remnants of the Northampton and Sherwood Foresters battalions which had been badly mauled in the offensive. The Canadians marched out to Estaires, a town about six-and-a-half miles behind the front lines. Their first stay of duty holding a divisional line on the front was at an end.[31]

From the time it had entered the trenches at Fleurbaix on March 4 to its departure, 16th Battalion lost ten men killed and eight wounded— a casualty rate deemed light and reflective of being posted to a quiet trench sector.[32]

Estaires, a major B.E.F. rest area a couple of miles east of the transportation junction of Hazebrouck, was congested with British and Indian troops. Having experienced severe snowstorms in the trenches the week before, the sudden outbreak of brilliant sunshine—although temperatures remained unseasonably cold—gave the town a holiday camp air. But the Canadians were not allowed to relax. Field parties were formed daily, marched toward the front, and put to work digging and improving rear communication trenches. Those not so employed were either engaged in combat training or route marches. On the last day of March the Can Scots spent the morning on entrenching duties forward and then in the afternoon completed a nine-mile route-march that Lt. Urquhart "enjoyed … very much."[33]

The Canadians would later look back nostalgically to their time at Estaires. Meals were regular with plentiful portions and the billets comfortable, so that soon everyone felt rested up. "This good time must finish, too good to last," one soldier scribbled in his diary. "Looks to me as though we are being fed up for the slaughter," an officer warily confided to another.[34]

So there was little surprise on April Fool's Day when orders transferred 1st Canadian Division to Second Army's recently formed V Corps under command of Lt.-Gen. Sir H. C. O. Plumer. One battalion after another, over a two-day period, marched to Cassel, about 17 miles west of Ypres, to take responsibility from two French divisions for the eastern section of the Ypres Salient.[35]

The Canadian Scottish made the move on April 7, rising at 0430 and marching off through light drizzle by 0645 in what soon became "a splendid day." Lt. Urquhart reported that they happily left "the flat country and got into rolling uplands.... Men stood march fairly well altho[ugh] about [half] dozen had sore feet." At 1400 hours, after marching about 17 miles, the battalion reached the Cassel billets from which it would spend the next week preparing to take over the French section.

Cassel's 3,000-strong population was overrun by French troops comprising a divisional headquarters, but also by an equally large number of men who seemed to have no unit affiliation. When Urquhart raised the matter with a French officer he learned that the majority of one regiment had been ordered to the rear after it broke because of collective cowardice. "What a fearful fate," Urquhart thought.[36]

April 14 saw the battalion on the move again, with 3rd Brigade in the vanguard of a Canadian divisional relief of the French 11th Division to be completed over a three-day period. The move began after dark, but the Can Scots did not enter Ypres until after midnight. Two large searchlights cut the sky with their harsh, wide beams and cast the place in an eerie incandescent glow. Ypres was "sadly battered," the historic Cloth Hall (built in 1200) shattered. Once through the ruins, the pace quickened and the men trotted over another three-mile stretch of road. A halt was then called and the battalion stood for forty-five minutes, men stamping feet to keep circulation flowing in the hard, cold night. Then they set off on the final leg of the journey to the trenches about three more miles away. "Flares were going up on all sides and again we seem to be on a salient. Passed through village of St. Julien which was shelled almost to pieces. Passed on to Reserve trench where we found Infantry officers of charming disposition and also discovered we were to relieve 79th R[égiment] of French Infantry. This officer was through all war and wounded on 20th August. Other officer attached from cavalry. He also had much experience and at Marne accounted for 8 Germans." Although most pleasant in their manner, the French officers had bad news for the battalion. There was no room in the trenches for them as the French were not yet ready to hand off to the Canadians. So the battalion trudged wearily back to Ypres. Here they remained for two days until finally going back up to the trenches on the night of April 16 on a cold, rainy night.[37]

While the rest of the battalion moved into the front line, No. 4 Company remained in reserve at St. Julien which, its houses destroyed by artillery, was a complete ruin. "A place badly shelled smells far from pleasant," Urquhart noted. Being in reserve entailed responsibility for carrying ammunition through the communication trenches to the front, and the job was not completed until 0500 hours.[38]

With the dawn, the Canadians looked about them in dismay at the parlous condition of the trenches. "The French must have slacked a great deal to leave trenches in such condition," Urquhart groused.[39] They soon learned that the forward trenches being so ill-constructed reflected a difference between British and French tactics. British doctrine held the front trenches must be defended at all costs and so they were constructed to withstand German attack. By contrast, the French only lightly manned front trenches in anticipation that when attacked a retirement to stronger lines behind would ensue. This enabled the 75-millimetre artillery to turn the front lines into a killing ground that created a "defence in depth." As they intended no final stand in the front trenches and wanted to avoid presenting the attacking Germans with good positions, the French built only minimal forward trenches. Consequently the field works, whether below or above ground, were unconnected in many places and lacked traverse lines to offer protection from flanking fire. As water was struck at just two feet of depth it was necessary to build breastworks of sod, mud, and sandbags to a height of four feet or more. While the French had carried this work forward to some degree, they had not thickened the walls to British standards and most were deemed incapable of stopping even a bullet's penetration. In some places the French had merely dug down to the waterline without erecting any form of breastwork above the shallow trench. Also lacking were Parados—low walls behind the breastworks that provided protection from shrapnel.

But not only negligent French fortification work disgusted the Canadians. More germane, one divisional report claimed, was that the defences were in a "deplorable state and in a very filthy condition, all the little broken down side trenches and shell holes apparently being used as latrines and burial places for bodies." Behind the Canadian Scottish position both the communication trenches leading to the rear and the open ground behind the front lines were littered with French dead, either half buried or left sprawling on the surface. Many times a soldier started digging only to disinter a French corpse.[40]

On that first morning in the Ypres Salient, Captain William Rae, who commanded No. 2 Company, looked over a parapet with binoculars toward the German lines and puzzled over oddities in the way the enemy frontage was constructed. "The whole top of it had been pulled about and altered, and there were various openings in it, unlike anything seen before." Rae reported his observations to battalion headquarters, which could make no sense of the German changes and so did not pass the intelligence up the line.[41] That the openings were points enabling hoses linked to poison gas cylinders to release their contents was never considered. Although intelligence gathered had alerted the high command that a chemical warfare attack might be imminent, nobody at the lowly level of 1st Canadian Infantry Division had been advised of the danger. So the Canadian Scottish set to improving their defensive works, fearful only of being struck down by shell or bullet as April 22 drew ever closer—when the division would face its first true battle in the most cataclysmic day the war had yet seen.

chapter three

Baptism

- APRIL 22–MAY 4, 1915 -

The British Expeditionary Force had no idea a German offensive was in the works. Instead, Brigadier Field Marshal Sir John French had confidently expected to wrest the initiative into his hands with a British assault on Hill 60 in the southern sector of the Ypres Salient on April 17. This 60-metre hill was really just a tailing pile created during construction of the Ypres-Comines railway in the 1860s, but standing atop the Messines-Passchendaele ridge crest it provided the highest point overlooking the salient, and its loss would deny German artillery spotters an ideal vantage.

To facilitate the attack British engineers had tunneled under Hill 60 and emplaced five mines each loaded with five tons of explosives. Just before the 13th Brigade of II Corps's 5th Division led the assault forward, the mines were set off in one earth-shattering detonation. The German garrison on the hill was decimated, many bodies and body parts hurled pin-wheeling through the air. Fifteen minutes later the British infantry started digging in on the smoking and hugely holed earth mound. German reaction was swift; the hill was subjected to withering artillery fire and repeated counterattacks that came close to throwing the British off. But they hung on tenaciously through four days of bitter fighting. Finally, 5th Division's alarming casualty rate became so severe that on April 21 Brig. Malcolm Smith Mercer's 1st Canadian Infantry Brigade was sent as reinforcements, warned to be ready to join the beleaguered troops on Hill 60 at only an hour's notice.[1] Mercer's 2nd and 4th Battalions were consequently standing by in forward trenches as the Germans put in motion a devastating attack they hoped would force the Allies to abandon the salient entirely.

A deep bulge thrusting about four miles into the German line, the Ypres Salient had been created at the end of October 1914. Salients are

45

naturally dangerous because the troops inside them are exposed to attack from three flanks. But they also require the opponent to commit sufficient forces to guard these three sides, meaning the Ypres Salient was tethering thousands of Germans in place who might have been committed to offensive operations elsewhere. This was precisely why the Allies saw it as strategically vital real estate to hold onto while the Germans equally sought its elimination.

Having lain in readiness since April 15, while waiting for the fickle prevailing winds that would carry the gas into the Allied lines to turn in their favour, conditions finally were right for the Germans on the morning of April 22. The German plan envisioned only two corps—the XXIII Reserve and XXVI Reserve—advancing across a four-mile front to Pilckem Ridge, which was delineated by the Boesinghe-Pilckem-Langemarck-Poelcappelle road. Here the Germans would dig in, their presence on the ridge expected to render it "impossible for the enemy to remain longer in the Ypres salient."[2] The decision to limit the scope of the attack reflected German ambivalence over the attack's purpose. While pinching out the salient was desirable, this offensive arose to achieve two other goals deemed more important. First, the offensive should divert Allied attention away from the Russian front where the Austro-German armies were concentrating for a major offensive in Galicia. Second, it would test the use of poison gas on the battlefield.

Although a signatory to the 1899 and 1906 Hague Conventions banning chemical warfare, Germany had started developing gas weapons in late 1914 for assaults on "positions which were constructed with all the modern methods of the art of fortification." Soon German scientists had the means to release "chlorine gas as a cloud, propelled towards the enemy by a suitable wind." Chlorine, a staple in the dye industry, was readily available and cheap, and could be confined as a gas in existing cylinders. By 1915 Germany was producing thirty-seven tons of chlorine gas daily. Just five days' worth of this production—loaded into 6,000 cylinders—was required for the attack. Although cheap and convenient to produce, chlorine gas remained a crude weapon. Much heavier than air, the gas was slow to dissipate and clung to the ground like a heavy fog, dependent on the all-important wind to carry it in the right direction. Chlorine gas, however, was a brutal weapon that attacked the lungs and immediately incapacitated anyone exposed to it. For the Germans

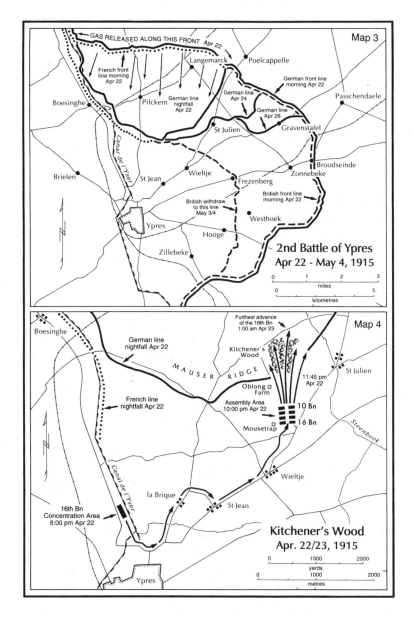

following behind, the gas would serve well. It left no noticeable residue in its wake, and being a visible green cloud, it was easy not to advance into its deadly wake.

The Germans had finished deploying 5,730 gas cylinders and the troops forming the assault wave across a 1,200-yard front running from west of Poelcappelle to a little east of Steenstraat eleven days before the winds finally permitted the attack to proceed. With each passing day, preventing the Allies from discovering the cylinders or concentration of soldiers became more difficult. The Canadian Scottish company commander, Captain William Rae, had not been alone in filing a report about the strange openings appearing at intervals along the German front. A couple of deserters also offered precise intelligence that predicted an imminent gas attack. But British high command gave the reports little credence and French Army general headquarters was even more dismissive, resorting to scolding one divisional commander who instructed his men to prepare themselves to withstand a gas assault. "All this gas business," the French officer was told, "need not be taken seriously." As a result, on April 22 the Allies were completely unprepared.[3]

The Canadian Division at this time held Second Army's left flank, a 4,500-yard front astride a low valley through which flowed the Stroombeek, a tributary of the Steenbeek River. Winding along at distances of one to 2,000 yards behind the division's front was Gravenstafel Ridge, which drew its name from a small hamlet close to the Canadian boundary line with the 28th British Division on its right. To the left was the 45th Algerian Division with the dividing line between these French troops and the Canadians being a road running south from German-held Poelcappelle to Ypres.

On this Thursday, 3rd Canadian Infantry Brigade was deployed next to the Algerians with 2nd Canadian Infantry Brigade to its right. The divisional reserve was provided by 1st Canadian Infantry Brigade, which was also on standby to possibly relieve the British troops embattled on Hill 60. The two brigades holding the front each had two battalions forward, one a short way back providing close support, and its fourth battalion stationed as divisional reserve on the northern outskirts of Ypres.[4] Brig. Richard Turner's 3rd Brigade had the 13th Royal Highlanders and the 15th (48th Highlanders) forward, with the 14th Royal Montreal Regiment providing close support. The Canadian Scottish were back in divisional reserve. Turner's brigade headquarters was in St. Julien.[5]

On this morning Lt.-Col. Leckie had his No. 3 and No. 4 companies placed around a little village called la Brique, which lay east of the Canal de l'Yser within a stone's throw of St. Jean. His other two companies were positioned on the northern edge of Ypres where a factory stood at the head of the canal. Turner's battalion headquarters was on the Rue Dixmude—a road paralleling the canal that led to city centre. When the Germans began shelling the French sector immediately west of the battalion, Leckie ordered the two companies at la Brique moved farther out on the flank so they were hard up against the canal's west bank just outside of Ypres, across the water from the nearest Algerian troops.[6]

Leckie did not act out of any sense of alarm. The tactical move was just a standard precaution in response to the German artillery fire. In the Canadian lines, the air was relaxed with the Canadian Scottish forming by platoons to receive their back pay and learn whether they were among the lucky few to be granted an extended leave period. As the day was milder than normal, some took the opportunity to bathe in the canal while others strolled off into the battered city of Ypres.

This seemingly peaceful day was shattered at 1600 hours by a "furious cannonade" that dropped shells immediately north and west of St. Julien and directly onto Ypres. No. 4 Company's second-in-command, Captain George Willis Jameson, and Lt. Hugh Urquhart rushed up to the top of the canal bank and endeavoured to make out "what sort of fight was going on, there could be no doubt that the enemy were advancing as the shrapnel bursts got nearer and nearer until at last the road east of the Canal from Ypres to Boesinghe was being shelled. We instinctively felt that it was necessary for us to 'stand to' and, on coming down to the billet, found orders for the Company to fall in. The order was carried out in quick time."[7]

Some officers had just been sitting down to a buffet tea at battalion headquarters when they "heard a huge shell coming in with the noise of an express train, such as one we hadn't ever heard before. When the terrific crash of the explosion took place I looked from under the buffet and some of the others were under the table. I consider we all acted with one thought and did excellent time.... We sat down to resume our meal and all was quiet again, when suddenly we heard the warning roar in the air. Again, like streaks of lightning we were in our corners. This time the crash was just outside our door. The glass blew in on the table and there was a crash of timber and falling brick-work. Then they started in earnest, shells, large and small, poured into the town. The cries of the people mingled with the crash of the houses falling to bits, the stampeding of frantic horses, and the shouts of the troops rushing to their quarters. There was the wildest confusion."[8]

Brigade quickly ordered Leckie to move his battalion up the side of the canal to a point just north of Ypres and hold there in readiness for an immediate advance. Once in position, many of the men took cover in an old trench system while those unable to squeeze in began digging slit trenches.[9]

At about 1730 hours, Brig. Turner received a report that "the French on our left were being subjected to heavy artillery bombardment, accompanied by the projection of a pale green cloud of gas of a peculiarly pungent odour. There was at the time some doubt as to whether the gas emanated from the Germans or from the French trenches, but it was shortly determined that it was being used by the enemy to overcome resistance."[10]

The Germans had opened the valves on their cylinders precisely at 1700 hours, releasing more than 160 tons of deadly gas over a period of six to eight minutes on the long-awaited northeasterly breeze. One gas cloud first seemed to be closing on the Canadian lines but it then shifted to drift across the Algerian front and joined with other green-yellow concentrations that created a towering, impenetrable, greenish-yellow fog.[11] Drifting steadily along at five to six miles an hour, the giant cloud was about a half-mile deep by the time it entered the Algerian lines and those of the 87th Territorial Division at its side. There was instant pandemonium, the gas burning men's throats and eyes, causing intense chest pains, and making it virtually impossible to draw breath. Soldiers began spitting blood and many collapsed dizzily and then suffocated. Those who survived fled the trenches.[12]

Advancing at a fifteen-minute interval behind the gas were the leading German infantry formations. Each man wore a primitive gas mask. There was no resistance in the forward trenches as the men stepped in their jackboots over the bodies of the dead and dying whose "faces were discoloured and contorted in grimaces of agony."[13] Within an hour the Germans had penetrated a full mile into the heart of the salient.

The first sign the Canadian Scottish had of the disaster playing out on their left was the sudden appearance of a stream of civilian refugees pouring "down the road, carrying with them their small personal belongings wrapped in bundles and then over the canal bridges came the French soldiers retiring, first by ones and twos and latterly a continuous stream."[14] The French troops were "breathless, bareheaded, without rifles or equipment." Mixed in among the fleeing infantry were French and

Belgian artillery limbers, "without guns, the drivers holding each other up as if they were wounded. The horses were being galloped amongst the refugees regardless of consequences." Canadian Scottish officers rushed to stop some of the men, trying to get information, but they were so panicked it was useless. "The infantry showed signs of acute distress and fear. They came back at the trot, coughing and spluttering, and, although shouted at, would not stop running. At any attempt to halt their retreat they threw up their hands, and between coughs, as they passed, gasped out, '*Asphyxié, Asphyxié!*'"[15]

Realizing the Canadian left flank was likely completely exposed, Leckie issued each man an extra emergency ration and two additional bandoliers containing a hundred rounds of small-arms ammunition. There was no way of knowing where the battalion might be sent or when any re-supply would be possible. For two hours the Canadian Scottish waited and then at 1940 hours received orders to move to brigade headquarters in St. Julien.

Although the direct route passed through St. Jean, the village and its crossroads were being battered by artillery. So the battalion took a roundabout route through la Brique and then on to Wieltje. It was a harrowing journey, shrapnel "bursting over all the roads, and across the parts which were badly shelled we doubled by small parties, escaping with no casualties." Once through Wieltje, Leckie led his men left off the St. Julien road for a fifteen-minute rest. "Our eyes and nostrils," Urquhart noted, "began to smart which we could not understand but realized later that it was by reason of the poison gas. It was now a matter of three or four hours after the original attack and we were a good mile and a quarter behind the trenches held by the French before the attack took place."[16] Nobody in the battalion suspected that the physical discomfort they suffered was caused by gas. They had no sense of why their throats were inordinately tight and dry.

At 2200 hours the battalion halted in a small field near brigade headquarters. Reporting to Turner, Leckie learned that his task was to support closely the 10th Battalion of 2nd Canadian Infantry Brigade in an attack aimed at driving the Germans out of a trench immediately south of woods known as Bois des Cuisiniers (later Kitchener's Wood), due west of St. Julien. Having cleared the trench, the two battalions would then recapture the entire wood.[17]

* * *

The localized counterattacks 1st Canadian Infantry Division was mounting to blunt the German offensive were organized spontaneously by Maj.-Gen. Edwin Alderson, for Second Army's command chain was thrown into confusion by the unexpected offensive. At his headquarters in Hazebrouck, Gen. Horace Smith-Dorrien only learned of the attack at 1845 hours, a full hour and forty-five minutes after the gas was released. Communications were in disarray, the German cannonade having so broken telephone lines across the entire front that passage of information ground to a standstill. Consequently, even after word of the offensive reached army headquarters, staff there were still trying to construct an accurate picture of the crisis facing them two hours later. Finally, confirmation was received that the two French divisions immediately adjacent to the Canadians had been driven back from both their first and second defensive lines, had lost all their supporting artillery, and no resistance was being offered anywhere to the east of the Yser Canal. Smith-Dorrien realized the French rout left Second Army's left flank fully exposed everywhere along an 8,000-yard front, except in the area where the Canadians were rapidly trying to stem the German tide. If the Germans quickly exploited the situation by driving into the yawing gap on the army's left they could overrun Ypres and cut off three divisions—including the Canadians.

Fortunately for the Allies, the German offensive had only met good success where the gas had been concentrated on its left flank—elsewhere the French had held firm. On the left, however, the 52nd Reserve Division of the XXVI Reserve Corps had penetrated deeply into the salient and won Pilckem Ridge by 1740 hours and rapidly carried on another mile to gain Mauser Ridge. On the extreme east of the German assault, 51st Reserve Division, after facing a stiff fight for control of Langemarck village, advanced out of it at 1800 hours with the intention to overrun St. Julien. By nightfall this division's forward elements had overrun Bois des Cuisiniers, later renamed Kitchener's Wood, captured four British guns, and established themselves in a trench line about three-quarters of a mile immediately west of St. Julien.[18]

Alderson, prompted by a series of hand-delivered messages sent by Brig. Richard Turner informing him that the Canadian front was now anchored on St. Julien, had sent an urgent message to 2nd Canadian Infantry Brigade "to hang on and take care of your left." The brigade's commander, Brig. Arthur Currie, had already grasped the severity of the situation and sent his 10th Battalion to reinforce 3rd Brigade. This enabled Turner to assign it to assaulting the German trench line in front of Bois des Cuisiniers with his Canadian Scottish in support. Currie, a Victoria militiaman instrumental in forming the 50th Gordon Highlanders and who had commanded that regiment's first contingent sent to Valcartier until being promoted to brigadier, displayed the canny grasp for tactics that would eventually propel him to the position as Canada's top soldier in the field. Having provided Turner with desperately needed reinforcement, he concentrated his 7th Battalion in the centre of Gravenstafel Ridge in a move that would further protect his threatened left flank should 3rd Brigade lose control of St. Julien.

Meanwhile, Smith-Dorrien had recognized that the frontage held by the Canadian division's two forward brigades was vital to re-establishing control over the situation. To bolster forces there, he released 1st Canadian Infantry Brigade from its role as divisional reserve and returned it to Alderson's command. The division commander immediately placed the brigade's 2nd and 3rd Battalions directly under Turner's authority.

Realizing that the Canadians were insufficiently strong to turn back the Germans without additional support, Smith-Dorrien reinforced Alderson with the 2nd East York Battalion from 28th British Division and promised him a free hand in both determining how to meet the offensive and calling up additional reinforcements as needed. Consequently, over the following two days, a total of thirty-three battalions would come at various times under Alderson's direct command.

The French also realized that the Canadians were pivotal to countering the German offensive. A liaison officer at Alderson's headquarters pleaded with him to immediately launch a counterattack that could serve to support a planned advance by the Algerian Division to regain Pilckem Ridge. Turner's assault on Bois des Cuisiniers, Alderson decided, would precisely serve this purpose as well as forestalling a German attack on St. Julien.[19] When Alderson asked for assurance that the Algerians would in fact attack, the liaison officer expressed dismay that there could be any doubt of this. So the Canadian plan developed in ignorance of the fact that the Algerian division had been effectively destroyed. The 10th and 16th Battalions would counterattack unsupported by any matching French effort.[20]

At 3rd Brigade headquarters, Turner, believing the French attack was about to begin any moment, was anxious to get the assault on the woods going. But he was worried about the fact that the Canadians lacked any experience in night attacks. The risk of the two battalions losing their way or becoming badly entangled with each other during the assault seemed all too likely, so Turner opted to simply have the two units advance one behind the other in a rigid formation. Such attacks were something the Canadians rehearsed so many times during training at Valcartier they could do so blindfolded—or at least on a pitch-black night. The 10th Battalion, Turner decided, would lead "on a frontage of two companies and with distances of 30 yards between lines" and the rest of the companies of the two battalions would follow in precisely the same formation.

The 16th Battalion lined up 30 yards behind the 10th with its No. 2 Company, under Captain William Rae, forward on the left and No. 4 Company, under Captain John Geddes, the right. Precisely 30 yards behind, Captain George Ross's No. 1 Company was on the left and Captain Cecil Merritt's No. 3 Company the right.[21] Together the two battalions numbered about 1,500 men, divided neatly into eight measured lines each of which would go forward with its men so closely aligned that their shoulders almost brushed. Just thirteen guns from four Canadian and British artillery batteries were available to support the hasty attack.

Assembled in their rigid lines, the two battalions stood in the darkness adjacent to a small farm called Mouse Trap Farm a short distance from brigade headquarters. Here, Turner's second-in-command, Lt.-Col. Garnet Hughes, walked up to give Leckie and his 10th Battalion counterpart, a tough Calgary rancher named Lt.-Col. Russell Boyle, last-minute instructions. The two battalion commanders congratulated Hughes on his thirty-fifth birthday, which most of the officers at brigade headquarters had been celebrating as the German offensive started. Hughes, who was Minister of Militia and Defence Sam Hughes's son, pointed dramatically toward the forest, advised them to follow the North Star, and then ordered them to advance when ready. While Hughes was giving his instructions, several 10th Battalion officers had been consulting their topographical maps and realized that 300 yards southwest of the woods stood Oblong Farm, which was likely in German hands. They asked Boyle to consider detaching at least a platoon to clear the farm to ensure it could not be used by the Germans to bring machine-gun fire against the Canadian right flank. Boyle brushed aside the advice. Instead, he turned to his men and yelled: "We have been aching for a fight and now we are going to get it."[22]

Leckie offered no rhetoric. In his usual conversational voice, Leckie simply told the Canadian Scottish to shed their packs and greatcoats and then fix bayonets. Everyone recognized the import of this order. They were "for it" and would be fighting with cold steel. As the minutes stretched, a solitary figure walked through the ranks shaking hands with each man he passed. This was Canon Frederick Scott, the 3rd Brigade's beloved fifty-three-year-old chaplain. "A great day for Canada, boys! A great day for Canada, boys!" he declared. Close by, a field battery fired a single round every five minutes into the wood to conceal the sounds of the infantry forming up. Then, at 2345 the Canadians advanced into the open ground that stretched between eight hundred and a thousand yards to the edge of the wood.[23]

* * *

The Canadians knew nothing about the strength or composition of enemy forces facing them, for there had been no time for any reconnaissance. Advancing in the dark, they could see neither the German trench nor any sign of enemy troops. All the leading Canadian Scottish could see were the shadowy forms of the 10th Battalion men ahead of them. Each company had two platoons ahead of the other two and, in No. 4 Company, Lt. Urquhart's 15 Platoon was leading on the left while Lt. Victor John Hasting's 13 Platoon was to his right. At first the orderliness of this formation held but, once the troops had advanced a short way, it became clear the ground was not as open as expected. Urquhart came to a ditch bordered by a hedge and saw that 13 Platoon was on the other side and moving away from the obstacle while his own men were following the line of the hedge, which veered to the right. In the dark the hedge seemed impenetrable, so the only option was for 15 Platoon to spring alongside the hedge until they came to a break. Passing through, they jumped the ditch and ran to catch up with 13 Platoon.

German artillery began falling on the field at a rate that suggested the gunners were still seeking the range, but several men were struck down by shrapnel. Before the attack began Urquhart and the other officers in the battalion had only been told by Hughes that they were attacking a wood across the field. Urquhart kept straining his eyes for some sight of trees, but all he saw ahead was "a dark blur." They had crossed about 500 yards and now seemed to be in a level pasture free of further hedges or ditches.[24]

Such was not the case for Captain William Rae's No. 2 Company. From the outset Rae's men had been forced to find ways through thick hedges, jump one ditch after another, and cut openings in several wire fences. Then a German flare arced into the sky. The Canadians were suddenly bathed by its harsh glare and, a second later, Oblong Farm erupted with tongues of flame as dozens of machine guns and rifles opened fire.[25]

There was no cover, nothing the men could do but keep advancing toward the woods as the Germans in the farm tore into their flank. Urquhart walked "over absolutely bare ground as [if] on a rifle range going from the Butts to the Firing Point with ceaseless angry zip, zip of bullets from rifles and machine guns. You could see the spit of fire from the rifles to our front and left. Then came the cries of those who were hit, the cracking of the bullets so close to our ears made them sing and it was impossible to make yourself heard."[26]

"I know now the meaning of a hail of bullets," Rae later wrote his mother. "I never dreamt there could be anything like it. At first I never for one moment expected to come through alive, but afterwards in some extraordinary way I made up my mind I was not going to be hit and went right on."[27] All around other men fell. They had been ordered to make no sounds. No shouting, no cheering as they advanced. But with bullets scything them down, with those coming from behind trying not to step on the fallen underfoot, with many of the wounded screaming in agony, the need for reassurance and to muster courage to keep going overcame this order. "Come on, Seaforths!" men in Rae's company cried. "Come on, Camerons," Urquhart's platoon shouted. "Come on, the 16th!" others bellowed as they realized all the Highlanders were in this together. One soldier broke from the line, screaming and tearing at his shirt which had burst into flame. Captain Geddes had been knocked to his knees with a mortal wound, but still urging No. 4 Company on he crawled forward a short distance before collapsing. Doggedly the ever-shrinking battalion made "for the spit of fire and flickering line of flame showing up in front against the darkness of the wood."[28]

Rae's company twice halted in the midst of this hell storm to straighten its line, the second pause coming while only about forty yards short of the woods. There was no set formation now, the 16th had overtaken the 10th and the two advanced the last part of the distance intermingled. Suddenly, with just yards between the Canadians and Germans the fire from the latter melted eerily away. The men let out a mighty cheer and then without Rae or any of the other officers shouting a command "rushed right at the German trench."

As they plunged in they found that "barely a few of them waited for us and these were shot or bayoneted at once. I jumped clear over the trench and rushed into the wood with some men. It was full of undergrowth and most difficult to get through but ultimately we came to the far side, the Germans flying before us. I cannot tell you everything that happened, but ultimately we established a line about 1000 yards back from the original German front."[29] Rae and the others who had spontaneously driven on through the wood rather than holding up at the trench began digging in where they were.

Moving through the woods one Can Scot "vaguely saw some Germans and rushed at the nearest one. My bayonet must have hit his equipment and glanced off, but luckily for me, another chap running beside me bayoneted him before he got me. By this time I was wildly excited and shouting and rushing into the wood up a path towards a big gun which was pointed away from us. Going through the wood we ran into several Germans, but I had now lost confidence in my bayonet and always fired."[30] The gun the soldier saw was one of the British field guns overrun by the Germans.

Urquhart, too, had plowed into the woods, firing his revolver at retreating Germans until it jammed. He scooped up a rifle lying next to a 10th Battalion man who had fallen seconds before right in front of him. Some horses were tied to trees in the wood and Urquhart noticed one "standing on three legs, holding one leg up as if it had been hit by a bullet. We rushed through the wood coming out on the further side from the German trench we captured. German flares were now going up behind us to the left and it looked to us as if we had broken through the

German line. We started to entrench on the far side of the wood.... Col. Boyle of the 10th I met on the right of the wood a short time afterward, also Col. Leckie.... Col. Boyle was wounded about this time. Col. Leckie was directing the digging in and giving orders that the 10th who were collected in a group near a house were to connect up from the hedge where we were digging in to the right where a further party of the 16th had started to entrench."[31]

Boyle had been asking a junior 16th Battalion officer about where the Canadian Scottish were deploying. Drawing out a map, Boyle turned on an electric torch, pronounced "he was satisfied with the information given," and then started walking back to his men. Moments later he was struck by a machine-gun burst. Five slugs shattered his thigh. Mortally wounded, the battalion commander died three days later in hospital.[32]

As far as Urquhart could determine, the 10th Battalion men were not digging in, possibly because its command structure was in disarray after Boyle's death. Hoping to help restore order, Urquhart approached the battalion's second-in-command, Major Joseph MacLaren, and relayed Leckie's orders about digging in. Seemingly distracted, MacLaren replied that "he was wounded in the leg" and headed toward the rear.[33] MacLaren was eventually loaded into an ambulance, but it was struck by an artillery shell while passing through Ypres and the officer was killed.[34]

Urquhart and the few officers who were left finally got the men of both battalions entrenching. The situation was dangerously confused, with no clear idea about where the Canadian flanks rested or whether they could expect any support or reinforcement. German fire was coming from several houses to the north of the wood.[35]

Leckie told Urquhart he was going back to find out whether reinforcements would be forthcoming and advised Rae that he was in command of the forward position. Back at the captured trench, Leckie looked around and estimated that the Germans had lost about 100 killed, 250 wounded, and 30 uninjured men taken prisoner. More Germans seemed to be milling in the woods attempting to surrender, but Leckie could spare no men to deal with them. He cautioned the men within hearing "against dealing harshly with prisoners." Tempers were hot as the battalions began assessing how badly they had been cut up. Leckie scribbled out a brief report and an urgent plea for reinforcements and sent it by runner to the brigade.[36]

About 0100 hours on April 23, one of 16th Battalion's machine-gun squads brought its Colt machine gun forward. The machine-gun officer, Lt. Reginald Hibbert Tupper, had the gun set out on the flank in an attempt to enfilade the German trenches in front of Oblong Farm and the area extending back from the farm to the southwest corner of the wood. This section of wood had yet to be cleared and seemed strongly held by the Germans, who often shouted that the Canadians had best surrender for they were surrounded. While the men could ignore the verbal harassment, there was nothing they could do to stop the deadly crossfire cutting into their lines from the German positions. The enemy fire from the southwest kept intensifying.

As the machine gunners ventured forth to try to meet the German fire with their own, Lt.-Col. David Watson brought two companies of his 2nd Battalion into the woods while sending a third company to directly attack Oblong Farm. Soon intense gunfire could be heard from the direction of the farm and then all fell silent, leading Watson to advise Leckie that he thought his men had succeeded in taking that position. The two battalion commanders decided these reinforcements should consequently try to clear the trenches in the woods, but the two companies had too few men to succeed at this venture. A thirty-minute assault launched at 0130 hours was finally repulsed. During the course of this fight, Tupper's machine-gun squad was "practically surrounded and subjected to intense fire." Tupper was "dangerously hit, and rendered so helpless that he was only able to drag himself back into the Canadian lines lying flat on the ground." When the 2nd Battalion attack failed, the Germans used the opportunity to charge and overrun the gun, taking two of its crew prisoner. But the crew managed to destroy its breach and block, rendering it useless. One gunner, who managed to escape, had his hand smashed by a bullet. Later, he discovered his kilt had been riddled by fourteen rounds.[37]

On the northern edge of the wood, the news that the flank remained exposed was sobering. Unless it was reinforced before morning, Rae considered his position would be untenable and that his men would soon be cut off from the rear. Rae ordered a withdrawal, just as the first glow of light touched the horizon. Leaving behind small groups of men to guard the recovered British artillery pieces, Rae led the rest of the battalion back. The men moved so quietly that the Germans failed to twig to what was happening, so the withdrawal neither attracted artillery fire nor any pursuit by infantry. When these troops arrived back at the trench on the edge of the woods, however, it was clear there was insufficient room for all of them. A large group was sent 150 yards out into the field to create a secondary trench line, which they finished digging just before dawn.

April 24 dawned clear and sunny, bearing the promise of an unusually hot spring day to come. A lull descended on the battlefield, few sounds of gunfire or artillery heard. In their trenches, the men of the 16th and 10th Battalions took stock of their situation and reflected on all that had happened in that night "which seemed like a life-time."[38]

One Canadian Scottish diarist noted that "the fellows looked frightfully tired and discouraged." As the light improved they saw on their left flank the German position in the woods that had subjected them to such deadly fire. Stretching back across the field they had crossed, rows of their dead lay strewn. "On certain parts of it the bodies were heaped; on others they were lying in a straight line as killed by the enfilade machine-gun fire. The men of the different companies of the 16th could be picked out by the colour of the kilt—the yellow stripe of the Gordons, the white of the Seaforths, the red of the Camerons, the dark green of the Argylls—with the 10th Battalion men in their khaki uniforms mingled everywhere amongst the Highlanders. [Despite the battalion officers having earlier decided that allowing the men to wear four different kilts would not do and a simple khaki one would replace the various tartans, the replacements had not yet reached the field so the men were still fighting in the tartans that identified their original regiment.] Slight movements of some of the bodies showed that life still lingered. Attempts were being made to get help to these men, but the spurts of dust, knocked up by the bullets hitting around the rescue party, indicated that the ground was under a fire. At last a stretcher-bearer was hit; he pitched forward on his face, whereupon the enemy's fire was much increased, and the relief work came to an end."[39]

With Leckie in command of both battalions, his brother Jack was responsible for 16th Battalion while Major Dan Ormond—the most senior surviving 10th Battalion officer—had charge of that unit. Fearing a counterattack was imminent, the officers began hurriedly regrouping their battered forces. The trench remained overly crowded and the first action was to put the dead up over the parapet and to dig small nooks into which the wounded could be sheltered. While some men began extending the trench on the right flank, others were sent crawling back through the cover of a mustard patch to Leckie's headquarters area in a trench about a thousand yards west of St. Julien. Within a couple of hours a coherent defensive line had taken shape.

Lt. Urquhart knew in his gut that they were in for a shelling like they had never seen before and so was not surprised when an aircraft appeared overhead at 0530, lazily circling, its Iron Crosses marking it as German. Surely it was an artillery spotter plane determining the coordinates of the trench. Shortly thereafter the first shells fell and with the plane still overhead to correct the fire the guns soon "got our mark. Some men were blown out of [the] trench, others injured by shrapnel, others killed by shock." From the left flank of the woods, machine-gun fire made any movement hazardous and hindered evacuation of wounded. "Difficult to get back to dressing station with wounded and some men hit in so doing," Urquhart noted in his diary, "so ultimately we had to forbid men to cross and kept wounded in trench, lifting dead over parapet. Very long day and glad when anxious time came to an end. All night we were standing to, every five minutes, and dawn was just as anxiously looked for as dusk."[40]

* * *

While the 16th and 10th Battalions endured a day of being battered by artillery fire, the Second Battle of Ypres raged on across an ever-widening front as more British and Canadian battalions rushed to close the dangerous gap created by the previous day's gas attack. Gen. Smith-Dorrien ordered V Corps to carry out an attack between Bois des Cuisiniers and the Yser Canal at 1440 hours, but then delayed it to 1626 while failing to notify the supporting artillery which duly began firing guns at 1445. Duly alerted, the Germans met the advancing battalions with withering fire from Mauser Ridge, attempting to deny heroic efforts that carried many troops to within 200 yards of the enemy trenches. Although unable to regain Mauser Ridge, the British troops established a strong defensive line 600 yards from the German forward trenches.

Although the initial impetus of their offensive had been blunted, the Germans were now committed to trying to destroy the salient. At

0400 hours on April 24 they attempted to create a new breakthrough at the salient's northern tip with a second gas attack directed at the 2nd and 3rd Canadian infantry brigades. As this attack struck well to the northeast of the woods, the Canadian Scottish were unaware of the cause behind the sudden crescendo of gunfire from that direction. Along with the remnants of the 10th Battalion, they were in the middle of being relieved from their forward position by the 2nd Battalion. Although the changeover was to have been completed before dawn, various delays resulted in the withdrawal taking place in full daylight. Their destination was 3rd Canadian Infantry Brigade headquarters, which was now situated about a mile to the south near the hamlet of Wieltje. Rather than risk trying to move in the open, Leckie led the men in single file along a shallow ditch bordering a narrow road that ran in the desired direction. Crawling on hands and knees along the mud-mired ditch to avoid the sniper fire cracking overhead, each man deepened the parallel grooves that had been created by those who had passed down its length ahead of him. At Wieltje, the 16th Battalion set up a defensive position in a series of dugouts near brigade headquarters.

Virtually the entire 1st Canadian Infantry Division sector was being subjected to a massive artillery barrage, so that movement anywhere in the headquarters area was hazardous. Crouched in their holes, the Canadian Scottish could glimpse "the advance of our troops under shell fire [but] also ... the advance of some of the Germans." Urquhart recognized that much of the artillery raining down consisted of "woolly bears, loud-noised, green-smoked shrapnel shells." He also heard "a constant rattle of musketry beyond St. Julien towards the north-eastern face of the Salient." Soon the gunfire spread to the woods that the two battalions had handed over to 2nd Battalion. It seemed the Canadians out on the sharp end were fighting for their very survival.[41]

And so they were, particularly where the chlorine gas cloud drifted into the lines precisely at the join between 2nd and 3rd Brigade's frontages, held respectively by the former's 8th Battalion and the latter's 15th Battalion. Issued cotton bandoliers with instructions to urinate on these and then cover their mouths in order to ward off the effects of the gas, the men duly followed instructions but many collapsed vomiting, blinded, and writhing in agony as their lungs were seared anyway. In 8th Battalion's sector the gas was less concentrated, which enabled some men to withstand its effects and still man their positions on the parapets, while the company farthest from the junction points was entirely unaffected. Consequently this battalion was able to maintain a rapid rate of fire despite many of their Ross rifles repeatedly jamming so that the men had to kick the firing bolts loose with their boots or the flat of an entrenching shovel. Faced with stiff resistance on this front, the German advance here foundered. But in the area held by the 15th Battalion the gas had killed the majority of the men or rendered them helpless. German infantry flooded through the resulting gap and drove toward Gravenstafel Ridge. By mid-morning the apex of the salient began collapsing inward and at 1500 hours St. Julien was overrun.

Yet remnants of 2nd Brigade still clung tenaciously to Gravenstafel Ridge and throughout Sunday, April 25, the slaughter continued as Canadian and British battalions frantically counterattacked the Germans, who were still seeking to keep the momentum of their advance going. For a week the battle raged until on May 3 the badly mauled Canadian division was pulled back. While the battle would continue almost to the end of May, the Germans were never able to regain the initiative, so the salient held. In those first few days, the Canadian division's holding "in the face of an enemy who by employing numbers of infantry supported by a preponderance of heavy artillery and machine guns attempting to exploit the advantage gained by his introduction of poison gas into modern warfare" saved the salient despite German advances in some sectors of three miles.

But the British Expeditionary Force's losses were staggering—59,275 casualties between April 22 and May 31. For its part, 1st Canadian Infantry Division reported 208 officers and 5,828 other ranks killed, wounded, or taken prisoner between April 15 and May 3.[42]

Few Canadian battalions had suffered more than the Canadian Scottish. "We had a terrible charge," Captain Rae had written his mother on April 28, "and it is only by God's mercy that I came out alive. 26 officers went in and only 9 came out unhurt. I lost all my officers."[43] Urquhart echoed Rae's dismay in his diary note of April 26. "What heavy casualties. 17 officers out of 26 put out of action. Captains [John] Geddes, [Cecil] Merritt, [Hamilton] Fleming, [James Herrick] McGregor killed. Captain [George Willis] Jamieson missing [and later found to have been killed]. Lieuts. George Ager, [John Gibson] Kenworthy, [Victor

Alexander] MacLean, [Angus] Armour, [Graham] Ainslie, [Edward] Gilliatt, [Reginald] Tupper, Captains [Sydney] Goodall and [George] Ross all wounded. Loss in men about 450 and in Camerons 117—what a terrible toll!"[44] Although Urquhart didn't know it, Captain Ross and Lt. Ager were also dead. Wounded, Lt. Victor MacLean had ordered his men to leave him where he had fallen in the woods as the Germans were but 20 yards' distant. "He had bade the men good-bye," so they could escape unimpeded. MacLean was taken prisoner.[45]

Merritt, who had suffered a desperate wound during the charge, had been dragged to the safety of the captured trench. When two of his men volunteered to carry the officer back across the open ground to safety, Merritt refused to expose them to the risk. Shortly before dawn, worried the Germans were going to counterattack, Merritt raised himself up and started issuing orders to get his men ready. A German sniper round struck Merritt in the head and he fell over dead.[46]

Fleming, who had predicted his inevitable death would come "early in the game," had been shot in the knee during the first moments of the charge. Pausing only a moment to bandage the wound with a handkerchief, he led No. 2 Company on to carry the trench. When fire from a German machine-gun post just in front of the woods threatened the tenuous Canadian hold on this position, Fleming quickly assembled a mixed force of men from both the 10th and 16th battalions. Jumping onto the parapet, Fleming led the men in a rush on the machine gun, but the fire from it was so intense that the force reeled back into the cover of the trench. Fleming carried on alone, disappearing into the darkness. Next morning, his body was found sprawled with one foot resting on the top of the post's parapet. Merritt, Fleming, and Geddes had been three of the battalion's original company commanders while the other, Major Lorne Ross, had died earlier on April 16. The loss of these four senior officers dealt the Canadian Scottish command chain a crippling blow.

The battalion's final casualty toll was 153 other ranks killed between April 22 and May 4, with another 239 wounded, and 30 lost as prisoners for a total of 422. Nine officers died, seven were wounded, and one was taken prisoner.[47] The Canadian Scottish had been effectively cut in half. But there would be no rest to integrate reinforcements. On May 14, after only ten days out of the line, the Canadian division marched urgently toward the Festubert-Givenchy area and a return to battle.

chapter four

Blown to Hell

- MAY 14–JUNE 13, 1915 -

During the eight months preceding the Second Battle of Ypres, the Canadian Scottish had overcome their initial distrust of those who wore different tartans or spoke with accents betraying differing roots or class backgrounds to become something akin to a family. Before that deadly charge on the night of April 22–23, casualties had been few and the Can Scots had often acted like older brothers to the replacements by helping hone their survival skills and teach them the tricks of trench life. By May 9, when Lt.-Gen. Edwin Alderson addressed the battalion by reading messages from all parts of the Empire that praised the stand the division had made at Ypres, the veterans stood among an equal number of strangers, and it was the distant rumble of artillery most of them heard more keenly than Alderson's voice. Out there in the distance somewhere men died and that "gave a warning of the chances of the future, which distracted their attention from listening to the praise of what had been done in the past."[1]

On the evening of May 14, as 3rd Canadian Infantry Brigade marched out of the salient, the survivors of Ypres kept a wary distance from the replacements. Most of these had joined the battalion on April 28, arriving from England as part of what was known as the Prince Rupert Company. Raised and commanded by Cyrus Wesley Peck, a forty-four-year-old businessman from the British Columbia coastal town, the company numbered 225 men. With a stout, egg-shaped body, and a thick, full moustache, Peck lumbered walrus-like about rather than strode, suffered asthma, and hardly looked a soldier. While Lt.-Col. Robert Leckie gave him command of No. 1 Company, he distributed the Prince Rupert men throughout the rest of the battalion. Leckie did the same with a 213-strong draft of reinforcements raised and sent overseas by the 50th Gordon Highlanders in Victoria when it arrived on May 7.

Not all the reinforcements sent to the battalion were newcomers. A small number drawn from the battalion's base camp in England had been brought over by the popular Seaforth lieutenant Roderick Ogle Bell-Irving. This contingent included nine other lieutenants, who were a welcome addition because many platoons had fallen under the command of sergeants or even corporals when their officers had been killed or wounded. The son of a prominent Vancouver merchant and benefactor of the city's Seaforth Highlanders, the twenty-four-year-old Bell-Irving had quit a clerking job when war was declared and quickly been posted as a Seaforth lieutenant. To his dismay, the young officer had been designated surplus and left at the training depot in England when the battalion moved to France. Bell-Irving had vowed that nothing would keep him from seeing front-line service now that he was back in the Canadian Scottish fold.

Just before midnight the Canadian Scottish reached their billets near Merville where the First British Army's reserve camp behind the Festubert lines was situated. Reporting to 3rd Canadian Infantry Brigade headquarters, Leckie learned that an attack was likely within twenty-four hours to support the French Tenth Army's staggering offensive in the area of the Artois Plateau between Lens and Arras.

The Artois Plateau sloped into the Douai Plain between these two communities, and here the German Sixth Army held a seven-mile-wide and four-mile-deep salient not unlike the Allied one at Ypres. Vimy Ridge, which formed a hard barrier cutting across five miles of the salient's tip, had been the primary objective of a French attack by three divisions launched on May 8. Although successful in breaking the German forward defences for a two-and-a-half-mile gain that almost won Vimy Ridge, the assault had been halted at the last minute when enemy reinforcements arrived before reserves could come forward from a holding position seven miles to the French rear. A slugging match ensued that a week later had inflicted 100,000 French and 75,000 German casualties.

First British Army had initially supported the French effort with a two-pronged offensive in the Neuve Chapelle area where its right flank adjoined Tenth Army's. This attack, later called the Battle of Aubers Ridge, had failed to gain ground. The French insisted the British either try again or extend their lines to free a Tenth Army division for redeployment on the Vimy Ridge front. Not wanting to have to attack

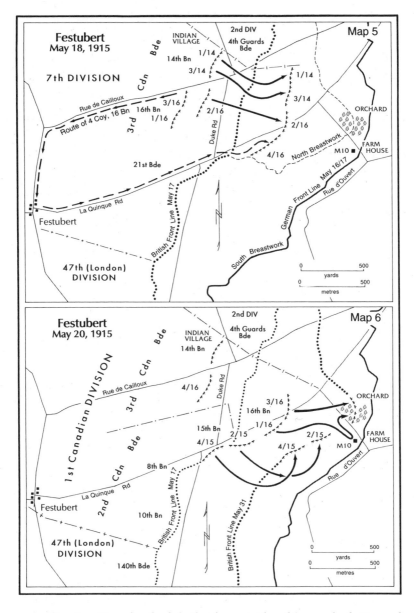

according to a French schedule that he considered too rushed, General Sir John French ordered 1st British Division to take over 5,500 yards held by the French 58th Division on May 15.

But the British general also intended to support the French by striking near Festubert across a 5,000-yard frontage west of Givenchy-lez-la-Bassée. The B.E.F. commanders decided to attack here primarily because the Neuve Chapelle area had been the focus of British operations for months before. Immediately north of the designated area lay Aubers Ridge, where the May 9 assault had gone awry. Responding to the repeated British operations here, the Germans had heavily fortified their lines so that barbed wire was arrayed in 50-foot-deep belts and a carefully integrated and overlapping system of machine-gun posts ensured every square inch of wire fell within a killing zone. The Germans had also dug deeper trenches than any Allied forces and turned some sections into bunkers with good overhead protection from artillery bombardment. With two to three mutually supportive trench lines, they were ready to defend in depth—a strategy recently picked up from the French and much improved upon.

First Army's Gen. Douglas Haig well knew of the German preparations, but had conceived a new tactic for overcoming them. Haig acknowledged the "defences in our front are so carefully and so strongly made, and mutual support with machine-guns is so complete, that in order to demolish them a *long methodical bombardment* will be necessary by heavy artillery (guns and howitzers) before Infantry are sent forward to the attack." Haig wanted to deploy 60-pounders and 15-inch siege howitzers with careful observation of every shot to ensure that the German strongpoints were fully destroyed before committing the infantry. While this methodical process would be a long one, Haig believed that such "a deliberate and persistent attack" would cause the enemy to "be gradually and relentlessly worn down by exhaustion and loss until his defence collapses."[2]

French was little impressed by Haig's idea. While he doubted surprise could possibly be achieved in the Neuve Chapelle area, a prolonged and surgically directed bombardment would guarantee the Germans were ready and waiting. But, hoping the sheer volume of artillery would batter the Germans senseless for a brief time, French limited the offensive goal to a mere 1,000-yard penetration—roughly one-third of the distance the British sought in the original Aubers Ridge attack. French—and Haig agreed—no longer considered winning ground of much value. Victory, the British generals had decided, would be won by the side that inflicted greatest attrition on the other. Literally, the only way to win the war was to kill and maim so many enemy troops until Germany could no longer man the front in sufficient strength to prevent a general breakthrough.

Haig began bombarding a 5,000-yard stretch of front north of Festubert on May 13. With methodical precision, 443 powerful howitzers slowly and deliberately saturated the German front with each firing fifty rounds every twenty-four hours at the enemy parapets and support and communications trenches. Meanwhile, a far greater number of regular field guns concentrated on tearing gaps in the wire and spraying the infantry with shrapnel. For sixty hours the guns thundered, firing a total of more than 100,000 shells.

On the night of May 15–16, the British attack began with two divisions—the 2nd British and the Indian Meerut—advancing under cover of darkness. At daybreak they were joined by the 7th British Division, which had been judged too unfamiliar with the ground to carry out a night assault. Despite the prolonged bombardment, Haig's hope that starting the offensive at night would catch the Germans off guard was partially realized.[3]

But after some initial gains the two British divisions proved unable to close a gap between them during the course of the day's fighting and at nightfall the Germans broke contact, except in the area of Ferme de Bois, where they held on to a series of stout outposts, and withdrew to a new line about 500 yards behind La Quinque rue.

Believing the German withdrawal meant they had been broken by the sustained bombardment, on the morning of May 17 Haig ordered his I Corps to establish a strong front astride La Quinque rue with the axis of advance directed southward toward La Bassée Canal. As the British divisions involved in the attack so far had come from this corps, Haig placed 3rd Canadian Infantry Brigade under I Corps command and assigned it as a reserve to the 7th British Division. All day long the British attacks were turned back by fierce German fire. That evening Haig ordered I Corps to try again in the morning and Brig.-Gen. Robert Turner was informed that his Canadians would lead the way.[4]

* * *

The moment Turner had received orders attaching his brigade to 7th Division, he had got the troops marching toward the front. Turner then hurried ahead to establish his headquarters in a farmhouse on the rue de l'Epinette, about a mile-and-a-half behind the British front line prior to the offensive's start. By 0915 on May 17, the battalions were deployed in nearby assembly trenches and their commanders sitting down in the farmhouse for a conference. Turner warned they could be sent into action at any moment, but their immediate job was to move the battalions to a position astride the former British front line around a cluster of houses called Indian Village. No roads connected rue de l'Epinette and Indian Village, so the men would march cross-country. Although each battalion hurriedly dispatched a reconnaissance party to map out respective routes, by the time they returned the brigade had been stood down. Then, at 2000 hours, each battalion marched through steady drizzle about five miles back to new billets—which for the 16th Battalion was located in the village of Essars, near Béthune. It took two hours to complete the march and not until 0100 hours on May 18 were the last troops settled.

Most were sleeping soundly when new orders arrived at 0400 hours demanding the brigade return to Indian Village. The Canadian Scottish got underway at 0645, with the officers noting that their men were "dead tired after so much running about and not fit for much work. It seems a funny proposition taking us back so far for such little rest."[5] The battalions did not reach Indian Village until 1600 hours because of the need to march cross-country. Almost immediately Nos. 2 and 4 Companies were ordered to assemble in a nearby field. Captain William Rae still commanded No. 2 while Captain Victor Hastings, who had been promoted to captain only two months earlier, had taken over No. 4 after Major John Geddes's death in the attack on the woods. In a quick huddle Lt.-Col. Robert Leckie told the two officers that No. 2 was to carry out a frontal attack alongside two companies of the Royal Montreal Regiment directed toward an orchard east of La Quinque rue. No. 4 Company would simultaneously "turnabout, make a detour through the village of Festubert, and move up la Quinque rue to the cover of the old British front line breastwork, where a British staff officer would be waiting. This officer would furnish further particulars of the advance, which in a general way was to proceed by way of a German breastwork communication trench, then to deploy, and attack the Orchard from the right simultaneously with the frontal attack. Both frontal and flank attacks were timed to converge on their objective at 5 p.m."[6]

Such a complex scheme conducted at night was obviously fraught with difficulties. Not only did the companies in the frontal attack have to advance over ground crisscrossed by deep drainage ditches, but they also had to clamber over several abandoned British and German breastwork systems erected because the shallow water table had made trenching impossible. There was no time to reconnoitre the ground. The Canadians would have to hope that the topography matched their maps, which, due to a printing error, were upside down so that north was at the bottom rather than the top. In an attempt to provide navigation markers for setting out a line of advance the British cartographers had assigned features such as hedges, trench intersections, and buildings numbers, but the ground had been so churned up and torn by artillery fire that the map bore little resemblance to reality. The challenge Captain Rae faced in keeping No. 2 Company headed toward its objective and in line with the two Royal Montreal Regiment companies was minor compared to the trek required of Captain Hastings. To gain the orchard, No. 4 Company faced a route march of 5,000 yards. Somewhere out there, a staff officer supposedly waited to guide them to their start line, but Hastings had to rely on a soldier from the British Queen's Own Cameron Highlanders to lead him to this individual. If the staff officer could not be found, Hastings had no idea where the company's start line was located.

Not surprisingly, the plan began unravelling from the outset. As the three companies began moving toward the objective in extended formation, the Germans zeroed in on the troops with heavy artillery fire. Most of the shells fell on the left and centre of the Montrealers, which caused them to begin shrinking to the right across the front of Rae's advancing Can Scots. All three companies became hopelessly entangled and lost all cohesion, so that finally the officers just herded the soldiers into hodgepodge clusters and led them onward. Finally the attackers were forced to ground by the withering fire about 500 yards short of the orchard with men scattered on either side of la Quinque rue.

No. 4 Company, meanwhile, had come under intense artillery fire while passing through the ruins of Festubert. Breaking into small groups to dodge through the gauntlet of shells, the company had gained a breastwork where the British Highlander assured Hastings the staff officer should be waiting. But there was no sign of the man. Hastings consulted his map, but was unable to accurately fix his location in relation to the orchard or the German communication trench the company was supposed to follow to gain it. They would just have to push out into the open and hope to find the communication trench where he thought it might lie. Realizing that they had a lot of ground to cover the orchard and would have to move rapidly to reach it on schedule, Hastings ordered the company to dump their 60-pound packs where they stood and then led them out into the open.[7]

To his relief, the company quickly stumbled on the communication trench. This proved to be intermittently either a trench or raised parapet that provided less cover than hoped. Hastings told Lt. Hugh Urquhart to take point with the bomb throwers assigned to the company close behind and the rest of the men following by rifle platoons in file. "We were still heavily shelled," Urquhart wrote later, "and the sights were pretty gruesome as many parts of parapet had been blown in, dead were lying round, their bodies terribly mangled. Found one part of trench blown in." He paused here, because the bomb throwers were balking at going further. Deciding the only way to keep them going was to lead by example, Urquhart clambered over the collapsed trench and dashed forward. Coming around a turn in the trench, the lieutenant stumbled upon a Wiltshire Regiment machine-gun post. The officer there said his men held the most advanced section of the British line and asked what Urquhart was doing there. Only then did he realize the bombers were not behind him. Quickly he scribbled a note that read, "Canadians to come on," and had one of the Wiltshires carry it back while he and the officer examined the map and confirmed that No. 4 Company was on track to reach the orchard. After a long wait the runner reappeared. "Canadians are all blown to Hell," he said. "There is terrible murder up there."[8]

Finally, three of the bombers appeared. Leaving two with the Wiltshires, Urquhart led the other on a reconnaissance toward a cluster of houses and trees he hoped might be the orchard. Only a few minutes out, the two stumbled upon a wounded Royal Montreal Regiment major, bleeding heavily through crudely applied bandages covering a multitude of wounds. Obviously dying, the major could only gasp that the frontal attack had failed. Ahead of him, Urquhart could now see dead and dying soldiers scattered inside and around the trench. Then an officer with strikingly fair hair came down the trench toward him and Urquhart recognized No. 2 Company's Lt. Ross Cotton, who reported the frontal assault's failure.

Urquhart headed back to confirm whether No. 4 Company had in fact been "blown to Hell" and soon found Hastings and what remained of his men coming slowly up the trench. When they reached the Wiltshire position, Hastings told the company to wait there while he and Cotton contacted either Captain Rae or the Royal Montreal Regiment commander, Lt.-Col. W. W. Burland. Finding the two men together, Hastings reported his company's situation. The three men agreed that the best the RMR and No. 2 Company could do was to stay in place while Hastings's men extended in a line from the trench to tie in with their right flank. Hastings was just about to take his leave when a runner arrived with orders from brigade to immediately attack the orchard. Burland quickly scribbled a note objecting to the idea that he and Rae both signed.[9]

Eventually a new message arrived from brigade that left their note unacknowledged and reported that the other two Canadian Scottish companies would take over their advanced position at dawn while the Royal Montreal Regiment moved to a position to the left on the south side of La Quinque rue. This would anchor the Canadian Brigade's left flank in with the 4th Guards Brigade of 2nd British Division. Meanwhile, to 3rd Brigade's right, the 2nd Canadian Infantry Brigade would be deployed.

Once these dispositions were fully in place on May 20, the two fresh Canadian Scottish companies would seize what had now been dubbed Canadian Orchard. At the same time, 15th Battalion (48th Highlanders of Canada) would advance to rue d'Ouvert, about 250 yards to the east. Shortly after dawn on May 19, the two beaten-up Canadian Scottish companies withdrew via a system of badly damaged German trenches. "Sight of these trenches was very terrible," Urquhart thought.[10] "Although in after years some of those who were present then … witnessed many desolate battlefields … none surpassed in grimness the scene they saw that morning at Festubert. It is true that later in the war, especially at the Somme and Passchendaele, the artillery battered buildings, villages and the earth into an unrecognizable pulp, but the completeness of this mutilation often served to cover up the human side of the tragedy which, at Festubert, stood revealed in all its nakedness. Smashed rifles, torn, blood stained equipment and clothing were strewn over the battlefield. The dead, mainly British, lay thick around. They were scattered amongst the multi-coloured bags, black, blue, gray and white of the breastwork, thrown broadcast by the bombardment. One man stood in the trench, in an eerily life-like attitude, the hand up to the head where the fatal bomb fragment had pierced, as if listening for the movement of an oncoming enemy; some were locked in an embrace of death with a bayonet through one or other of the bodies."

A couple of men discovered among the scattered equipment a pack covered in blood that had "Denholm" marked on it, and the insignia of the Royal Scots regiment. Knowing that the brother of their sergeant, Alexander Denholm, served in that British regiment, Denholm's comrades carefully steered him past the spot so he would not be left worrying about his sibling's fate. Later it was learned that the Denholm brother had been evacuated to England where he was recovering from wounds.[11]

From Festubert, Urquhart looked toward the German wire and defences and saw more British dead lying thick on the ground, "as if mown down by a scythe; the occasional man had fallen against the wire in the kneeling position, ready for the final spring which death had denied him. And there were more hanging over the ditches, half in, half out, killed as they attempted to cross; or in the open, in all sorts of contorted attitudes. Burial parties were making little headway, and in the muggy, wet morning the many corpses lying on the sodden, red-stained earth, gave forth a sweet, pungent odour which was almost overpowering."[12]

The scene was utterly dispiriting. "Add to this the fact of it being a wet morning, tired feeling and [it] will be understood how terrible our sensations were. No. 4 Company's casualties for this attempt 44." The company had lost almost a quarter of its strength in an action where not a man fired a shot or even got close to the enemy. Adding to the misery their packs had been rifled where they had been dropped during the night march. Urquhart had everything stolen but a blanket. Finally, back in a trench at Indian Village, they bedded down with what gear remained. "Tried to sleep but too cold and wet," Urquhart scrawled in his diary.[13]

* * *

In preparation for the planned attack, Lt.-Col. Leckie established a battle headquarters in a trench in front of Festubert and from here a telephone line was strung along the communication trench to the forward companies. Hoping to gain some appreciation of the lay of the land and

German defences around the orchard, two patrols were sent toward the orchard after nightfall on May 19. One patrol crept eastward along a trench that cut through a marsh close to La Quinque rue to a shattered house that proved empty. Lying less than 100 yards from the orchard's southwest corner, Leckie decided the house provided perfect cover and stationed two Colt machine-gun teams in it before dawn so they could protect the attack's left flank.

May 20 dawned warm and sunny. An uneasy quiet pervaded, as if each side waited for the other to renew the violence. Leckie spent the morning drafting and submitting a detailed plan of attack that he proposed initiating at 2215 hours. Brig. Turner quickly approved Leckie's proposal, but a short time later divisional command said the attack was off altogether.

Moments after learning this news, Leckie's headquarters was bracketed by a heavy German bombardment that began pounding Festubert at noon, but escaped damage. The telephone wire to the forward companies, however, was knocked out. Despite the heavy fire still lashing the communication trench, L/Cpl. Duncan Stewart and Pte. George Hardwick crawled along it and fixed all the broken sections.

After about four hours, the German artillery finally lifted and a runner reported to Leckie with instructions for him to meet Turner at Indian Village at 1530 hours. When Leckie arrived the brigadier said the Canadian Scottish would attack the orchard with a single company while on their flank the 48th Highlanders would also be advancing. The assault was to go in at 1945.

Leckie protested because the attack would be in broad daylight with one company advancing over exposed ground against a heavily entrenched enemy. Why not go in after nightfall? Turner agreed that would be preferable, but it was also true that after the failed night attack at Aubers Ridge the British high command considered that the ability to control troop movement during daylight outweighed the disadvantages of exposing them to more accurate fire. Turner said the orders were there and they must comply.

With Zero Hour less than four hours away, Leckie raced back to Festubert and summoned Captain William Rae. Despite the fact the officer was still exhausted from the failed earlier attack, Leckie handed him command of the new assault because neither Major Cyrus Peck nor Captain Frank Morison, who respectively commanded No. 1 and No. 3 companies, had combat experience. Normally overall command of the assault would have fallen to the battalion second-in-command, Major Jack Leckie, but he was away on ninety-six hours' leave. Leckie never doubted that Rae was up to the task, for following the officer's performance during the attack on the woods in the Ypres Salient he had promoted him to major. But the promotion had yet to be approved at higher levels—a frustration for Leckie that led him to alternatively refer to Rae in the Canadian Scottish war diary by either rank.

The attack, Leckie told Rae, would be delivered by No. 3 Company with Peck's No. 1 Company supporting it by covering a communication trench that ran directly north from the battalion's forward line to the orchard. If No. 3 Company succeeded, Peck would then advance to where the trench entered the orchard and hook hard right from there to clear a fortified house designated as M10 on the maps.[14]

Since the two companies had taken up their forward positions they had been engaged in a fruitless effort to dig a defensive trench in the open ground between La Quinque rue and the communication trench No. 4 Company had tried following earlier to gain the orchard. Just two feet below the surface, the shovels cut into muck and water quickly filled the shallow trench to the brim. Only on the right flank where their front abutted the communication trench's meandering course was the semblance of a trench possible. On the left, meanwhile, their flank mired in a marsh that was so deep with mud that a gap existed between them and the Coldstream Guards stationed on its opposite side.

In the late afternoon, Rae set up an advanced battalion headquarters in a house on the south side of La Quinque rue about 150 yards behind the Canadian Scottish front line and summoned Morison and Peck. Already the operation was lurching into motion. As the two officers walked in, a short artillery bombardment began softening up the orchard. Rae conducted a hurried briefing and then sent them back to their companies. They had just minutes to form up their men in a long, strung-out line before the guns lifted and the Canadian Scottish began walking forward. Each man was spaced two paces apart. There was no cover. They simply walked stiffly into the face of a storm of machine-gun and rifle fire that one man later described as being "like sleet." Another saw a terrified rabbit scurry past and shouted, "Oh, look at the bunny! Look at the bunny, will you!"

There was no covering fire from the two Colt machine-gun teams stationed by Leckie in the house. They got off just one burst before German artillery zeroed in and obliterated the place. Both guns were destroyed and their crews either killed or wounded.[15]

No. 3 Company's left platoon, under Lt. Espine Montgomery Pickton-Ward, wandered lost through the marsh and out in front of the Coldstream Guards. The British troops started shouting directions, but Pickton-Ward was struck dead before he could re-organize his command.[16] Sgt. John Cochrane calmly took over, received some directional advice from a Coldstream officer, and then ordered his men to come about sharply ninety degrees. As the advance was renewed, he moved along the line dressing it back into a smart parade-ground formation despite heavy enemy fire. Cochrane was shot five times, but never faltered until the orchard was gained. Only then did he let the stretcher-bearers carry him away, but upon reaching headquarters he slid off the stretcher and personally reported to Rae.

The other platoons in Morison's company gained the road opposite the orchard only to find a deep ditch bordered by a hedge that was impassable except for a couple of narrow gaps. As Morison was about to run through one of these, a bomber yanked him back. "Bombers go in front of officers, Sir," he barked, jumped the ditch, and ducked through the gap with the rifle platoons following hot on his heels in single file. Charging through these two gaps, the company quickly overran the orchard and swept it clear of the few Germans stationed there. At the orchard's southern edge, Morison ordered the men to dig in behind another hedge. Fifty yards beyond, a facing trench was held by the Germans, who could be heard shouting excitedly back and forth in surprise over the loss of the orchard.

The battalion's first objective gained, Major Peck's No. 1 Company began the drive toward the fortified house south of the orchard. Barring their advance was a German parapet, but the two leading platoons found a narrow gap and dashed through. "Immediately these men cleared the gap, several machine guns opened fire on them, and they were at the mercy of the enemy. The garden round the house was covered with a network of barbed wire, and between the breastwork and the house was open ground. A number of the men were killed as they cleared the breastwork and as many more in an attempt to storm the wire. A few of the latter group shammed death and lay in front of the wire until darkness fell, hoping they might then get into the house, but as the attack of the 15th Canadian Battalion ... had been unsuccessful, they finally withdrew, without attempting to get into the objective." Seeing the fate that had befallen the two leading platoons, the rest of the company remained behind the breastwork. In the opening mêlée, Major Peck had been wounded and evacuated. No further attempt was made to take the house. In capturing the orchard, the Canadian Scottish achieved the deepest penetration of the German line by British First Army during the Battle of Festubert. Canadian Orchard would remain in Allied hands until the great German offensive of April 1918.[17]

At 0200 hours on May 21, the 13th Battalion (Royal Highlanders of Canada) began relieving the two Canadian Scottish companies and, at dawn, they marched to Indian Village. Here the rest of the battalion had listened anxiously through the night to the fierce fight. When the two companies marched in, Urquhart was shocked at how cut up they were, "No. 3 only having 56 men left and No. 1 [Company] about 85." Captain Don Moore, Pickton-Ward, and Lt. Gordon MacKenzie were dead. Peck, Lt. Arthur Morton, and Lt. Andrew Gray wounded. "The fellows seemed all done but the work accomplished was immense." Urquhart was saddened by how Pickton-Ward met his fate. "Poor Ward," he wrote. "Body was buried by Coldstreams." The battalion quartermaster knew what was needed and Urquhart heartily agreed. "Gave a good dose of rum to men and then they had a sleep. It was a terrible strain on them. You could see they were simply done."[18]

In less than two weeks since the slaughter at Ypres, the battalion had again been shredded. Three officers dead, another three wounded. Sixty-eight men killed and 203 wounded for a casualty toll of 277.[19] The Canadian Scottish moved immediately to new duties, alternately standing in reserve in the area of Essars or putting in trench duty east of Givenchy-lez-la-Bassée. Here they remained while the spring of 1915 gave way to a hot summer. Although the trenches were by no means safe and each deployment to the front yielded casualties, the passing weeks gave opportunity for the battalion to slowly nurse its wounds and heal again.

The 16th Battalion was far from alone in the heavy casualties suffered for no gain during the Festubert offensive. Over the course of five separate assaults on as many days 1st Canadian Division had advanced a mere 600 yards at a cost of 2,468 casualties. This, so close on the heels of its losing half its fighting strength at Ypres, created a reinforcement crisis.[20]

The only good the Canadian Scottish could see in the results of the fighting of early 1915 was one welcome casualty of war. On June 13, Canadian Headquarters ordered the Ross rifle withdrawn from active service and replaced it with the Lee-Enfield that was the standard rifle of all Commonwealth forces except the Canadians. The Can Scots, Urquhart noted, had "found this weapon quite unsuitable ... in the field, and many ... during the Ypres and Festubert battles, discarded it for the Lee-Enfield. It jammed from heat expansion after the firing of twenty or thirty rounds. Men were to be seen stamping on the bolt in an attempt to open it, cursing bitterly with tears of rage in their eyes, and, finally, when all efforts to draw it had failed, flinging the rifle away."[21]

A couple of weeks later another issue of new kit arrived that soon sparked the Battle of the Kilts. Although the decision had been made to supplant the four regimental tartans with one of khaki, it had taken some time for these to be manufactured. When they arrived, it was immediately evident their manufacturer knew nothing of kilts. Depending on whether a man was small or large, the kilts might wrap twice around and drag on boot tops or barely cover his loins. "Lemonade rags," the men called them.

To a man the Gordons of No. 1 Company refused to wear them, declaring that they "wished to retain their tartan." Leckie responded by placing some of the company's sergeants under arrest. Then Regimental Sergeant Major David Nelson objected to the kilt as an "outrage" and was also arrested. Finally the khaki issue was withdrawn for modification and the men continued wearing their varying tartans. This resulted in the battalion being garbed in an erratic assortment of clothing as reinforcements arrived, with or without regimental Highland kit, and attempts were made to jury-rig appropriate clothes on the spot or secure them from regimental aid groups back in Canada.[22] After one late June parade before Col. Turner, Leckie noted with some despair that, although the parade had gone well, "the diversity of uniforms had a jarring effect!"[23]

Eventually the matter would be resolved with the battalion agreeing to wear the Mackenzie tartan, although a khaki kilt finally became available that proved suitably constructed. Over time the khaki kilt was commonly used by the Highland troops when not on parade. By that time, however, the Canadian Scottish would have gone through several bloody battles that inflicted such losses that the continued identification of the four companies by regimental affiliation had been rendered moot as men sent to fill the ranks were being drawn at random from reinforcement pools.

chapter five

Trench Warfare Drudgery

- JUNE 1915–MARCH 1916 -

On June 24, 1ˢᵗ Canadian Infantry Division moved about 16 miles from Festubert to the Ploegsteert sector, coming again under British Second Army command and being assigned to Lt.-Gen. Sir W. P. Pulteney's III Corps. The division was assigned a 4,400-yard front between Messines and Ploegsteert, where it would remain for three months of comparative quiet.

The bloodletting of the first five months of 1915 had left both the Allied and German armies so depleted that an uneasy stalemate descended on the Western Front. With Germany removing troops to reinforce the Eastern Front, the British high command felt confident that no major enemy offensives would be forthcoming. This ensured time to strengthen forward defences and rebuild the British Expeditionary Force with little German interference.

Rebuilding proved more troublesome for the Canadian division than was true of its other Commonwealth counterparts due to manpower supply shortages. Minister of Militia and Defence Sam Hughes had neglected to create an efficient system for raising and training reinforcements to replenish the contingent he had so erratically formed in the fall of 1914. The heavy losses of April and May had completely drained the division's entire reserve pool in England, which had only numbered 2,000 men. This forced the dissolution of entire battalions stationed in England as part of the Canadian buildup there that were then fed piecemeal to the division. Even this measure failed to provide enough troops to bring the line battalions up to strength.

Consequently, the Canadian Scottish—like most other battalions— had only half their assigned complement at the beginning of July and Lt.-Col. Robert Leckie decided three larger companies would be more useful than four that were greatly reduced. Amalgamating Nos. 1 and

3 Companies under Captain Frank Morison's command also helped account for a grave shortage of officers, with each company still only assigned one or two apiece. The manpower shortfalls did not mean any lessening in divisional expectations. Each battalion remained responsible for the same trench frontage it would normally be expected to man, which left officers and men trying to fill the shoes of two people. Morale plummeted.[1]

Fortunately, the Ploegsteert line was "a real rest front" where Germans and Allies maintained an unofficial quasi-truce. Rarely did either side fire artillery or machine guns. But even a so-called rest front remained deadly for the unwary or merely unlucky. Snipers plied their trade, targeting exposed positions or crossing points in the facing breastworks. Both sides vigorously patrolled No Man's Land, seeking prisoners or ambushing enemy patrols. Twenty-nine-year-old Lt. Wallace Chambers, the battalion's machine-gun officer, was fatally shot while on a July 6 reconnaissance in No Man's Land.

Stalking snipers and roving German patrols in the darkness of No Man's Land unsettled reinforcements and made even veterans trigger happy. This led to several incidents where men forgot to challenge troops coming through the wire into the trenches from No Man's Land for the password and shooting first. One officer died bringing a patrol in when the party deployed in the trench specifically to cover its return opened fire from a range of just 10 yards. When another patrol slipped out of the pre-dawn darkness into a trench where Pte. Jules Mondoux was digging a trench with his back turned, the notoriously jumpy veteran spun and struck the lead soldier in the head with the flat of his shovel. Paraded to Company Headquarters, Mondoux said: "I don't know why—I am sorry—but it is my nature." Thereafter, returning patrols approached cautiously to within calling distance and entered only once assured it was safe to do so. Lt. Hugh Urquhart believed these incidents proved that almost everyone had, in the parlance of the trenches, their "wind up," or "in ordinary language … were nervous and excitable."[2]

It was a happy day on July 23, when a draft of Cameron Highlanders from Winnipeg arrived and the battalion was suddenly brought up to full strength. The day was also one of major command changes for 3rd Canadian Infantry Brigade as Richard Turner was promoted to major general and left to head up 2nd Canadian Infantry Division. This division was readying for deployment to the mainland from England. Brigade command went to Robert Leckie, with John Leckie assuming leadership of the Canadian Scottish and Major Cyrus Peck becoming his second-in-command. Although the two Leckies were extremely close, their personalities differed markedly. Jack, as he was called by friends, had none of Robert's shyness and consequent air of aloofness. Instead, he was dashing and impulsive and thrived on action and adventure. Where his brother was slender, Jack was stocky and possessed of great physical strength. He treated the men like equals and, in the role of battalion second-in-command had won their trust and respect, so that his advancement to command was welcomed. "We liked the way he talked, and the way he walked," one soldier wrote.

Not a disciplinarian, Jack Leckie would chat cheerfully with men sentenced to field punishment. Coming across a habitual offender, Cpl. Edward Gallagher, scraping mud off boardwalks, Leckie was once heard to say: "Well, my lad, that's better than shovelling snow in Canada." Gallagher tilted his head to one side, considering the matter, and chuckled. "Quit your kidding, Major," he responded.

One soldier was even moved to verse, penning a poem entitled "Major Jack" that appeared in the battalion's trench magazine, *Brazier*:

> Come call your boys together,
> Major Jack,
> They will follow to the death,
> Where you lead them, when you need them,
> Major Jack.
> For they know you're tried and true,
> Major Jack,
> And they'll each along with you
> Do their whack.
> In your heart no thought of fear,
> On your lips a word of cheer,
> Ever ready, cool and steady,
> Major Jack.[3]

Not everyone was so enamoured of either Leckie. Urquhart had never warmed to the brothers and, at the news of their promotions, confessed to his diary of having "very mixed feelings when of all those men who are now gone and who were treated so badly by him [it's unclear whether he was referring to Robert or Jack Leckie]. Yet there they are lying under the ground and those two who are far inferior to what they were [are] getting all the honours." August 13, the day after this entry, was Urquhart's birthday and also marked exactly a year since his regiment had mobilized. "I remember wondering then if I should be alive to-day and how it would feel to look back on experiences. I am very thankful at being permitted to be alive and that I was allowed to go through these experiences. I don't know that I have done my best as I should have. Perhaps I will be forgiven for this. Why should I be left alive when such men as John Geddes and Merritt are killed? They made such sacrifices and had so much to live for. Very disappointed at many things and think we have not yet reached climax of misfortunes simply because our inefficiency so great. But the thing to look back on with gratitude is splendid courage and devotion of men."[4]

At the company level there were also changes. When the redoubtable Captain William Rae was evacuated ill to England, No. 2 Company passed to Captain Roderick Bell-Irving. Illness also struck Captain Morison, so No. 3 Company was taken over by a newly arrived Cameron named Captain John Hall. The reconstituted No. 1 Company came under the command of Captain Stanley Wood. An American from the Deep South who had enlisted in the Canadian Army as a private at the war's outset, Wood had won a commission and joined the battalion in May 1915. When Captain Victor Hastings was also evacuated with an illness that saw him returned to Canada, Lt. Urquhart was promoted to captain and awarded command of No. 4 Company.

The Canadian Scottish also lost their regimental sergeant major, Davie Nelson, when he was badly wounded on July 11. The only surviving company sergeant major after the spring fighting was Jimmie Kay from No. 4 Company, who moved up to try to fill Nelson's shoes. Kay knew this would be tough, for Nelson had been less the battalion's senior non-commissioned officer than an "institution." The former Seaforth Highlanders of Canada's sergeant major, Nelson had always provided a steadying hand for the officers and men through every battle.

Although Nelson's combat days were ended by a wound, the RSM had been obviously past his prime—a fact that plagued many of 1st Division's senior officers and non-commissioned officers alike. One of the reasons so many company commanders were falling to critical ill-nesses was that they were older men. Nelson, who had once been the Seaforth's champion light-weight boxer and had a lean, wiry build, was already "slightly bent" when the battalion reached Europe. Many Can Scots thought nothing but sheer determination of spirit kept the RSM going during the ensuing months of combat and trench duty. Often he was to be seen standing outside his tent, shifting his pipe from side to side in his mouth, gaze fixed toward some faraway point, and nobody could hazard what he was thinking during these moments.[5]

* * *

While 1st Division had been rebuilding, its role in the B.E.F. was also changing due to the buildup of Canadian forces in Europe as part of the nation's commitment to supporting Britain. The arrival of 2nd Canadian Infantry Division fulfilled a government pledge on October 6, 1914, "to place and maintain in the field a second contingent of twenty thousand men." The arrival of those troops led Britain's War Office to agree to the formation of a Canadian Corps in which the two divisions and all sub-sequent Canadian divisions would serve. This represented a departure from normal British military doctrine where little emphasis was placed on committing divisions to particular corps service. Rather divisions were shifted from one corps to another as deemed necessary—precise-ly the experience of 1st Canadian Division during the spring operations. But a precedent for some Commonwealth powers keeping their troops together had been set earlier by Australia and New Zealand, who insisted that all their divisions be permanently retained inside an ANZAC Corps. The British now agreed that Canada should adopt this innovation.

Initially Sam Hughes wanted to be ordained corps commander, claiming Canadians desired this. But he lacked both military and gov-ernment support. Nor was the unrepentant Anglophobe able to inject a Canadian officer into the post. Instead, 1st Division's lieutenant general, Edwin Alderson, got the job. On September 13, 1915, corps headquar-ters opened for business at Bailleul, about 15 miles behind 1st Division's front on the Ploegsteert line. With Alderson's promotion the die was cast: henceforth, Canadian divisions would be commanded by Canadian offi-cers, with the promotion of Arthur William Currie to major general.

Currie had been instrumental in raising the 50th Gordon Highlanders as a militia unit in Victoria. Six-foot-four, weighing 250 pounds, and possessed of a voice as robust as his size, the forty-year-old former realtor had entered the war with no professional military experience. But his handling of 2nd Canadian Infantry Brigade during the Second Battle of Ypres had been so masterful that B.E.F. commander-in-chief Field Marshal Sir John French had declared him "as the most suitable of the three [Canadian] brigadiers" for divisional command. French had wanted Currie to guide the inexperienced 2nd Division through its combat learning curve but Hughes, backed in this by Prime Minister Robert Borden, intervened in favour of Turner in a blatant show of political cronyism.

At the end of September the newly operational corps boasted a total strength of 1,354 officers and 36,522 other ranks.[6] If Hughes was not to have its command, nothing would keep him from constantly meddling with its operation. While basing himself in England, he shuttled regularly to the mainland to lobby for an enlarged role for Canadian officers at corps headquarters. But neither the British War Office nor Field Marshal French considered the Canadians sufficiently experienced in such demanding staff work, and so most corps positions were staffed by British officers. At every opportunity Hughes would review and address the troops. When the Canadian Scottish drew the dubious honour of parading for him, Captain Urquhart's acid comment was that Hughes delivered the "usual foolish bombastic speech…. Men took it as a sort of joke."[7]

For the 1st Division battalions, the time spent waiting for the corps to become fully operational ensured that it remained posted in a quiet sector. But this meant that the men "had, therefore, to content themselves with the … drudgery of trench warfare" in increasingly "dreary surroundings" as summer gave way to fall. More importantly it provided time for the division to adjust to and incorporate a number of tactical innovations conceived as a result of the spring fighting.

British infantry tactics in early 1915 had been little changed from those the army had followed for a hundred years. There were two simple and important weapons—the rifle and the bayonet. Accordingly, battalions had a straightforward organization consisting of a headquarters section and four rifle companies. When machine guns and signalling equipment were added to the roster, a section responsible for each was created, but these were attached to and controlled by headquarters. As the war had devolved into one of deadlocked trench fighting, new sniper, gas specialist, and bomber sections were created that also remained under headquarters control. The role of the companies was still to provide simple riflemen.

But the spring fighting had shown that these specialist sections were too estranged from the companies they supported, sometimes—as had been the case in the first attack on Canadian Orchard—balking at commands given by junior officers under whose authority they did not strictly fall. Communication problems also resulted in headquarters often not sending the specialists to where they were most desperately required. Recognizing these issues, the British high command ordered more battalion troops trained in one or another specialization with the intention that in most cases some specialists would be integrated directly into a company. Each company commander was instructed to select his best men for specialist training, but this drew protests that the companies were being gutted of the self-sufficient men who could most be depended on in combat. "Why so many first-class men?" the Canadian Scottish company commanders grumbled to their battalion adjutant, which as this post was being rotated between officers until Major Gilbert Godson-Godson returned from hospital after being wounded on April 22, happened to be Urquhart. "How is it possible to make specialists out of inefficient men?" Urquhart snapped back and the duly selected men were sent off to be schooled in their new duties.[8]

Two classes of snipers, company and battalion, were created. The first were put on a company's strength and practiced their deadly trades from positions along its front. Battalion snipers operated "from specially built shelters in the front trench or from ruined houses, trees, haystacks or other posts which gave them cover and a view of the enemy territory behind his front line." While company snipers were not excused from ordinary company duties, nobody seemed to know who commanded the Canadian Scottish battalion snipers. Lacking an officer's oversight, they tended to either hunt alone or in co-operation with a couple of their peers. Whether by nature or design, battalion snipers—armed with their special telescope-mounted rifles and lugging along a host of ancillary camouflaging and spotting gear—were considered loners and left to ply their deadly trade as they saw fit so long as the often intricately camouflaged firing posts posed no hindrance to company movement within the trenches.

Company troops generally valued gas experts more than snipers, because the former could save their lives while the latter might draw undue attention of German snipers or even artillery should his presence in a nearby section of trench be noted. Gas experts were easily recognized by their black and red armbands, but their specialty often seemed as mysterious as alchemy. For their job was not only to identify when a gas wind—one blowing from the German lines toward their own—prevailed, but also to detect when the Germans were deploying the means to deliver a gas attack. At first small flags were strung along the trench to monitor wind currents but soon—often aided by anyone in the battalion possessed of carpentry skills—the gas experts erected small weathervanes or miniature windmills that looked incongruously like toys in the grim trench environment. Detecting an attack before it was launched generally proved impossible, but once a gas cloud was sighted the specialists sounded a warning by blowing klaxon horns, banging gongs, or ringing bells. All down the trench men would don the recently issued Smoke or Hypo helmet. Invented by Major Cluny McPherson of the Newfoundland Medical Corps, this "consisted of a piece of thick grey flannel ... impregnated with hyposulphite, soda and glycerine solution kept in bulk at the quartermaster's stores; and fitted with mica eye pieces. This cloth could be drawn over the head, tucked under the tunic, and gave good protection against [chlorine gas]." It was also claustrophobic and heavy and limited vision to the point that there was a temptation to tear the helmet off despite the risk of gas exposure.

The formula of chemicals with which the helmet was impregnated changed regularly as the Germans introduced new types of gases. Phenates were initially added to counter phosgene and later hyomine added yet more anti-phosgene protection while also combatting prussic acid. In November 1915 the Hypo helmet was replaced by the "P" Helmet, which had a rubber tube fitted with a valve to allow breathing. A year later, the "PH" Helmet added a small box respirator.

While gas helmets provided individual protection, the specialists also ensured that dugouts had army blankets soaked in anti-gas solution at the ready to cover entrances during gas attacks. They also roved the trenches carrying small portable spray tanks filled with the solution to smother pockets of gas that lingered in hollows within the trenches following an attack.[9]

It was the job of the gas specialists to train a company's officers and non-commissioned officers in proper helmet use so these could in turn train the soldiers they commanded. A form of live-fire training was also practised whereby the specialists would pump a section of trench full of gas and then guide men in small groups through the misty clouds to safety on the other side. Urquhart found this training proved the helmet "very effectual," but when one soldier inexplicably "lifted his helmet and got slightly gassed," he collapsed unconscious. After resuscitation, the man confessed to deliberately lifting the helmet out of curiosity over how breathing in gas would feel.[10]

Gas experts and snipers were trained in the summer of 1915, but bomber specialists had come earlier to the battalions—fighting at Ypres and Festubert. Their weaponry had been crude, mostly "jam pot" bombs. Developed in the early weeks of the war, the formula for building a jam pot bomb was simple. "Take a tin jam pot, fill it with shredded gun cotton and ten-penny nails, mixed according to taste; insert a No. 8 detonator and a short length of Bickford's fuse; clay up the lid, light with a match, pipe, cigar or cigarette, and throw for all you are worth," stated one recipe. Their other weapon was the Mark 1 grenade, which was canister-shaped and weighted to ensure it landed nose-down to ignite a 16-inch fuse. As dangerous to the throwers as to the enemy, their weapon led to bombers often being described as members of a suicide club.

The hazardous nature of their trade had contributed to the decision to keep the bomber section under headquarters' command and they were only sent as required to support a company during offensive operations. Usually advancing ahead of the rifle companies, they attempted to chuck bombs into the German trenches as the riflemen closed in and once inside the trenches raced along their length throwing bombs into every dugout passed to wipe out any pockets of resistance.

Regulations strictly forbade non-bombers from using or even touching bombs unless directed by a bomber, which fostered men in the section to assume an air of self-importance and elitism that irritated everyone else in the battalion. It little helped that the bombing officer was usually a junior subaltern who operated independent of company command. In

May 1915, the elitist nature of the bombing trade began to diminish with the introduction of the Mills bomb. Weighing one-and-a-quarter pounds, with a serrated shell that fragmented on detonation and fitted with a four-second fuse ignited by pulling a safety pin while holding down a strike lever, the Mills was the precursor of most modern grenades. A model was also developed that could be fired from a rifle. As Mills bombs became prevalent, it was decided to increase the number of bombers by training men within the companies to perform this task. The result, Urquhart noted happily, was that the bombers, "who used to stroll through company trenches dictating to company men with an air of authority, were shorn of their privileges by absorption into the companies."[11]

* * *

During the late summer of 1915, 1st Division had continued to maintain its presence on the Ploegsteert front even after the Canadian Corps assumed overall responsibility for the 4,400-yard line on September 13. Coinciding with the corps being declared operational, the division's front was actually extended northwestward from Ploegsteert Wood across the Douve River valley to Wulverghem–Messines road. Six days later Second Division began a four-day relief of British formations on the left that broadened the Canadian sector northward three miles to the Vierstraat–Wytschaete road. This road marked the divide between the Canadian area and that of V British Corps. Three divisions of II Bavarian Corps stood opposite the Canadian line where the opposing trenches wriggled along at distances ranging from a maximum of 500 yards to an easy stone's throw apart. From the Messines–Wytschaete spur rising up on the Douve's left bank to intersect the 15-mile-long Messines Ridge the entire Canadian sector lay exposed to enemy observation.[12]

As Lt.-Gen. Alderson completed his dispositions of Canadian Corps on September 23, he learned that a major Allied offensive was set to begin in just two days' time. Once again the British participated only at French insistence. With the Gallipoli Campaign in the Dardanelles in full swing, the British were overextended to the point that further reinforcing the B.E.F. was predicted to be problematic until early 1916. There was also a grave munitions shortage for both British and French artillery, also not to be rectified until the new year. Until then, the War

Office preferred to keep casualties to a minimum by remaining on the defensive. No autumn offensive was anathema to the French, however, and the British government reluctantly acquiesced. Two thrusts would be delivered against either side of a large German salient that reached its apex at Noyon. To the south near Champagne, France's Second and Fourth Armies would advance northward while the French Tenth Army and British First Army drove eastward at Artois—the intent being to cut off and destroy the three German armies holding the Noyon Salient.

The brainchild of Chief of Staff Gen. J.J. Joffre, the offensive rejected the stalemated reality of the Western Front. Joffre believed the salient could be pinched out through a massive commitment of forces—in the French case, fifty-three divisions supported by 5,000 guns.

Although, initially, some ground was gained, a swift German response poured reinforcements into the line and the battle soon conformed to rote until officially cancelled on November 4. The Allied casualty tally was about 60,000 British and 200,000 French, while the Germans lost 150,000. The Noyon Salient remained largely unchanged, with the British having gained only two miles on a two-mile front that left them inside their own difficult-to-sustain salient around Loos, while the French retained only a three-mile penetration at Champagne that left their forward troops dangerously exposed on flats facing ridges in German hands.[13] Criticized for his handling of the offensive, particularly a failure to feed in reserves at what was later considered a decisive moment, Field Marshal Sir John French was shunted out of B.E.F. command in favour of Douglas Haig.

Canadian Corps played no part in this offensive except to conduct several demonstrations intended to prevent the facing German divisions being drawn away to reinforce the salient. Largely, the sector remained quiet and the troops were more bothered by October's weather conditions than enemy action. Each day it grew cloudier and colder, with a clammy mist descending after nightfall that clung to the low ground well into the following morning. Then, on October 25, the skies opened and thereafter the rains carried on incessantly, turning the ground into muddy mire and causing streams to flood.

The Douve River overflowed its banks and inundated the valley behind the Canadian front lines, leaving the men there cut off from the rear as the communication trenches either filled with water or collapsed.

A link was re-established in 3rd Canadian Infantry Brigade's sector only when engineers built a web of wooden walkways made by interlinking sections of two six-foot lengths of two by fours. These shaky structures lacked handrails and as each man, heavily burdened with packs full of supplies for the front, passed along their length the boards became heavily greased with slippery mud. Soldiers routinely skidded off into the watery and mud-soaked morass—sometimes nearly drowning before being hauled to safety. On the front line, the Canadian Scottish on the battalion's right flank watched helplessly as their breastwork crumbled when the sandbags making up its walls became so sodden they burst and the sand gushed out in a muddy stream. Things were no better on the left flank. The trenches dug where the water table had allowed it were transformed into canals running knee-deep with liquefied mud.

At brigade reserve, in an area designated as Red Lodge, huts erected over the summer months leaked like sieves and the mud caking the floors dried hard as concrete. All roads were lost beneath the shifting flow of silt-laden river water and oozing mud. Only when the battalion was withdrawn to the divisional reserve area with its leak-proof huts were the men ever to get dry. The closing weeks of 1915 were largely spent by the Canadians in fruitless efforts to create workable drainage systems.[14]

Throughout the fall and early winter, the Canadians and Germans routinely harassed each other almost daily with artillery fire. Snipers stalked the unwary and nightly patrols prowled No Man's Land looking for weaknesses in the opposing defences. Barely a day passed when the Canadian Scottish were in the line that the war diarist failed to record that at least one man had been wounded or killed. The journey to and from the front was looked upon as being even more treacherous. On December 4, Urquhart wrote that—there being no usable communication trenches—the men had "to come back [by] the dreary road overland across the Douve. Fell into various ditches and got soaking wet." The narrow bridge spanning the river lacked handrails and the water roaring underneath was clearly "very deep." With the men moving so slowly across such open ground, Urquhart feared being spotted by the Germans. Caught by artillery fire the Canadian Scottish, he knew, would "certainly have heavy casualties."[15]

* * *

Each battalion spent five days in the trenches and then five days in the rear. The Canadian Scottish generally rotated duty with the 48th Highlanders while the Royal Montreal Regiment and the Royal Highlanders of Canada did likewise. This was not an altogether happy arrangement for the Can Scots, as they felt the 48th Highlanders seldom worked on trench maintenance and improvement during their stints at the front. "As usual 15th did no work," Urquhart confided to his diary in one of all too many similar comments.[16]

The 48th Highlanders appeared no more impressed by the Canadian Scottish, though, with their battalion war diarist regularly recording that upon returning to the front lines work parties had to be immediately formed for "building new dugouts and draining trenches."[17]

Badly mauled in the Ypres Salient fighting, the 15th Battalion had also been plagued initially by poor leadership. Its first commander, former Member of Parliament and personal friend of Sam Hughes, Lt.-Col. John Currie (no relation of Arthur Currie) had little military experience. In the midst of the Second Battle of Ypres he had fled the front under the pretence of rounding up stragglers and ended up taking shelter at 2nd Canadian Infantry Brigade headquarters from which he was forcibly ejected. Lt.-Col. John Creelman eventually reported that Currie wound up at his 2nd Canadian Field Artillery headquarters clearly in a drunken condition.[18] While the incident was largely covered up, Currie was soon sent back to Canada and Lt.-Col. William Renwick Marshall headed up the 15th Battalion as of June 28, 1915. A Royal Regiment officer from Hamilton, Marshall rebuilt the battalion from the ground up over the summer months and re-instilled its pride.

The 48th Highlanders relieved the Canadian Scottish on December 20 so, on Christmas Eve, the Canadian Scots returned to the front. Just before the Battalion marched off, Lt.-Col. Jack Leckie had taken his company commanders aside and advised them that a sergeant from Royal Montreal Regiment had deserted "to the enemy this morning," while another soldier from that battalion had disappeared the previous day from a listening post in which another man had been found mysteriously shot dead. This was part of a pattern, Urquhart thought, whereby the 14th Battalion was always having "extraordinary things happen."[19] Of immediate concern was the sergeant's knowledge that a battalion rotation was underway. If the Germans gleaned that intelligence from him they could either heavily bombard the lines of approach from the rear or even attempt to overrun the forward changes while the changeover was under way.[20]

The brigade's only non-Highland battalion, the Montreal-raised battalion had a reputation for severe disciplinary problems. Already the Montrealers were on their third commander, with Lt.-Col. F. W. Fisher having taken over in October. Fisher was having no better luck enforcing discipline than had his predecessors, the problem exacerbated by the fact its No. 4 Company was entirely French-speaking while most of the battalion's officers spoke only English. Both deserters were from that company. The first deserter had clearly murdered the man standing guard with him in the listening post and then fled to German lines while the sergeant had slipped over the parapet in broad daylight in view of many men who made no effort to prevent his leaving.[21] Desertion was a serious matter that normally warranted much analysis, yet the battalion's official war diary made no mention of these incidents. Instead, the five pages forming the entire month of December's entries were most often marked by nothing more than a shorthand entry for ditto—"do, do, do."[22]

A hard rain fell that Christmas Eve as the Canadian Scottish marched toward the front. Word was that the Douve had swept away its bridges and might have to be waded—ensuring everyone would get drenched and that some men might be caught up and drowned. Fortunately one bridge still stood. Nor did the enemy make any moves with either artillery or infantry raids, so the handover was achieved peacefully.

By the time the men settled into the trenches, the rain lifted and the night proved clear and lit by a three-quarter moon that softened "with subdued light the scars and unsightliness of the battlefield into a picture of shades and shadows and still, stark forms." About fifteen minutes past midnight a German soldier in an outpost facing the battalion's left flank stood and shot off a Very light that bathed No Man's Land in a ghostly light. "Guid Nicht, Jock, and a Merry Christmas," the man shouted, turned his back to the Canadians, and walked nonchalantly back to the German trenches. About forty-five minutes later 1st Canadian Division's Maj.-Gen. Arthur Currie and 3rd Brigade's Brig. Robert Leckie arrived and the men formed shoulder to shoulder in the trench as the two officers passed down their line, pausing to personally wish many "a Happy Christmas."

Christmas Day dawned cloudy and proved "as strange as the preceding night." There was no fighting. Instead the Germans milled about openly behind their trenches—looking "well fed and well clothed, having on a great variety of uniforms, slate colour, green, khaki." Some ventured beyond their forward parapets, waving bottles of wine and cigarettes to tempt the Canadians into joining them. When some of Urquhart's company began singing Scottish songs while others started walking out into No Man's Land, the officer barred their way and ordered them back into the trench. But he had "great difficulty keeping men down." Later an artillery linesman dashed over to join the Germans and then the irrepressibly ill-disciplined Cpl. Edward Gallagher from No. 3 Company went out and exchanged cigarettes with one German—an act that drew cheers from both sides. When Gallagher refused demands by his company's acting commander, Lt. David Bell, to return, Lt.-Col. Leckie lost his patience and ordered both Gallagher and Bell arrested. Urquhart saw little sense in this. Rather, he admitted to having a "strange feeling looking at these fellows in perfect friendship and shooting at them next day. What an insane thing."[23]

Leckie and the other senior battalion officers were increasingly nervous that the situation threatened to get out of hand, for what happened if the men became too friendly with the Germans? Before they could decide a plan of action, however, a machine gun somewhere on the front burned a long burst into the air and "everyone ran to cover like rabbits, and all social intercourse came to an end."[24] In the future there would be no uncertainty about whether to permit Allied soldiers to fraternize with their German counterparts at Christmas, as sufficient shelling, sniping, and patrolling was scheduled to ensure No Man's Land remained too dangerous.

The Canadian Scottish spent New Year's Day out of the line and enjoyed a fine dinner. January also brought improving weather that allowed for repairs on many of the defensive works and communication trenches destroyed by the rains. On February 3, the brigade moved to a rest area at Meteren, a town about one mile from Bailleul. The Ploegsteert tour was winding down for Canadian Corps, but there remained several weeks of front-line duty. And the front remained hazardous, a fact rammed poignantly home to the ranks of 3rd Brigade when Robert Leckie was badly wounded in both thighs by shrapnel from an artillery shell on the night of February 17–18.[25]

A few days later the command went to Brigadier George Tuxford. Welsh-born, the newly married twenty-year-old Tuxford had immigrated to Canada in 1890 to take up ranching near Moose Jaw, Saskatchewan. In 1898 he drove a herd of cattle across the Rockies and up to the gold miners at Dawson City, Yukon, for what was then the longest cattle drive in Canadian history. Back home, he joined the 16th Mounted Rifles as a militia officer in 1910 and when war broke out went overseas as commander of the 5th (Western Cavalry) Battalion of 2nd Canadian Infantry Brigade. At Second Ypres he had led this battalion with distinction through a desperate fight that prevented the division's right flank being turned.[26] Tuxford would prove a highly capable brigadier.

Little more than a week after Tuxford assumed command of the brigade, Canadian Corps left the Ploegsteert front toward one that held little in the way of good memories for the men of 1st Division—a return to the Ypres Salient. On March 28, as the Canadian Scottish marched into the salient they "could hear ahead heavy gun fire, and in front of us shell bursts could be distinctly seen." This was the "dreaded front" that they remembered from the bitter spring of 1915.[27]

chapter six

Return to the Salient

- MARCH 28–AUGUST 9, 1916 -

The Ypres Salient was reputedly the most miserable, dangerous place on earth. Abandoning it entirely had been advocated repeatedly as this would straighten the Allied line through the ruins of Ypres and eliminate being overlooked from three sides by German guns on the ridges. But Chief-of-Staff Gen. J.J. Joffre summed up the prevailing French and British belief when he declared it was better his *poilus* "be killed in their tracks rather than draw back." The salient had become a symbol of defiance sanctified by the blood of the thousands who had died there. To abandon it would render those deaths meaningless.[1] Captain Hugh Urquhart had another theory—pure bloody British doggedness refused to let go of anything. Only the tenacity of the soldiers caught in its maw prevented its "unpardonable" loss.

But none of the veteran Canadians welcomed returning, wondering instead "what move fate would now make for or against them in this place, where the odds were so heavily piled against the soldier." It was a feeling Urquhart thought shared by "all infantrymen, who were compelled to renew acquaintance with this spot." Seconded to 3rd Brigade headquarters, Urquhart was fairly confident of surviving despite having to regularly shunt back and forth from the battalion to brigade on various errands. Unlike a company officer or a lieutenant leading a platoon, whose lives were often measured in minutes from the moment the whistle sounded for an advance, Urquhart faced a reasonable probability of being killed or maimed by a chance shell or sniper's bullet.

What made the Ypres Salient so dangerous was that the Allied troops there were trapped "inside a sort of saucer having but a precarious hold on the edge, with the enemy close up peering over on three sides, hurling destruction from the complete assortment of his weapons." In such a place, Urquhart ruefully noted "it requires great tenacity and a bit of humour to hold on."[2]

After the First Battle of Ypres wound down, the crescent-shaped salient had stood about eight miles wide at its base with a six-mile-deep apex. The Second Battle of Ypres had shrunk those dimensions, but only a little. Its citizens had long ago abandoned the once glorious Flemish capital of Ypres when the German artillery came into range. Soldiers still thronged like rats amid the city's ruins, billeting inside half-destroyed buildings and cellars. The city's long-destroyed streetcar line terminus on Menin Road near a north-south junction was so frequently shelled it was nicknamed Hellfire Corner. To hide the movement of men and supplies, the British had circled Ypres with huge tarpaulins to obstruct the view of German artillery observers who responded by regularly drenching known routes of movement with shellfire.[3]

The Canadian Corps arrived three divisions strong with another slated to deploy in August 1916. But lacking the 4th Canadian Infantry Division, and with the newly deployed 3rd Canadian Infantry Division short of its own artillery, the latter was supported by gunners from the Indian 3rd (Lahore) Division. Fifty-six-year-old Maj.-Gen. Malcolm Smith Mercer, who had formerly commanded 1st Division's 1st Brigade, headed up 3rd Division.[4]

A hiccup in the relief plan saw Canadian Corps beginning to take over from V Corps precisely at the same time that its British 3rd Division was scheduled to put in an attack on the village of St. Eloi. An extensive artillery bombardment was to precede the assault, but hopes for success were really pinned on a scheme to detonate six massive mines that would destroy a 600-yard section of German frontage. Noting that the British division was badly worn out and depleted by casualties, Lt.-Gen. Edwin Alderson suggested that 2nd Canadian Infantry Division assume responsibility for the attack. But, as the British troops had specially trained for the operation and there was no time to similarly train the Canadians, it was decided to go ahead as planned. Once St. Eloi was captured during the March 27 operation, 2nd Division would take over the objective.[5]

Tunnelling under enemy lines to sow mines was an increasingly common tactic, and the predominantly clay soil in the salient made it an ideal area of operation. Engineers had started the tunnels running from the British front to St. Eloi in August 1915, working at depths ranging from 50 to 60 feet. By late March, six mines, sized in accordance to the destruction desired on the given section of German trench overhead, were deployed in a matching number of tunnels. One contained only 600 pounds of ammonal while another held a massive 31,000 pounds. Detonated in combination, the mines were expected to obliterate the German defenders so that the attacking infantry could then plunge through the gap and advance about 300 yards.

At 0415 hours the attack began with an opening artillery salvo and detonation of the six mines followed over an interval of only a few seconds. The British Official History described that "it appeared as if a long village was being lifted through flames into the air."[6] Lord Beaverbrook (Sir Max Aitken), serving as the General Representative of Canada at the front, wrote in his 1917 *Canada in Flanders* that it was "like the sudden outburst of a volcano."[7] The explosions were felt and heard in southern England.

At Ground Zero the results exceeded anticipations alarmingly. Existing landmarks were decimated and some British trenches collapsed as well as the German targets "like packs of cards." Two German infantry companies were annihilated and the previously important piece of tactical real estate known as The Mound was reduced to a gaping hole. A tailing pile from a brickfield, the thirty-foot-high Mound had covered a half acre. Heavy shelling over many months had whittled away half its height, but now The Mound was entirely gone.

At first the attack went well with the first three craters on the right quickly overrun and the British troops managing to bull their way through to the German third line 200 yards beyond. On the left flank, however, devastation from the explosions rendered landmarks unrecognizable. Confused, the assault troops halted in a large crater designated as Crater 6 in the mistaken belief they were on the assigned objectives of Craters 4 and 5. For three days the fighting raged with neither British nor German troops taking command of the two craters. But then German troops set up a machine-gun post inside Crater 5 and the British matched this with one of their own in Crater 4. On April 3, the British managed to overrun Crater 5 and the week's fighting drew to a close with all assigned objectives but one taken. The sole objective remaining in German hands was Point 85, a height of ground in No Man's Land the Germans immediately began using as a forming-up point for counterattacks.

At noon the following day, 2nd Canadian Infantry Division took over the front, finding its original trenches all but destroyed by the mine explosions and the 1,000-yard new line running in front of the craters defended by a trench no deeper than a drainage ditch. Bloated corpses and body parts protruded out of the mud or floated in the watery pools inside the craters. Tactically the position posed a nightmare to garrison—the ground so disturbed that the water table had risen virtually everywhere almost to the surface making trench digging a futile enterprise. Four of the craters were so closely clustered they formed an impassable barrier that forced troops moving from the rear to the front to carry out a wide detour around them. Crater 5—part of this cluster—was 50 feet deep and 180 feet across. The earth blasted from its heart formed a massive rampart that rose between 12 and 20 feet above ground and spilled outward for 50 yards in all directions. The Canadian Official Historian later declared that rarely had any troops been required to take over a "less advantageous position."[8]

* * *

1st Canadian Infantry Division held the front lines immediately north of 2nd Division, but its troops had little idea of the precariousness of the situation to their south. The sounds of bombardments and counter-bombardments clearly indicated a fierce contest was underway, but with the Ypres-Comines Canal cutting between the divisional lines, 1st Division could play no useful role there.

The Canadian Scottish found their area of operations—so familiar to the veterans—difficult enough. "There stood 'The Snout,' 'Hill 60,' the village of Wytschaete perched on the northerly shoulder of our old friend, the Wytschaete–Messines Ridge, and the ruins of Hollebeke or Blue Château on the banks of the Ypres-Comines Canal at the foot of it.... Prostrate before the gaze of the watchers on those ramparts, lay the city of Ypres, the hub of the salient, which radiated derelict canals and railways, and the roads and paths over which hastened the specks of humanity.... Even the rest camps in distant areas were at the mercy of the enemy, for every trace of habitation—the smoke or the dust by day, or the glimmer of light by night—lay open to his observation."[9]

South of Ypres, behind the Canadian front, stood 511-foot-high Mont Kemmel, the eastern anchor for a range of hills stretching westward across the otherwise flat Flanders plain to the sea.[10] But Kemmel and the rest of the range was too far back to serve as an observation point or defensive position. Their heights only reinforced the sense that soldiers in the salient lived inside a saucer. Movement by daylight was safe only for men moving warily in ones and twos. Anything larger drew immediate artillery or mortar fire. This meant conducting all supply and unit movement at night, but knowing this the Germans subjected all likely routes to sporadic artillery fire from dusk to dawn.[11]

Night in the salient was surreal, the flash and rumble of the German guns giving the impression of an endless sheet-lightning storm. Very lights and other flares bathed No Man's Land in a ghostly light under which the barbed wire aprons glimmered. Nowhere was safe from shellfire, the shriek of incoming rounds usually heard too late for those struck by it to find cover. "When your number's up ..." the soldiers declared.

No Man's Land was routinely subjected to untargeted searching fire by German machine guns, and snipers were always lurking and ready to shoot at the slightest movement within their range. At night, the racket was worse than during the days, so soldiers had to learn to sleep through it as best they could. And always there was the cold and damp that pervaded the trenches.

Dawn brought a welcome respite. Urquhart noted then that "nature, as if aware that she would be left undisturbed, reasserted herself. The haze of the night's bombardment still floated around; the smell of the high explosive still tainted the air; but the skylark mounted up singing gaily. The fragrance of the blossoming hedges, the scent of flowers in the neglected gardens, the freshness of the morning air mingled in a draught of sweetness and advanced bravely to defeat the poison of death. The sun peeped over the summit of Wytschaete and gilded Kemmel with its tints; the war and its carnage dissolved for a fleeting moment into a mirage of beauty and peace."[12]

With its right flank anchored on the foot of the hill known as The Snout and its left running along the summit of Mount Sorrel with Observatory Ridge—which was the last height of ground between Ypres and the Germans and so tactically vital to both sides—the 16th Battalion occupied a notoriously bad sector for drawing the fire of artillery and snipers positioned atop The Snout. One 60- to 70-yard chunk of open real estate just 500 to 600 yards from The Snout was routinely covered by the snipers there and could only be crossed at great peril in a headlong dash. Urquhart witnessed Major Cyrus Peck making such a dash, moving in a "hop and skip at a pace hardly in keeping with his ample proportions." Lt. Gordon Tupper, who accompanied the major in this crossing, received a flesh wound while Peck's batman, Pte. James Metcalf, later found a bullet lodged inside the case holding his safety razor. The Snout's snipers were skillful and quick to recognize when senior officers came within range. Brig. George Tuxford had a bullet hit his newly issued steel helmet, circle clean around inside it, and then pass out like a momentarily trapped bee might without causing him the slightest injury.[13]

At first the German artillery concentrated its full fury on 2nd Division's lines, but on April 4 the guns subjected the entire corps front to an almost continuous bombardment despite marking St. Eloi as the bull's-eye point. The two forward 2nd Division battalions were badly mauled and their trenches so damaged that the men were exposed to deadly fire from machine guns ranging in from just 150 yards' distance. By the evening of April 5, an attempt to relieve one of the battalions began despite the heavy shellfire. This relief was still underway when two German battalions counterattacked at 0330 hours on April 6 and, in less than three hours, the Canadian troops lost all the gains won by the British on March 27. The fighting would seesaw back and forth until April 19, when 2nd Division and British Second Army's Gen. Herbert Plumer—who had ordered repeated counterattacks—were forced to admit defeat. Canadian casualties totalled 1,373 in exchange for 483 Germans killed.

"It seems extraordinary, yet if one thinks of it quietly and calmly, it is not very likely, but almost a natural outcome of the conditions under which your Division took over the line," Lt.-Gen. Edwin Alderson wrote Maj.-Gen. Richard Turner. "Our Army Commander, gallant gentleman as he is, has taken it well, though he is probably most hit, because the Army originated the situation."[14]

Plumer took the loss anything but graciously. He sacked the chief of staff and an assortment of officers from 3rd British Division, whom he believed botched the initial offensive. Then he turned on the Canadians, demanding the heads of Turner and Brig. H. D. B. Ketchen—whose 6th Canadian Infantry Brigade had been driven back. Knowing he could save only one of the men, Alderson drafted a report that made Ketchen the scapegoat. On reading it, Turner refused to endorse what he considered a pack of distortions. Furious at this rebuke by an officer he held in little esteem, Alderson asked Field Marshal Douglas Haig to dismiss Turner. Haig, cautioning that he sensed "some feeling against the English" among the Canadians, demurred and decided to axe neither Turner nor Ketchen. Mistakes were to be expected, he declared, and the Canadians had all done "their best and made a gallant fight."

None of this quelled Plumer's fury and, backed into a corner, Haig announced that Alderson faced too many "administrative and political questions ... in addition to his duties as commander in the field" and also "reluctantly" concluded that he was "incapable of holding the Canadian Divisions together." Responding to a War Office request, Prime Minister Robert Borden and his Cabinet approved replacing Alderson on April 26. Within a month he was shuffled off to a face-saving appointment as Inspector General of the Canadian Troops in England.[15] Thoroughly baffled, Alderson went to his largely redundant new posting believing his insistence on replacing the Ross rifle and equally problematic Colt machine gun with British weapons the summer before had so infuriated Sam Hughes that he vengefully masterminded his ouster. Although the move had enraged Hughes, who had watched with despair as the Canadian Corps set aside the Ross for Lee Enfields and the Colt in favour of a medley of Vickers and Lewis machine guns, he had played no role in Alderson's removal.

Ottawa left it to Haig to appoint a successor and he selected Lt.-Gen. Julian H. G. Byng. The fifty-three-year-old Byng, known as "Bungo," had been commander-in-chief of the British Army of Occupation in Egypt when the war broke out. Recalled to command 3rd Cavalry Division, he had led it through the First Battle of Ypres and more recently overseen the British evacuation from Gallipoli before taking command of XVII Corps on the Western Front. Both as a divisional and corps commander Byng had established a reputation as a "master of tactics," who was practical, thoughtful, and unafraid of innovation.[16] This had surprised many colleagues who had seen him as a stereotypical cavalryman—jaunty, cheerful, but not overly bright.

Perhaps fearing it meant he was being sent into the wilderness of obscurity, Byng lamented: "Why am I sent to the Canadians? I don't know a Canadian. Why this stunt?"[17] Initially his fears seemed valid as Canadian Corps was directed to take over a larger frontage in the salient so that Haig could withdraw British divisions for transfer to the Somme where the next great summer offensive was to occur.

* * *

The new alignment of the corps left 2nd Division still before St. Eloi, 1st Division operating with two battalions forward in a frontage centred on Hill 60, and 3rd Division extending its full four battalions in line from Hill 60, past Mount Sorrel to Hill 61 and nearby Hill 62, then northwards to Sanctuary Wood, and into The Gap—as the ruined village of Hooge was called. Branching off for a thousand yards west of Hill 62— nicknamed Tor Top—was Observatory Ridge. The Germans had long desired this ridge, because from its heights they would be able to mount accurate artillery fire against any target deep behind the Allied front, which might well make retaining the salient untenable.

In early May, the Canadians began to suspect the Germans were getting ready to make their move when patrols discovered German engineers pushing saps forward on either side of Tor Top. By month end, a trench dug 50 yards forward of the German front line and just a hundred yards from the Canadian wire on a lateral line to the saps tied them together. Similar saps were found in front of Mount Sorrel. The Royal Flying Corps also reported that a curious trench system had appeared that served no tactical purpose, but identically matched the Canadian positions near Tor Top. Was this a rehearsal area? Nobody knew. But the sense that something was afoot grew.

Just after nightfall on June 1, the German artillery fell silent all along the Canadian front. Not another shell was fired for the remaining seven hours of darkness. Unbeknownst to the Canadians, German infantry was at work in No Man's Land, cutting gaps in the wire in front of 3rd Division. Rising suspicions that the artillery silence meant the Germans were up to something were allayed when the guns resumed their harassment fire shortly before dawn. At 0600 on June 2, Maj.-Gen. Malcolm Mercer and Brig. Victor Williams of the division's 8th Canadian Infantry Brigade were strolling the front-line trenches that ran from Mount Sorrel to Tor Top just as the Germans opened up with a "veritable tornado of fire [that] ravaged the Canadian positions from half a mile west of Mount Sorrel to the northern edge of Sanctuary Wood." What followed, the

War Office later declared, was "the heaviest [bombardment] endured by British troops up to this time."[18] Unable to drive the Allies out of their forward trenches with poison gas, the Germans had now decided to mirror Allied tactics by attempting to blast them out through sheer weight of shells fired from a massive concentration of guns positioned immediately behind the infantry being sent into an attack.

Smack in the vortex of this bombardment was 8th Brigade's 4th Canadian Mounted Rifles and, in minutes, "their trenches vanished and the garrisons in them were annihilated." Of 702 officers and men, only 76 emerged unscathed. Mercer and Williams were both gravely wounded—the former's eardrums shattered. Nobody could move, there was no question of evacuating the wounded or rescuing the two senior officers from where they lay. On Mount Sorrel's reverse slope an underground gallery offered some shelter and here most of the survivors huddled until it too collapsed. The barrage raged for seven hours. Then the Germans detonated four mines close to the trenches on Mount Sorrel and four infantry battalions advanced with eleven more standing in reserve. "In bright sunlight the grey-coated figures advanced in four waves spaced about seventy-five yards apart," wrote the Canadian official historian. "Afterwards Canadian survivors spoke of the assured air and the almost leisurely pace of the attackers, who appeared confident that their artillery had blotted out all resistance."

They met virtually no resistance, for 1st Canadian Mounted Rifles— the other 8th Brigade battalion on the front lines—had also been shattered by the shelling and reduced to scattered bands that could only fight and die or surrender. Meanwhile, 3rd Division's commander was struck in the leg by a bullet and then finished off by a spray of shrapnel. Williams was captured. In minutes the division and brigade under attack were rendered leaderless. From a few isolated fortified positions, Canadians fought back only to be immolated by Germans armed with flamethrowers. After piercing 600 yards into the Canadian lines, the storm troops leading the assault halted per their instructions and began digging in despite being astride Observatory Ridge with little between them and the ultimate prize of Ypres. This gave the beleaguered Canadians a breathing space to reorganize and establish a blocking line.

Brig. E. S. Hoare-Nairne of the Lahore Divisional Artillery assumed temporary command of 3rd Division while Lt.-Col. J.C.L. Bott of the 2nd

Canadian Mounted Rifles took over 8th Canadian Infantry Brigade, re-establishing a command structure. Byng, meanwhile, issued orders at 2045 that "all ground lost to-day will be retaken tonight" in a counterattack at 0200 hours. With 3rd Division in disarray and reeling from its devastating losses, Hoare-Nairne was given two of 1st Division's brigades for the counterattack with 2nd Canadian Infantry Brigade to operate against Mount Sorrel while 3rd Canadian Infantry Brigade struck Tor Top.[19]

Because 3rd Brigade had been in corps reserve and 16th Battalion's Lt.-Col. Jack Leckie was away on leave, Major Cyrus Peck commanded the Canadian Scottish. Peck had been at brigade headquarters when the initial bombardment of 3rd Division began and for far too long the news received was contradictory and confusing. Finally, he had returned to battalion knowing little other than a crisis was at hand. Rumours were flying that the entire salient was collapsing.

Not until 1630 hours was Brig. George Tuxford summoned to 1st Division headquarters and told 3rd Brigade would be attacking. Even then Maj.-Gen. Arthur Currie could not tell him what objectives he was to aim for. Tuxford decided all he could do was get the brigade moving toward the front, but this had to be undertaken cautiously as he had no idea how far the Germans had penetrated.[20]

Peck had anticipated events, earlier confining the Canadian Scottish to their camp while "the wagons, with the entrenching tools, reserve small arms ammunition, and grenades were brought from the transport lines."[21] Consequently, when orders arrived at 1700 hours, the battalion was able to move immediately. Because of the way the brigade had been billeted, the Royal Montreal Regiment and 48th Highlanders of Canada were closer to the jumping-off point than the other two battalions, so Tuxford decided they would put in the attack with the Royal Highlanders of Canada and the Canadian Scottish standing in support.

While his men marched, Tuxford reported to Brigadier Hoare-Nairne for final instructions. He was dismayed to be kept loitering outside 3rd Division headquarters until 2145 hours because the acting divisional commander was off discussing details at corps headquarters. Finally, Hoare-Nairne returned and gave Tuxford written instructions that in "conjunction with the 2nd Canadian Infantry Brigade on the right and the 7th Canadian Infantry Brigade on the left, the 3rd Brigade would attack and recover trenches 52 to 59 inclusive, comprising Hills 61 and 62."

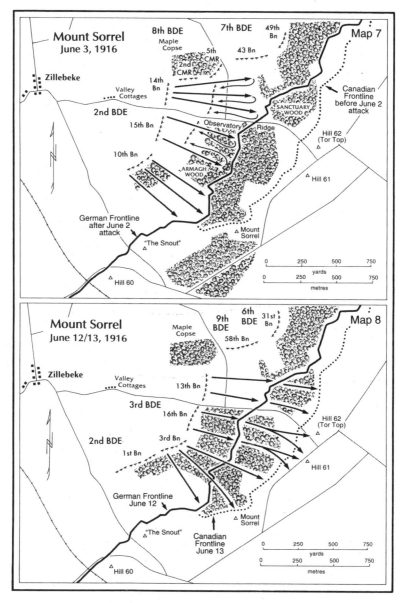

With the brigade still 11 miles from its dawn attack position, Tuxford realized he was in "a race against time." Fortunately a 3rd Division staff officer had sped things up with a telephone call to 3rd Brigade headquarters. Advised of the plan well before Tuxford, Captain Urquhart had acted on his own initiative and ordered the battalions forward a mile to an assembly point near Zillebeke.²²

Urquhart remained uneasy, fearing reported "strong masses of Germans ... moving up towards Mount Sorrel" indicated that enemy reinforcements had so strengthened the enemy positions the counterattack would fail. By the time Tuxford returned, all the headquarters staff, except for Urquhart and the brigade major, had gone ahead. Horses saddled and ready outside the small hut, the three men huddled for a final consultation over a large trench map showing the southern portion of the salient spread on a table before them. Suddenly a car pulled up and Gen. Currie stomped in. "Towering above them all and pointing to the map ... he explained in a quiet, decisive way the involved situation, urged all speed with the assembling of the troops, and ended his appreciation by the statement: 'We can't tell what the enemy's intentions are, and, for all we know, he may be planning to drive us from the Salient before the morning.'"[23]

By this time the battalions were marching across open country with their objectives visible in the distance. The Germans were sending up massive volleys of Very lights, "orange, red and green," so that the low ground before the slopes of Hill 60 and Observatory Ridge was clearly illuminated. Both sides had artillery firing continuously, the sounds of guns echoing back from the hills. Hearing the ground in front of Observatory Ridge was free of enemy, Tuxford ordered the leading 14th and 15th Battalions to assemble at the ridge's westerly foot just in front of Zillebeke and facing a cluster of houses called Valley Cottages that lined the road running up the ridge. The 14th was on the left, the 15th on the right with the 16th close behind it in support. The Canadian Scottish slipped a little to the south of where the 48th Highlanders were forming and found shelter in some old trenches dug behind a hedge near a main communication trench called Fosse Way. Off to the left, the Royal Highlanders of Canada had set up about 200 yards farther back behind a copse of trees between Fosse Way and Zillebeke Lake.

Six green rockets fired from 3rd Division's advanced headquarters were to signal Zero Hour at 0230 on June 3.[24] Impatiently Tuxford watched as first his second hand and then minute hand ticked past the appointed hour. It was a miserable night, a cold heavy rain falling. The troops stood or sat in the open, growing colder and wetter with every passing minute. Soon Tuxford looked away from his watch. Minutes turned to hours with still no signal. At 0445 Tuxford

assured 3rd Division his brigade was ready to go, but there was no re-
ply.[25] Finally word came that the 7th Battalion from 2nd Brigade and the
49th Battalion of 3rd Division's 7th Brigade were still on the march. The
attack had to wait on their arrival. Dawn came and, with it, instructions that the attack would begin at 0700.[26]

A twenty-minute bombardment that Tuxford thought "exceptional-
ly weak" preceded the attack. Ten minutes after the shellfire ceased the
rockets shot skyward. Urquhart wondered if they really were the rockets, for they just looked like "puffs of smoke in the sky. There was a pause
of doubt. Then the two attacking battalions after a short interval moved
off."[27] The officers of the 7th and 49th Battalions never saw the rockets at
all. They held their troops where they were and watched as the two 3rd
Brigade battalions advanced out of the centre of the Canadian line toward Hill 61 and Tor Top "with the greatest coolness" and straight into
a hailstorm of artillery, mortar, and machine-gun fire. Had the four
battalions gone forward as one the fire could not have been so concentrated, but due to the uneven start the Germans saturated the Montreal
and Toronto troops with fire and then meted out the same punishment
in turn against each of the other two leading battalions as they lurched
forward at different times.[28]

The Royal Montreal Regiment excelled this day, advancing into
the withering fire at a steady pace that kept it right in line with the 48th
Highlanders. Both battalions disappeared from view, swallowed by the
gunsmoke cloaking the battleground. Two hours passed before a runner
came back with word that they had advanced 2,000 yards, going through
Valley Cottages and on to Rudkin House. This put them within 1,000 yards
of the forward trenches. But the runner said they could advance no further because of the intensity of artillery fire. Instead they were digging in
and would hold despite the fire, their heavy losses, and being subjected to
enfilading fire from Hill 60 and The Snout. The 7th Battalion, meanwhile,
had been blocked in front of a heavily manned trench in Armagh Wood
while the 49th Battalion fared better, gaining a section of trenches almost
on its objective.[29] All four battalions were badly disorganized and some
men, in each case, unaware the attack had stalled out, had continued on
to the final objectives only to be killed or taken prisoner.

Urquhart was out in the smoke trying to precisely locate the two
3rd Brigade battalions. Finally he located the Montrealers and was led to

Major A. T. Powell. Although wounded, the major said he was in command and that all the other senior officers had been killed or injured. The battalion was digging in and badly cut up.[30] Once the forward line appeared stabilized, Powell passed command to Lt. R. A. Pelletier and was taken to the rear for treatment. Pelletier would be twice "blown up," with one blast knocking him unconscious for a while. But he refused to relinquish command until the battalion was relieved.[31]

Once assured the Royal Montreal Regiment's position was as secure as it could be, Urquhart had set off southward along a trench running through a small wood of shattered maples appropriately named Maple Copse to find the 48th Highlanders. He soon found things "in a bad state there.... Many wounded and dead in terribly mangled conditions." At the battalion's headquarters dugout he learned "they were badly hit, losing a number of officers."

Returning to brigade headquarters, Urquhart advised Tuxford that neither battalion was close to its final objectives. Nobody knew for sure, but in both cases some isolated groups might have got through and would now be cut off. Supporting this theory was the fact that each battalion was missing a number of full platoons. Urquhart warned that any attempt to renew the advance beyond where the forward battalions were dug in would entail crossing wide-open ground, dominated by heavy fire from commanding positions. Tuxford realized that he would have to wait until nightfall before passing his two support battalions through. But the question was whether the attempt should be made at all.[32]

The Canadian Scottish and Royal Highlanders, meanwhile, had spent most of the day being hammered mercilessly by German artillery. Men died or were wounded while huddling in shallow, muddy holes. At dusk, it was decided that continuing the attack was fruitless and the two support battalions were set to work digging a defensive trench with orders to meet the expected renewal of the German offensive where they stood. Casualties continued to mount as the shellfire never relented and, by dawn, the survivors were exhausted from a terrifying night spent carving some semblance of a trench out of the mud-soaked earth.

Tuxford had been busy, too, securing more men by having 1st Canadian Infantry Brigade's 2nd Battalion placed under his command. He planned that these fresh troops would relieve the Montreal and Toronto battalions while his other two battalions put in a renewed counterattack. But it was not to be. For the next seventy-two hours both sides pounded the other with artillery, but neither advanced. Each day, Tuxford received orders to prepare to send the Canadian Scottish forward only to subsequently receive a postponement. On June 7, Currie informed him that the attack "would now definitely be temporarily postponed." The brigade was replaced by battalions from 2nd Division's 5th Brigade and moved to billets in the rear. Their rest was to be short; the battalion commanders warned that 1st Division was teeing up a better-planned attack.[33]

Standing in support had taken an unusually heavy toll on the Canadian Scottish for such duty. Three officers had been killed and one wounded. Twelve other ranks had died, another seventy-nine been wounded, and eight reported missing. But the two attacking battalions had suffered far higher losses. The Royal Montreal Regiment reported two officers dead, fifteen wounded, and one missing. Among the Montrealers' other ranks 42 were killed, 207 wounded, and 129 missing and presumed taken prisoner. Three 48th Highlander officers had been slain and nine wounded. The Toronto regiment's other ranks lost 21 dead while another 175 other ranks fell wounded. A further seventy-seven men were missing.[34]

* * *

Tuxford later wrote, "This action did not recover the lost trenches, it resulted in consolidating an advanced line connecting the 3rd Division in a due southerly direction via RUDKIN HOUSE, with the 2nd Brigade of the 1st Division. This ground was entirely wide open to the enemy at the time of the advance, which also denied OBSERVATORY RIDGE to the enemy." But the Germans still held valuable ground just two miles from Ypres that posed a constant threat to the entire salient. Field Marshal Haig ordered them expelled, but—because of his plans in the Somme—offered Canadian Corps nothing more than supporting artillery and one British infantry brigade. Perhaps, he said, the attack could be made with less infantry if they were sufficiently supported by more gunnery. Accordingly the artillery consisted of the greatest number of guns the British had ever concentrated on such a narrow front—218 in all. These guns were soon arrayed and pounding both the German incursion zone and its support lines. The Germans reported that casualties among the 26th Infantry Division and 120th Regiment, which held most of the disputed ground, "mounted in horrifying numbers."[35]

Trained as an artilleryman, Currie carefully monitored the gun plan and added a twist of his own. At his insistence, a four-day bombardment began pounding the German lines on June 9 at intervals of twenty to thirty minutes. Each time the guns lifted, the Germans, who had taken shelter in dugouts back from their forward trenches to escape the torrent of shells, would tumble forward to man their positions only to be caught in the renewed shelling. Their losses mounted and yet no Canadian infantry came at them.

Currie would do the same thing on June 13, but this time put in the attack. With his battalions all badly depleted, Currie regrouped them into two composite brigades. On the right, 1st Brigade's Brig. Louis Lipsett would attack with 1st, 3rd, 7th, and 8th Battalions, while on the left Brig. Tuxford would head for Hill 61 and Tor Top with the 2nd, 4th, 13th, and 16th Battalions. Lipsett would have just one battalion out front—the 3rd— while Tuxford placed his trust in the battalions of his brigade—the 13th and 16th. On the far left, the 9th Brigade's 58th Battalion would also join 1st Division's assault. This time, there would be no confusion about objective locations. Currie had acquired accurate aerial photographs of the enemy's lines and codenamed each trench with the name of a Canadian city. The front of the German line was Halifax, the next line Montreal, the following one Winnipeg with the final objective—the Canadian front line of June 2—dubbed Vancouver. In 3rd Brigade's case, Vancouver included both summits of Hill 61 and Tor Top.[36]

On the night of June 11–12, the infantry moved through heavy rain to their forming-up positions. The Canadian Scottish returned to the Fosse Way trenches, now partially flooded, that they had occupied the previous week. Here they passed "a wet, cheerless day, a steady, misty drizzle soaking the clothing of the troops who, during those hours, lay in the open." A prisoner brought in boasted that the Germans expected a counterattack, news that little raised the men's spirits. Another worry was that the ground was a quagmire. An intelligence report declared the "shell holes deep and wide, filled with water. The fallen trees in Armagh and Sanctuary Woods form serious obstacles to the advance of heavily laden troops."[37]

Stuck in the open and enduring a day of misery ensured the men were all tired before they even began, but there had been no choice in the matter. The only bright news anyone could give Lt.-Col. Jack Leckie was that an old trench ran parallel at a hundred yards' distance from the German positions at Halifax. This would serve as a good assembly point for a quick dash into the German front line while still being far enough back to not fall within the artillery's kill zone. Leckie decided to put the platoons of the leading wave into the trench and then position his second wave in shell holes about 50 yards farther back. The third and fourth waves would remain at Fosse Way. It was a risky plan because of the likelihood of discovery while moving so close to the German front, but Leckie hoped the stormy night would conceal the first wave.

Nos. 1 and 2 Companies under Captains Stanley Wood and Roderick Bell-Irving respectively would lead with two platoons forward and two in support. They would attack in two waves, each consisting of two lines spread out in extended order. Two bomber sections numbering twenty men would be on the left and right flanks. The line of advance would take the Canadian Scottish across the front slope of Observatory Ridge, into the hollow of shattered Armagh Wood, and on to the final objective.

Wood and Bell-Irving led their men off at 2200 hours on June 12. Because of the need for stealth and the slow progress over badly torn ground, it took three hours for them to cover 1,000 yards and gain the old trench line and shell holes.[38] But they arrived undetected and still had thirty minutes to prepare for the 0130 attack, which would go in the moment the ten-hour-long artillery bombardment lifted for the final time. But forty-five minutes before the guns ceased, the tempo of shelling suddenly surged to a terrific crescendo. When the guns stopped, with ears still ringing, the Canadians went over the top, advancing through a dense smokescreen and lashing rain that reduced visibility to mere feet.[39]

Each Can Scot carried a rifle with fixed bayonet and 270 rounds of ammunition, two grenades, one iron ration, a full water bottle, and three empty sandbags that would be used to create a defensive parapet at the objective. Every third man also carried a shovel. Behind the two infantry waves followed consolidating parties consisting of one hundred engineers and pioneers, seventy-five men tasked with carrying support materiel, and twenty-five wire-laying signallers. These men had a shovel for every second man while the tenth man in a section was loaded down with a pick, an axe, and bags of nails. One man in each party had a cross-cut saw for cutting trees, branches, or available lumber into usable lengths for parapet construction. The officers in the front ranks carried a multi-tude of flares—white to fire when Halifax fell, red when Vancouver was gained, and green to report that the attack was held up. Red flags would be raised on the flanks of the battalion at each objective.[40]

Right out on the front edge of their companies, Bell-Irving and Wood headed through a rain of German bullets that scythed men down on every side. Men lost their footing in the treacherous mud and, within seconds of going over the top, most were covered head to toe in gooey slime. Rifles and revolvers became clogged and rendered use-less.[41] Between the start point and Halifax, Wood—the southern gen-tleman from America—was killed by a bullet through the heart. Two lieutenants, Charles Cecil Adams and Howard James McLaurin (the latter commanding the second wave No. 4 Company), were mortally wounded in the charge. McLaurin's brother, Pte. Douglas C. McLaurin, had also served in the Canadian Scottish and been killed on April 5, 1916. On June 7, Lt. McLaurin had suffered an earlier wound but re-fused to go to hospital because the battalion was so shorthanded. If there was to be an attack, he had said, it was his "duty to stay with and lead his men in it."[42]

Advancing with the riflemen for the first time were sections of men armed with the Lewis gun which, along with the Vickers, had replaced the Colt. One man could carry a Lewis, which weighed 26 pounds, and match pace with the infantry. It was still a heavy weapon to lug across No Man's Land and the complicated firing mechanism offered an "astonish-ing variety of stoppages."[43] Because of the gun's complexity and its rapid rate of fire, the gunner—designated No. 1—was supported by a crew of three to four men. The No. 2 man's job was to reload the weapon while two or three others carried spare magazines in special canvas bags. Each round-pan magazine was loaded with forty-seven .303-calibre cartridges. Eager to prove their worth, the Lewis gunners suffered heavily. The crew of No. 1 gun was chopped down to two men even before it stepped out into No Man's Land. Five times during the advance, other men pitched in to help operate the gun only to be killed, but the first two survivors made it all the way to Vancouver. No. 5's gun crew all died.

Despite the heavy resistance, the leading companies gained Halifax, the bombers blasting the trench with one grenade after another. Their ri-fles rendered useless by the mud, most of the infantrymen also resorted to chucking the two grenades they carried at the enemy. Once the explosions ceased, the men plunged into the trench and went at the Germans with bayonets. At the sight of the approaching steel, the majority of the enemy either surrendered or took to their heels. Clearly the artillery had done its job. Many Germans seemed dazed and incoherent—wandering about with no rifles or other equipment. Entire sections of Halifax had been obliterated and bodies were strewn everywhere.

Bell-Irving had just fired the white flare declaring Halifax taken and was rallying the men for a charge on Montreal when a machine gun opened up from a nearby wood and men began to fall screaming. Flashes from "a black jumble of fallen trees" betrayed the gun's location. Immediately a group of men rushed the position only to be driven to ground by its deadly fire. Suddenly the attack began to falter. Seeing a clearing to the left of the position that could be crossed quickly, Bell-Irving dashed alone into it and came at the gun from the flank. His revolver had been jammed earlier by mud, but he had snatched a rifle with fixed bayonet from a casualty. Now he leapt over the machine gun's parapet into the midst of the gun crew and in quick succession bayoneted three Germans. The fourth managed to grab Bell-Irving's rifle, threatening to wrest it away from the tiring officer, when reinforcements arrived and someone shot the German down. Still clinging to the rifle, Bell-Irving stood panting over the corpse. Then he tossed the gun aside, scooped up a new rifle with fixed bayonet, and calmly led the battalion toward Montreal.

Nos. 1 and 2 Companies moved out in line, no longer strong enough to form two waves. Close behind were the other two companies. As they left Halifax, the artillery finished working over Montreal and lifted. It was so dark, finding the way without straying either to left or right was almost impossible. They clambered over tangles of dead and wounded, shattered trees the artillery had felled as cleanly as an axe, slipping in the oily mud, tripping over webs of branches and stumps. Rifles still jammed, they threw grenades at any German position encountered. It was a dangerous practice as in the blackness they could easily grenade their comrades. More than a few men were wounded by shrapnel from a grenade thrown by a nearby friend. Montreal fell easily and the battalion paused to reorganize with all four companies now strung into one ever-shrinking line.

Before them the ground proved open, passage easier. Winnipeg fell in a matter of minutes and from there it was a quick dash to Vancouver where the enemy "offered no fight; the Battalion walked unmolested into its final objective." It was 0215 hours. Major Cyrus Peck arrived minutes later, having kept the battalion's forward headquarters close on the heels of the rifle companies. Not until 0310 did his message reporting the news reach Leckie's headquarters. As with all the other objectives, the trenches here had been smashed by the artillery. In one small section a "stretch of the fire step was left upstanding giving a resting place to the crumpled bodies of its defenders, whose blood tinged with redness the water at the bottom of the trench."

As dawn lit the sky, Lt. Pete Osler ignited the red flare that signalled success, mounted the parapet, and walked back and forth "waving it on high like the fiery cross of old." But the battle was not over. Groups of Germans could be seen near the trenches attempting to rally a counterattack. Seeing this, and also spotting a German machine gun nearby, Cpl. Hugh Arthur Rees, a machine gunner with No. 2 team, brought the weapon into action. For the next four hours, as Vancouver was increasingly pounded by German artillery, Rees kept the gun in operation and broke up one attempted counterattack after another even when it became clear the enemy artillery was attempting to zero in on him. Finally a shell found the mark and the crewmen with him were all killed while Rees was badly wounded. It was the first act of heroism that would see the British-born twenty-three-year-old awarded a Military Medal for valour.

In the light of day, the Canadian Scottish looked back from the heights they held at the battleground crossed during a bloody night. Through "the blur of rain," they saw "a dreary waste of desolation—sodden earth, water-logged shell-holes, shattered tree stumps, and limp, bedraggled groups of men cautiously picking their way back over the morass into a curtain of watery mist, which entirely obscured the rear area." They had won at a terrible cost. From June 3 to June 14, the loss of officers—with ten killed—proved the highest number the battalion would sustain in any engagement over the course of the war. So many were dead or wounded that three non-commissioned officers—Gus Lyons, Jas Russell, and J.R.M. Ellis (all given commissions only the night before the battle)—ended up in senior positions—two commanding rifle companies and the third being second-in-command of one.[44] During the period June 11–14, 16th Battalion lost five officers killed and four wounded. Other rank casualties totalled 23 dead, 155 wounded, and 65 missing.[45]

The other battalions suffered similar casualty rates and all achieved their objectives at about the same time, so that the Battle of Mount Sorrel was mostly concluded in just a little over an hour. The Germans effectively lost all the ground won on June 2 and the lines were restored as before. During the twelve days when the salient's survival had hung in the balance, Canadian Corps suffered almost 8,000 casualties while the Germans sustained 5,765. The Canadians and Germans glared at each other for the rest of the summer, in trenches lying 150 yards apart.[46] On August 9, the Canadians left the salient and moved to the rear for a short respite before once again marching toward battle.

In 1915, the Canadian Scottish had spent only three weeks in the salient. This time it served four and a half months. Both sojourns had been costly, but the latest had brought two hundred more casualties than the first and a greater loss of "trusted leaders." As the Canadian Scottish marched away they timed their step to a new piece of doggerel:

> Far from Ypres I long to be,
> Where the Allemand cannot get me;
> Think of me crouching where the worms creep,
> Waiting for Sergeant to sing me to sleep.
> Sleep? Sergeant—sleep?
> Does anyone sleep?
> They certainly sleep; everyone sleeps,
> But not surely—surely not, Sergeant!
> Not in the Yeep-pres Salient.[47]

On September 28, 1914, less than two months after Canada's declaration of war against the Axis powers, 16th Battalion shipped out from Quebec aboard *Adania*. This rare but underexposed image, taken from the ship deck, shows members of both the 14th Battalion (in caps) and 16th Battalion (glengarries) looking back toward Quebec.

The dilemma over how to merge four Highland regiments into one is clearly illustrated in this photo taken on the Salisbury Plain in 1915. Although the distinctive tartans are hard to make out, the differences in glengarries are plain to see.

Although his shyness led to a seemingly aloof manner, Robert Leckie's experience leading Canadian troops in the Boer War helped him to bind the Canadian Scottish into a cohesive battalion ready for its first experience of combat. This photo was taken after Leckie's promotion to Brigadier.

King George V (next to officer waving arm and carrying cane) reviews the 16th Battalion on November 5, 1914.

The Canadian Scottish raise their headgear in a salute to the King as he departs Salisbury Plain by car.

Canadian Scottish move toward the front lines in Flanders. Note the use of handcarts to move supplies.

Canadian Scottish having lunch on a section of front line where the digging of trenches was impossible, so sandbagged emplacements were created instead.

Canadian Scottish examine a crater created by a 17-inch shell fired in the Ypres Salient.

16th Battalion retake the guns in the orchard during the Second Battle of Ypres.

In July 1916, John Leckie was promoted to the command of the Canadian Scottish. More gregarious than his brother, he proved a popular commander.

Ploegstreet Church in the Ypres Salient during the summer of 1915.

Emplacements captured by Canadian Scottish in Sanctuary Wood.

Canadian Scottish soldier examines No Man's Land from an observation post.

Even when the front was stalemated during the early months of 1916, units were still sent over the top on raids and limited attacks that yielded only more casualties.

No Man's Land on the Somme, a landscape so devastated and exposed that collection of the dead proved impossible.

By June 1916, Armagh Wood had been reduced to a wasteland.

A trench on the Somme.

A tank lumbers forward during an advance in the Somme.

chapter seven

Crisis in the Somme

- AUGUST 9–OCTOBER 11, 1916 -

The River Somme bisects France's great northern plain, following a northwesterly course along a broad, marshy valley that leads to the English Channel. South of the river is lowland, while to the north high, rolling chalk grassland is cut laterally by tributaries. In the summer of 1916, the river generally stood between the two combatants with the Germans enjoying the benefit of possessing the higher ground. Between Peronne and Amiens, an eight-mile-long, 500-foot-high ridge running from Thiepval to Morval divided the watersheds of the Somme and its Ancre tributary that drained into the parent river east of Amiens. The Allies called this Pozières Ridge, after a village holding the highest point. Before the war this had been a gentle, bucolic land where farmers retained a somewhat medieval lifestyle—still clustering together in large villages from which they ventured during the day to work the land. Cattle grazed the rolling hills while grain, fodder, and sugar beets sprouted richly from the fertile plains and reclaimed marshes. The forests had been cleared long ago, so only a few scattered woods remained. The valleys created by the Somme and Ancre were home to wide, untamed marshes because both rivers regularly overflowed their banks.

Summer of 1916 saw this land gripped in the fury of war. In late August, the Canadians began their march to the Somme. The news coming out of the Somme battleground had cast the veterans into a fatalistic mood that even the most naïve reinforcements, those who still believed war a place where heroism and glory could be found, were unable to shrug off.

There had been no glory found on the Somme since the British Expeditionary Force's greatest offensive of the war began here on July 1. Despite its grand scope, Field Marshal Douglas Haig's purpose had been quite limited—to take pressure off the French who were being cut apart at Verdun by killing as many Germans in one place as possible. Slaughter had been the goal.

The Somme had not been Haig's first choice for the killing ground. North of the River Lys near Messines some strategic advantage might be won, beyond attrition, if the Germans to the north could be cut off and eliminated. But the French would have had no role to play in an offensive near Messines, and Field Marshal J.J. wanted Tommies and *poilus* attacking side-by-side. On the Somme, the French would be on the British right flank, and Joffre had won the argument by assuring Haig he would send two armies forward to fight beside the British so that the entire advance would span an incredible 60 miles. Haig distrusted Joffre, had heard such promises before. But the French were allies he could not ignore. Acceding to the Somme strategy, Haig suggested delaying until August 15. The British would have received badly needed reinforcements and alleviated their ammunition shortage by then. There would also be the tank, which the British hoped might loosen the damnable chains of trench warfare.

No delays, Joffre had shouted. "The French Army would cease to exist" before August.[1] They were bleeding to death at Verdun where the Germans had struck the massive fortress on February 1916 with no greater purpose than to kill three Frenchmen for every German. If the fort fell, the way would be open to the Marne River. The French, as German Chief of Staff Gen. Erich von Falkenhayn had known, were forced "to throw in every man they have. If they do so the forces of France will bleed to death."[2]

Bleed the French had, but the Germans had spilled equal amounts. The Verdun battlefront stalemated, with both sides so heavily invested that neither could give way. France met counterattack with counterattack, but by early summer its armies were faltering. Haig must attack. July 1 was agreed.

By then French losses had become so severe Joffre reneged on his grand promise. He could send only the Sixth Army, comprising eight divisions. Six of these would strike across a six-mile front with the other two in reserve. The modest French commitment made the Somme primarily a British show. Haig committed new troops—the so-called Kitchener's Army—thirteen Fourth Army divisions with five in reserve and a three-division strong corps from the also newly formed Third Army. To a man,

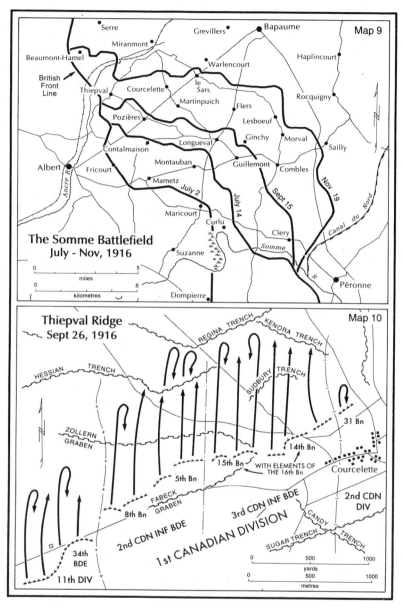

Map 9

The Somme Battlefield
July - Nov, 1916

Map 10

Thiepval Ridge
Sept 26, 1916

Kitchener's Army were volunteers. Droves of them had enlisted in early 1915, swelling British army ranks to more than a million men. Organized into units by geography, most were familiar with the men they served alongside. Sometimes a single company had all walked off the same factory floor together to the recruiting halls. Untainted by the fatalism of veterans in their midst, they headed for the trenches exuding optimism.

That same optimism prevailed in the other new units assigned to serve in the two new armies. These were the Territorials from various colonies and included the 1ˢᵗ Newfoundland Regiment.

Because of the French reductions, the offensive's front was cut from 60 miles to 28, with its northern flank facing Beaumont-Hamel. Running south from there, the British sector cut across the Ancre River, passed behind Thiepval and Pozières and in front of Albert before curving tightly through the ruin of Fricourt to meet the French boundary at Maricourt. The French line passed through a large marsh on the Somme's northern bank southward past Dompiere. Facing the Allies were three consecutive trenches protected by two vast wire entanglements, each 30 yards wide. Separating the trenches were 150-yard-wide kill zones. Following the crest of Pozières Ridge at distances ranging from 2,000 to 5,000 yards behind the forward position, a secondary line boasted equally impressive wire obstacles with dugouts 20 to 30 feet deep that could each shelter twenty-five men from artillery bombardment. Although formidable, the defences were lightly held by just five full divisions.

Fourth Army's assault would strike a 16-mile-wide front to the left of the French while, on the right, Third Army's three-division corps would attack five miles north at Gommecourt to pin the German forces there and hopefully serve to decoy reserves away from the main thrust. Fourth Army's geographic objective was the heights of Pozières Ridge, but Haig's major aim remained to fix the German defenders in place and butcher them with artillery.[3]

To this aim, a seven-day bombardment, which threw in regular discharges of poisonous gas along with the firing of 1.5-million shells, preceded the July 1 attack. Then, at 0730 hours, the troops went over the top only to find the Germans on full alert and seemingly unscathed by the massive bombardment. Kitchener's Army advanced into a maelstrom of machine-gun fire and all but a few perished in a single day—57,470 men killed, wounded, or missing. The Newfoundland Regiment was decimated in its attack at Beaumont-Hamel, taking 684 casualties, 310 of whom died. Only the French, having fired so few shells that the Germans expected no attack from their quarter, gained their objectives and at relatively little cost.

For the ensuing two months the battle raged, the British making painful gains that finally gave them a toehold on the ridge when its namesake village was captured by I Anzac Corps in late July. But every inch of ground was won at a staggering cost. By August's end, the British had suffered 200,000 casualties and the French 70,000. The Germans, ordered to surrender not a single inch of ground, had taken 200,000 casualties.[4] Attrition remained the goal but, as Canadian Corps entered the trenches on September 1, the rate of casualties on both sides seemed tipped moderately against the Allies.

* * *

Haig hoped to re-invigorate the offensive in mid-September with "fresh forces and all available resources." While Canadian Corps was arguably far from fresh, it was attached to Gen. Sir Hubert Gough's Reserve Army. This new unit had taken over the northern Somme battlefront so that the badly reduced Fourth Army could shorten its lines. The Canadian front was 3,000 yards wide. To enable 2nd and 3rd Divisions to prepare for their role in the forthcoming offensive, Lt.-Gen. Julian Byng fed only 1st Canadian Division into the line. This extended from Fourth Army's left flank westward along Pozières Ridge to a point 700 yards west of Mouquet Farm to the east of Thiepval. During their time on this front, the Australians had repeatedly tried wresting the farm—a stronghold anchored on a cluster of deep dugouts—from the Germans without success. Although a last-gasp attempt on September 3 had been repulsed, the Australians had seized a 300-yard-long chunk of Fabeck Graben Trench, which stretched northeastward to Courcelette.

The 2,000-yard stretch of front that became 3rd Canadian Infantry Brigade's responsibility included the ground before Mouquet Farm and the piece of Fabeck Green. It was poor country for warfare. "Valleys and ridges, broad and narrow, ran into and across each other at all sorts of angles and grades." A "broad, rough ditch of tumbling chalk zigzagging down the valley, was the wreck of the German trenches; the heaps of ruins on both sides of the Albert-Bapaume road was la Boisselle; the mounds and bare tree stumps to the left, Ovillers; the crater to the right, so huge that a large house might have been easily placed in it, was a mine blown by the British on July 1st.... The hollow, in which la Boisselle lay, ran parallel to the front; Sausage Valley to the right of the village, ran straight toward the trenches. It closed into a bottle neck at the top of the slope, and spread out again into more valleys, pits, and sunken roads, which gave excellent cover to the guns and men defending the area, and made the task of attacking troops difficult and costly."

Two forward Canadian Scottish companies entered this hellhole by burrowing into mine craters while the two in reserve set up alongside battalion headquarters in la Boiselle. Somewhere ahead were Australian troops waiting to be relieved, and the gunfire and explosions from that direction meant they were still engaged. Taking over a hot front was a bad scenario. The village was rubble, so acting-commander Major Cyrus Peck and his staff took over a three-storey, fifty-foot-deep German dugout that had served the Australians before them. Although amply furnished with tables, couches, and upholstered chairs, the place was also damp, filthy, and fetid. Peck worried it was too distant from the front lines to properly control the battalion, but nothing closer was suitable. Streams of Australian ambulances, followed by walking wounded, flowed down the muddy road past the dugout, which did little to lift Peck's spirits as he set off late on September 3 to hear how the relief was to be carried out.

The meeting took place at the Australian brigade headquarters. Peck learned that the location of the Australian troops on the front was uncertain because conditions "were chaotic. The enemy was systematically sweeping the area backward and forward with a field-gun barrage. He left no part of it untouched. The ground was churned up beyond recognition by shellfire. The only distinguishable landmarks on it were the mounds of bricks and earth representing Pozières, and "Gibraltar," the ten-foot-high German observation post on the Bapaume road at the southwesterly edge of the village. None of these features was of assistance in determining front-line positions. There were four badly smashed, second-class roads intersecting the area, but they, if anything, added to the confusion."[5]

To the left, 1st Canadian Infantry Brigade reported having successfully relieved its Australian counterparts the night of August 31. Back at his headquarters, Peck could only send the battalion groping almost blindly through heavy rain toward map co-ordinates where the last Australian positions had been identified. The Canadian Scottish companies soon lost contact with each other, each continually bumping into apparently randomly scattered parties of Australians.

Back at the dugout, a patrol reported finding a better location for headquarters about a mile closer to the front. But if they moved now, Peck would be out of contact for some time both with brigade head-quarters and his own companies. He decided to stay put until the re-lief was complete.[6]

Morning found the 3rd Brigade still relieving the Australians, but the Germans seemed to overlook the opportunity the intermingling of troops might have presented them. The shelling tapered off and no attack materialized as finally the brigade's three forward battalions deployed within a roughly triangular-shaped front. The Royal Highlanders held the left side, the Canadian Scottish the apex, and the 48th Highlanders the right side. Things were less tidy than the dispositions sounded, for the Can Scots had no contact with the Toronto battalion and nobody knew the width of the gap between.

The gap still existed the following night when the Germans hit the brigade with a heavy artillery barrage that covered patrols probing its front. Three patrols trying to pierce the Canadian Scottish lines were re-pulsed. No. 4 Company's major, George Lynch, observed that he saw a silver lining presented by these actions, believing they "saved the mo-rale of our men, for, however demoralizing the shellfire, directly the sen-tries called 'they're coming over' all were on their toes." But the shelling was deadly and continued through the ensuing day without relent. By the evening of September 5, Lynch's company had been whittled down from 135 to 53 and many men still standing nursed light wounds but re-fused evacuation because the situation was so dire. There were "stretches of line … forty to fifty yards long and not a man in them, and our posts consisted of but two to three men."[7]

Again nightfall coincided with intensified shelling and the Can Scots grew desperate. What was left of No. 4 Company had gone three days now without any fresh supply of food or water. They could ward off the hunger by munching a stale and dry bread ration carried into the trench-es with them, "but the thirst was the awful thing." "My throat and mouth felt parched and cracked," one infantryman wrote his family.

On the battalion's left flank, No. 3 Company was hanging in the wind next to the gap and being harassed by German fire from that quarter. Then a shell destroyed the trench facing that direction, killing or wound-ing all but twelve of the platoon there. That appeared to be the signal for a German bombing attack that tried to overrun the entire company and was only narrowly repulsed. With his shrinking company headquarters section in tow, Major John Hall was forced to duck through one collapsing shelter after another to stay ahead of the marauding Germans. Finally he got word back to Peck that the company needed reinforcement, for if the Germans got serious about this, "the line could not be held."[8]

Peck's other two forward company commanders were making similar pleas, but he had only one No. 1 Company platoon and sixty-eight men from No. 2 Company in reserve. Committing them required brigade approval, but Brig. George Tuxford refused with the argument that the Can Scots already had too many of their troops in the front lines.

At 0230 hours on September 6, the battalion intelligence officer, Lt. Edward Hart reported to Peck after a personal reconnaissance forward. Not only had they taken terrible casualties, Hart said, but the Canadian Scottish were holding a front 350 yards longer than assigned. Peck passed the information to Tuxford with the additional argument that his company commanders would not seek reinforcements unless they were needed. Tuxford relented and, by 0330, those men of No. 2 Company held in reserve were on the move.[9] Thirty minutes later the divisional artillery began engaging suspected German gun positions with a fire rate of ninety shots per battery.[10]

The Canadian gunners were shooting blind, however, at only suspected targets. Their German counterparts had observers on the high ground who were able to see the Canadian Scottish positions and, throughout the day, they pounded them with artillery and mortar fire. One exploding shell killed a company runner while wounding Lt. Harold Strang and CSM Bernard Lunn with shrapnel. Six other men died instantly when a shell landed right on their position. Having observed these men's deaths, the German spotters were able to direct a squad of infantrymen to seize their position. The Can Scots only took it back by mounting a bayonet charge. A No. 4 Company Lewis gun team was then wiped out while trying to mount their gun on a parapet. All attempts to remount the undamaged gun resulted in it being blown back down by a shell.

Lt. Hart came forward at dusk to take a head count. He discovered No. 3 Company had been reduced to Major John Hall, CSM George Palmer, and twelve men. No. 4 Company counted fewer than twenty. The battalion's grip was desperately weak with one platoon from No. 2 Company spread across a long stretch on the right flank and the other broken up to bolster the ranks of these two badly reduced companies. When this information was passed to Tuxford, the brigadier ordered the 16th Battalion relieved that night by companies from the 14th and 15th Battalions. Heavy shelling turned the relief into another drawn-out affair, concluded only on the afternoon of September 7. One Can Scot, with the battalion from its 1914 formation, declared that "Mouquet Farm was the most nerve-racking, hellish time I ever put in; a lifetime in three days, I shudder at the thought of my experiences there."[11]

The day after the Canadian Scottish left the line, so too did the rest of 3rd Brigade, with 2nd Canadian Infantry Brigade taking its place. Such confusion reigned because of artillery fire that control of the Fabeck Graben Trench section was lost to a hasty German attack. What was to have been a simple period of front-line duty served the brigade a butcher's bill worthy of outright battle—970 killed or wounded.[12] The fallen included 349 Canadian Scottish, with one officer killed and eight wounded plus 97 other ranks dead and 243 injured.[13] Except for Second Ypres, the battalion had never suffered such a loss. Added to the men killed or suffering from physical wounds were those diagnosed with shell shock. Most galling was the fact that almost every casualty, whether physical or psychological, resulted from artillery fire. This aptly reflected the prevailing tactical belief of late 1916 that "the artillery captures the ground; the infantry occupies it." But Pozières Ridge typified "the worst stage of [this tactic's] evolution; a battle where two were playing at the game of attrition; an artillery duel where men, as the victim and plaything of mechanical forces, were subjected to the tortures of the damned."[14]

* * *

In mid-September, 1st Division moved into corps reserve as the other two divisions took over in readiness for the coming British offensive. Two full armies this time would concentrate on a 10-mile section of ground with Fourth Army immediately right of the Canadians putting in the main thrust that Haig hoped would break through all the way to Bapaume, a gain of about six miles. The Canadians would protect Fourth Army's left flank with an advance across a 2,200-yard front directed at Courcelette. Along the Albert-Bapaume road immediately adjacent to the Fourth Army, 2nd Canadian Infantry Division would launch the main assault, while 3rd Canadian Infantry Division would concentrate on overrunning Mouquet Farm and the most westerly portion of Fabeck Graben Trench.

A bloody fight was certain. Included in the first objective was a thousand-yard-long section of Candy Trench, which extended southeast from Courcelette to pass in front of Martinpuich, and lay a thousand yards from the Canadian lines. Securing the trench's left flank was the heavily fortified ruins of Sugar Factory, about 500 yards south of Courcelette. Sugar Trench trended southwest from behind the factory toward Mouquet Farm which, at 400 yards' distance, was the closest point to the Canadian front. These trenches and any nearby ruined buildings bristled with machine guns. Courcelette itself was a fortress, its cellars augmented by countless dugouts and large underground galleries that transformed it into a deadly rat's nest.

But the British had a couple of innovations—one entirely new and the other a refinement of past tactics—that they hoped would give them the advantage. First was the tank Haig had been awaiting. The Mark I was a massive waddling 26.5-foot-long hulk—trailing two heavy wheels intended to reduce shock and aid steering that added yet another six feet to its length. It was 14 feet wide and 7.5 feet high and weighed 28 tons. Its eight-man crew (four of whom operated the complex drive mechanism) was armed with either two naval 6-pounder guns or four 7.62-millimetre Hotchkiss machine guns mounted on either side. Powered by a six-cylinder, 105-horsepower Daimler engine, its top speed was 3.7 miles an hour, but over the heavily shelled ground of No Man's Land that speed was effectively halved. Caterpillar tracks provided traction and its awesome length meant the tank could span a ten-foot-wide trench without tipping in.[15] Forty-nine tanks were available, but only seven were assigned to the Canadians—all going to support 2nd Division with one held in reserve. Each leading brigade would have three tanks.[16] Five infantrymen were detailed to each tank, their task to pull wounded comrades out of the way to prevent their being crushed.

Mechanically undependable and few in number, the tanks were not considered a decisive force. Because of this, Haig's trust was weighted to the artillery, but this time adding a new twist as to how it was delivered. The July offensives had proven it was "fallacy" to expect "that nothing could exist at the conclusion of the bombardment in the area covered by it" and infantry would stroll in and take over.[17] Long waves of infantry being butchered by machine guns left untouched by the artillery proved this. The solution was for the infantry to advance behind the shelter of a "creeping barrage." For Canadian Corps this meant "the first large-scale rolling barrage ever ... fired by Canadian gunners." At Zero Hour the guns would rain shrapnel on a sector 50 yards in front of the German trenches. Sixty seconds later the barrage would lift to directly flail the trenches for three minutes. Thereafter each lift would advance a further 100 yards at three-minute intervals, creeping ahead of the advancing infantry until they reached the final objective. These objectives, including Candy Trench, would be saturated for six minutes before the artillery advanced again in three more lifts, staged three minutes apart, until reaching the end point for the creep directly between Courcelette and Martinpuich—a full 3,000 yards from the Canadian start point.[18]

On September 15 the artillery arrayed to support the Canadians numbered sixty-four heavy and 234 field guns—their wheels literally brushing each other in the gun pits behind Pozières. It was the same elsewhere so that literally "mile upon mile of batteries of all calibres [were] massed along the front."[19] For the past three days these guns had been relentlessly battering the German lines. Now the guns fired in unison at 0620, the concussion and explosions making the ground tremble.

As the assaulting battalions went over the top, they could hear none of the shouts or whistles of the officers over the din of shells roaring overhead and the explosions ahead. But words were unnecessary. The men were well briefed. In seven minutes, the first of the seven successive waves sent forward reported being on the first objective. The forward German trenches had been obliterated, their occupants mostly killed by shrapnel injuries to the head. A German counter-barrage began cutting down Canadians as they renewed the advance but, at 0700 hours, 4th Canadian Infantry Brigade reported it was inside Candy and Sugar trenches with the 6th Brigade reaching its objectives forty minutes later. Brutal hand-to-hand fighting cleared Sugar Factory with 125 Germans surrendering.

The contribution the tanks made to this success was forever shrouded in the fog of war. Some said they were pivotal in suppressing German fire from the Sugar Factory, but only two were known to have got anywhere near the place with three of the others becoming stuck and a fourth breaking down. The two that remained operational withdrew soon after Sugar Factory's capture.[20]

Lt.-Gen. Julian Byng ordered the attack renewed at dusk, and a two-day street fight ensued in Courcelette, with the bayonet figuring as the prominent weapon. It ended with the town taken. Meanwhile, 3rd Division had gained control of a significant portion of Fabeck Graben and, to its left, II British Corps had pushed forward 400 yards. Within a few days 3rd Division declared Mouquet Farm taken but, when it was relieved by British troops on the evening of September 16, they discovered Germans still hiding in the deep tunnels there. Close fighting cleared them out. The week-long fight cost the Canadian Corps 7,230 casualties.[21]

Despite Fourth Army's being the main offensive effort, it had fared less well than the Canadians. Although Martinpuich fell on September 22, the attack then ran out of steam and the Germans quickly formed a new defensive line running from Morval past Gueudecourt and the Albert-Bapaume road at Le Sare about a mile north of Courcelette.

Rain mired the battlefield at the end of September and both sides spent the interval of poor weather readying for another round. On September 18th, 1st Canadian Division relieved 2nd Division. The plan was to renew the offensive on September 26, with 1st Division putting two brigades up front on the left while the slightly rested 2nd Division returned its 6th Brigade to the northern outskirts of Courcelette. First Division had its 2nd Canadian Infantry Brigade on the left and 3rd Canadian Infantry to the right, with its shoulder touching the lines of 6th Brigade. In this formation, Canadian Corps would drive northward on a 3,000-yard front to break the defences atop a low spur projecting eastward from the Thiepval Ridge. Three trenches stood in the way—Zollern Graben, Hessian, and Regina. Branching off to the southeast toward Courcelette from the latter was Kenora Trench. Intelligence reports warned Kenora was "one of the deepest and strongest trenches … ever seen." Regina was farther away, though, about 1,000 yards from the start point.[22] The Canadians were not attacking alone. On the left were the 18th and 11th Divisions of II Corps from the Reserve Army. This meant the offensive spanned a 6,000-yard front, stretching from Courcelette to Thiepval. Haig's intention was to gain control of Thiepval Ridge, which would deny the Germans the ability to overlook the British rear areas.

* * *

After being briefed at 3rd Brigade headquarters, Lt.-Col. Jack Leckie led his officers and non-commissioned officers to the top of Pozières Ridge for a look at the ground. To the east they could see the German lines. Leckie pointed out Kenora Trench, which from this distance "did not appear to be of any particular strength. It had an excellent field of fire, but there was little wire in front of it. The 16th parties were confident that it could be captured with ease. The ground beyond was open country untouched by shell fire; the fields looked fresh and green. The towns of Pys and Miraumount in the distance seemed intact." While Canadian Corps headquarters had received sound intelligence on Kenora's defensive strengths, this information was not passed down to divisional level. So Leckie and the other Can Scots could only draw conclusions on what they saw from the ridge.

Two days before the attack scheduled for September 26, Brig. George Tuxford told Leckie his battered battalion would play a minimal role—advancing one and a half companies behind the Royal Montreal Regiment to clean up any pockets of resistance it bypassed.[23] While the two men talked, the supporting artillery began to thunder. Until the assault, the guns would fire continuously, drenching German positions with explosives intermixed with a generous dose of gas shells.

As night fell on September 25, No. 2 Company's senior surviving officer, Lt. Henry Duncan, led his men and half of No. 4 Company toward 14th Battalion's lines. The Montreal battalion had sent a guide who quickly became disoriented. After several hours blundering about in the darkness, he brought the party unintentionally to the Courcelette's outskirts. German artillery suddenly began shelling them, and as the Can Scots moved warily into the ruins, a soldier ran toward them.

"What's all the rush, fellow?" called one of Duncan's sergeants.

"Wait, and you'll damn well soon see," the man shouted over a shoulder as he sprinted out of the village. The sergeant advised Duncan they should get through Courcelette as quickly as possible and trotted forward. Duncan signalled for the others to match the pace and they "were hardly out of the village when a hurricane of five point nines swept into it, letting us know what we missed." The guide remained disoriented, leading them on a wander into No Man's Land that ended only when he tripped upon a sap (an enemy-dug trench providing the Germans with a concealed approach to the Canadian lines) that led to the Royal Montreal Regiment's forward trenches. Dawn was breaking and Duncan figured it a miracle their sojourn in No Man's Land had not brought them into contact with any German patrols or drawn their fire.[24]

Zero Hour was set for 1235 hours, so Duncan and his men took up a position in a trench behind the Montrealers. All along the front, 3rd Brigade's troops were packed tightly into jumping-off trenches so shallow they had to crouch. Just before the whistles sounded, officers signalled them to stand, straighten their gear, and fix bayonets. Suddenly bullets, like so many thousands of bees, buzzed overhead causing many of the men to reflexively crouch back down until they realized the fire was going outward. For the first time, Canadian gunners manning Vickers machine guns were firing their weapons indirectly in hopes of catching any reinforcements in the open before they could reach the forward trenches.[25] A minute after the machine guns opened fire, eight hundred artillery pieces unleashed a barrage of shrapnel and explosive shells. Those shells were roaring overhead as the first wave surged forward. This was quickly followed by a second, and then the Canadian Scottish detachment headed into No Man's Land behind the Royal Montreal Regiment.[26] Brigadier Tuxford thought the Royal Montreal Regiment and 48th Highlanders putting in the attack were "moving well" and that the supporting "barrage [was] beautiful."

Between the start line and Kenora, the Germans had constructed a 250-yard-long trench codenamed Sudbury, which angled to the east off Courcelette-Grandcourt road. This trench formed the boundary between the two 3rd Brigade battalions, but neither bothered clearing it of enemy troops. That job fell to Duncan's Can Scots.

Approaching the trench they came upon "a gruesome spectacle." Inexplicably the Germans had abandoned the trench in favour of lying out in the open on its front slope where they had been flayed by shrapnel. A long line of bodies dangling head down over the trench parapet indicated most had realized the error too late to return to its cover. The trench itself was clogged with others who had either succumbed to wounds or who were still dying. Forty to fifty surviving Germans offered a stiff fight until the Canadian Scottish killed them. Another forty had offered no resistance, waiting meekly to surrender.

Dead or alive Duncan, was surprised to see that all these troops were "of excellent physique" and wore new uniforms. The trench was well stocked with "soda water, small bottles of brandy, wine, and boxes of cigars." Leaving the trench behind, Duncan led his men along a sunken road to clean out a series of dugouts. Rather than breaking into each dugout to engage the Germans with rifles and bayonets, Duncan's men instead threw phosphorous bombs—a "jam pot" bomb filled with phosphorus—inside. The bombs released a "white pungent vapour, sufficiently powerful to overcome any man still taking refuge underground." Dugouts cleared, Duncan declared the mopping up over and returned his men to the cover afforded by Sudbury.[27]

The two assaulting battalions, meanwhile, had gotten separated when the 48th Highlanders met heavy resistance from dugouts in No Man's Land. Speeding on alone, the Royal Montreal Regiment plunged into Kenora Trench, where most of the defenders opted to surrender rather than fight, and reported the objective secure at 1322 hours. They began sending large groups of prisoners back. Just as the Montrealers began to relax, however, the Germans struck back by counterattacking from both flanks and German artillery precisely targeted the trench. Casualties mounted alarmingly and, twice, the battalion was driven out of Kenora entirely. Each time it was regained in vicious hand-to-hand fighting.

It was mid-afternoon before the 48th Highlanders advanced out of No Man's Land into a gap between Hessian and Kenora Trenches and dug in on the slope of Thiepval Ridge about 150 yards short of Regina Trench. On the left, 2nd Canadian Infantry Brigade had gained its objectives on the ridge's summit but was fighting off repeated counterattacks. II British Corps had gained a toehold in Thiepval village and captured the western half of Zollern Graben Trench. But between its flank and that of Canadian Corps a gap had opened and the Germans still controlled most of Thiepval Ridge.

Lt.-Gen. Byng's intention for the morning was that his 2nd Division would secure the German front northeast of Coucelette while 1st Division seized Regina Trench. Tuxford, however, was worried that 3rd Brigade's heavy casualties were such that even "to hold position taken, I may require considerable reinforcements." The brigade's ability to reinforce the captured front with its own men was limited, the 48th Highlanders reporting they had sent "all available men to hold this line" and desperately needed more troops from other units to help them hold on through the night. By nightfall, the 48th had every man it could find up front and still counted only 150 troops stretched in a thin line that was unable to tie in with the Royal Montreal Regiment on its right. This battalion controlled a 200-yard stretch of Kenora Trench but was constantly engaged and also plagued by friendly artillery fire that kept chewing up one of its flanks. A fragmented signal to Tuxford reported that the Montrealers had "taken over German bombs and can use them.... Will hold position until further orders. Kindly send up reinforcements. Have fairly good trench, 2 M.Gs., very little ammunition. Great number of wounded between here and [Battalion Headquarters]." A following message sent at 1840 reported thirty percent casualties, but morale remaining good. Again, reinforcements were urgently requested—as "we now have every available man in the line."[28]

All Tuxford could do was to send some piecemeal sections of the Canadian Scottish forward. No. 3 Company under Major John Hall was assigned to the 14th Battalion while the 15th Battalion would be reinforced by Major Sydney Goodall's No. 1 Company. Both units reached the front by 2100 hours. All his fighting troops now attached to other battalions, Lt.-Col. Leckie sent his unneeded headquarters staff to the rear and joined the brigade's forward headquarters to monitor events.[29]

When No. 3 Company arrived, it was met by Lt.-Col. R. P. Clark who told Hall to send two platoons—Nos. 11 and 12—under his only remaining officer, Lt. Gordon Tupper, to reinforce the Royal Montreal Regiment's No. 3 Company at Kenora Trench. As Tupper headed toward Kenora, Clark further ordered Hall to send No. 9 Platoon under CSM George Palmer to a strongpoint just back of Kenora, while Hall and No. 10 Platoon remained in reserve at battalion headquarters.[30]

Having lost two-thirds of its strength and all its officers other than Lt. W. J. Holliday, 14th Battalion's No. 3 Company had by this time withdrawn with all its wounded from Kenora Trench and taken cover in Sudbury.[31] Unaware of this development, Tupper and his men were still headed for Kenora Trench—following a 14th Battalion guide who led them astray and almost into the midst of a heavily manned German trench. Spotting the silhouettes of German coal-scuttle helmets, Tupper hurriedly turned his men about and beat a hasty retreat just as the enemy opened fire. Only a few men in the two platoons were hit, but No. 11 Platoon's sergeant, George Slessor, ended up alone and lost in No Man's Land. He eventually stumbled into an unoccupied section of Kenora Trench and took refuge there. He would be found the next morning, "sound asleep, with his head pillowed on a dead German."[32]

Finally the guide came upon Holliday's men in Sudbury Trench. Heartened by the reinforcements, Holliday mustered the seventeen men in his company still capable of fighting and charged back to Kenora Trench. The Germans had managed to get only a few men in place there and these were quickly driven off with about six being taken prisoner. Tupper then brought his men forward and the small force "consolidated as far as practicable."[33] Shortly thereafter, CSM Palmer, having failed to find the reported strongpoint that had been his objective, led No. 9 Platoon into Kenora to bolster the number of its defenders.

At dawn the Germans saturated Kenora Trench with shellfire, inflicting many casualties. But repeated counterattacks were thrown back. Slowly the number of defenders dwindled as the day wore on. In the late afternoon, Tupper and Holliday "decided that it would be wise to vacate this isolated position." They fell back to Sudbury Trench and then reported their action to battalion headquarters.

Lt.-Col. Clark's signal to Tuxford that Kenora Trench had been abandoned arrived at the same time that the division—pressured by corps—issued instructions intended to secure both Kenora and Regina Trenches. Once again 3rd Brigade's 15th and 14th battalions were to seize Kenora, while 2nd Brigade's 5th and 8th Battalions would go for Regina.[34] Tuxford went forward to personally assess 14th Battalion's condition. Including the Canadian Scottish from No. 3 Company under Major Hall, he counted just seventy-five men capable of going into action. How that number of men could succeed he had no idea but, as ordered, he sent the brigade forward at 0200 hours on September 28. They moved out into the muddy battlefield under heavy rain but the cover this offered was quickly lost as illumination flares pinned the Canadians in the open. In thirty minutes, the attack was shredded by German fire. The Royal Montreal Regiment calculated its losses since the beginning of the offensive at 10 officers and 360 other ranks.[35] In this last action Hall's casualties were not recorded, but they included ten men from one section led by Sgt. Ivor Burgess. The twenty-four-year-old sergeant from Winnipeg was among the men killed.[36]

Late on September 28, what was left of 1st Division was relieved by brigades of 2nd Division and the Battle of Thiepval Ridge closed. Field

Marshal Haig admitted it had largely been a failure. The ridge's now blood-soaked northwestern flank remained in German hands and Regina Trench seemed impregnable.

The Canadian Scottish—officially only being in support for the preceding nine days—lost one officer killed and three wounded with forty-one other ranks dead and another ninety wounded.[37] Added to the 349 casualties suffered in early September, these losses left the battalion desperately needing time to rebuild—a story that was true of all the division's battalions.

* * *

Withdrawn to a rest area at Warloy-Baillon, about five miles west of Albert, Major General Arthur Currie thought his 1st Division would be given sufficient time to incorporate reinforcements. Almost all raw recruits, they lacked even the most rudimentary skills of trench survival. There was a desperate shortage of officers. Few of those posted to the Canadian Scottish had any former combat experience.

Yet, even as the Battle of Thiepval Ridge was declared over, General Haig decided to renew the offensive on October 12. This time there would be an advance of two miles across the breadth of Fourth and Reserve Armies' fronts. Reserve Army would make two thrusts, which would converge at Miraumont. One thrust, made by Canadian Corps, would drive northward from Thiepval Ridge through Grandcourt to Miraumont while the other followed the western bank of the Ancre River through Beaumont Hamel and then headed east to the point of convergence. Before this plan could rise beyond the theoretical, however, Regina Trench must be taken because it was to serve as the Canadian start line.

On October 1, 2nd Division went for the trench at 1515 hours to no avail and a cost of several hundred casualties. Byng decided he had no choice but try again with 1st Division supported to the right by 3rd Division. Heavy rains forced a postponement, but Byng knew time was short, for the Canadian Corps had to be in possession of Regina Trench by October 11 in order to carry out its role in Haig's offensive. While waiting for the rain to let up, Byng drafted a plan of attack with sights set on a two-mile section of Regina Trench stretching from a point 500 yards west of Kenora Trench to where Canadian Corps lines met Fourth

Army's left flank. Each division was assigned half this frontage and would advance two brigades with two battalions forward so that eight battalions would simultaneously overwhelm Regina Trench. Currie assigned 1st Division's share in the attack to his 1st and 3rd brigades. For his part, Brigadier Tuxford recognized that the Royal Montreal Regiment and 48th Highlanders were currently too beaten up for combat duty. So the Royal Highlanders and Canadian Scottish would have to lead.[38]

Regina Trench lay on Ancre Height's reverse slope and could only be examined by aerial reconnaissance, which the rain made impossible. Hidden behind the heights, it presented a difficult artillery target requiring blind fire. Great banks of wire entanglements protected its front, and although the artillery daily ripped holes in it, each night the Germans repaired the damage by packing the gaps with coiled bales of concertina wire. The German defenders were mostly proud naval marines.

Finally the rain let up and, at dusk on October 7, 3rd Brigade moved to assembly positions inside some abandoned German training trenches northeast of Courcelette. Directly in support of the brigade were two trench mortars, which would each fire 120 rounds.[39] The Canadian Scottish would advance on the brigade's right with the Royal Highlanders to its left and 1st Brigade's 3rd Battalion on its other flank. Artillery support had been promised, but it seemed strangely desultory and the officers distrusted the assurances that the wire fronting the trench had been broken. Having had no opportunity to send battalion scouts to reconnoitre the ground, they used flashlights to examine their maps and hoped these matched reality.

Initially the night "was fine and peaceful with moonlight so clear that a man's shadow showed up dark and well defined. As the hours moved on, high, fleecy clouds overspread the sky, and the brightness became subdued; soon afterwards the moon sank down and, at zero it was quite dark." The battalion was arranged so that Major Sydney Goodall's No. 1 Company was on the right and No. 4 Company, under Major George Lynch, was on the left with No. 2 Company, still commanded by Lt. Duncan, behind Goodall and Major John Hall's No. 3 backing Lynch.[40] Each platoon leader had an extra water bottle filled with rum to provide his men with a little liquid courage just before the attack.[41]

At 0100 hours on October 8, the first wave slipped into No Man's Land and dug in about 120 yards in front of the training trenches to shorten the distance it must cover while the second wave occupied the trench system. Regina Trench lay 700 yards distant, its position clearly indicated by the numerous flares the Germans fired into the sky. A few minutes before Zero Hour—0450 hours—the artillery on both sides ceased and an unnatural quiet settled over No Man's Land. Then, precisely at Zero Hour, the Canadian Corps guns spoke again and unleashed the creeping barrage.

The guns firing signalled the Canadian Scottish to stand and advance. Each company's platoons went forward in two waves spaced 50 yards apart, so the battalion advanced in four orderly lines. Major Lynch, Captain David Bell, SM Arden Mackie, and No. 4 Company's piper James Richardson walked into the open and watched the shells fall for a couple of minutes. Then Lynch, Mackie, and the piper bade Bell adieu for he was to lead the company's second line. Lynch blew his whistle and the three men walked ahead of the leading line with Richardson to Lynch's left, Mackie his right.

Lynch had planned to leave Richardson behind, thinking a piper unnecessary for a night assault. But the twenty-year-old had demanded to be paraded before Lt.-Col. Leckie and begged to accompany the troops. Leckie had overruled Lynch.

The ground free of craters, the battalions were able to keep their lines properly dressed. Halfway to Regina Trench Mackie asked Richardson why he was not playing the pipes. Richardson replied he was to await Lynch's order. On they went, taking little German fire and men began to hope their luck might hold. Then they passed over the crest of the hill and began descending toward the wire. With a sense of dread Mackie "was astonished to see it was not cut. I tried to locate a way through but could find no opening. When the company came up the enemy started throwing bombs and opened rifle fire. Seeing a big shell-hole on the left I ran over to Major Lynch to ask him to get in there until I could get the wire cutters to work on the wire, but as I got up to him he fell—shot in the breast. I knelt to bandage him but saw he was breathing his last. Piper Jimmy Richardson came over to me at this moment and asked if he could help, but I told him our company commander was gone."[42]

The company was completely bunched in front of the wire. Some men threw bombs toward the German trench while others tried to beat down the wooden stakes supporting the wire with their rifle butts and then trample it into the mud. The German grenades generally fell short as they were throwing uphill, but their rifle fire was "deadly accurate." Casualties mounted. Unless something were to be done quickly, Mackie realized that No. 4 Company would be wiped out.

Suddenly Richardson turned to the sergeant. "Wull I gie them wund?" he asked calmly. "Aye mon, gie 'em wind," Mackie barked back.[43] Coolly, the young smooth-faced soldier marched back and forth in front of the wire, playing the pipes while a storm of fire swirled past him on either side. "The effect was instantaneous," reads his Victoria Cross commendation. "Inspired by his splendid example, the company rushed the wire with, such fury and determination that the obstacle was overcome and the positions captured."[44]

On the battalion's right flank, No. 1 Company's situation proved less perilous, for the artillery had "smashed gaps in the wire" and the men charged through and gained the trench. Working rightward to join up with the left flank of 1st Brigade, the two companies here commanded by Major Goodall and Lt. Duncan met fierce resistance from the marines who neither asked for nor granted any quarter. Goodall was mortally wounded and Duncan killed on the spot.

On the left flank, Sgt. Mackie had taken the head of No. 4 Company after Captain Bell was killed shortly after Lynch. Commissioned from the ranks in 1915, Bell's competence had been such that just before the attack he was offered a temporary staff appointment at brigade headquarters. In refusing it, Bell had said to leave before an attack was akin to desertion. While leading the second wave through the wire, a bullet pierced his helmet and he fell dead.

Major Hall had also been wounded at the wire. While waiting for the stretcher-bearers, he had jotted a note to Leckie: "My compliments to the Commanding Officer, and tell him I'm awfully sorry I am not able to carry on." Hall died after being hit a second time while the stretcher-bearers were carrying him to the rear.[45]

Daybreak found the battalion locked in a fierce mêlée. Every commanding officer was dead. All its bombers were dead or wounded. Some men were throwing German bombs for everyone had exhausted their supplies. The right flank was in contact with 3rd Battalion from 1st Brigade but, on the left, there was no sign of 13th Battalion. Only a small Royal

Montreal Regiment section led by a junior officer had managed to gain Regina Trench. They joined the Canadian Scottish. Sgt. George Slessor's platoon held that flank and they hurriedly barricaded the trench with sandbags and hammered together bits of lumber ripped from the doors leading to German dugouts.

A quick count revealed ninety-eight Can Scots had reached Regina Trench. These included four officers and five non-commissioned officers. Looking back they could see the rest of the battalion hanging dead or wounded in the wire or scattered on the ground before it. Just two Lewis guns remained. Everyone was desperately low on ammunition, stripping it from the wounded. Lt. Edward Hart commanded. To advance beyond Regina would be suicidal, he decided, so they would dig in and hang on to the 360 yards of trench they had won.

Hart doubted that would prove possible, for the Germans busted through the barricade on the left and Slessor was wounded. A bloody bayonet charge regained the barricade, but the naval marines only went back a few feet and kept pressing forward at the slightest opportunity. No fool, Hart knew the Germans would inevitably break through. Lt. Charles Bevan was the only other Can Scot officer standing. He and Hall worked opposite ends of a line that kept shrinking as men fell. At 1500 hours they decided "to fall back." Hart later wrote: "We had by this time no more than seventy-five all told in the trench. . . . It was apparently impossible for me to get messages back to Battalion Headquarters or for Headquarters to get messages to me. Therefore, I took the responsibility rightly or wrongly of ordering the Battalion to retire. Retirement was effected with light casualties, the men being passed back a few at a time to the jumping off trench."[46]

Piper Richardson was among the few who did not reach safety. In the trench, Richardson had set his pipes aside and first joined the bombers before serving as a stretcher-bearer. About 200 yards from the trench, Richardson paused and announced he had forgotten his pipes. Refusing to be dissuaded, he headed back toward Regina Trench. He was never seen again. First declared missing, he was registered as presumed dead a year later. On October 22, 1918, Richardson was posthumously awarded the Victoria Cross.

The October 8 attack ended in disaster with neither division succeeding. This failure marked the end of 16th Battalion's Somme operations.

On the morning of October 11, its remnants—numbering the strength of a single company—marched to the rear. En route they passed the men of the 72nd Battalion (Seaforth Highlanders of Canada) from 4th Canadian Division advancing to their battle christening. The Seaforths among the Can Scots greeted their fellows affectionately, but one observer thought the contrast between them "pathetic. The new Battalion, smart and buoyant, flushed with the prospect of meeting the enemy in its first engagement; the old one, shattered, faced for the second time with the task of rebuilding battalion esprit and organization from the ground upward."[47]

Vimy
- OCTOBER 12, 1916–MAY 4, 1917 -

Canadian Corps suffered 1,364 casualties in the October 8 attack with 344, or roughly twenty-five percent, of this total coming from 16th Battalion. Eight of the battalion's 13 officer casualties died while 131 other ranks were killed. This was a staggeringly high percentage of men killed, slightly more than a third.[1]

Overall, Canadian Corps casualties in the Somme led to its full withdrawal from that sector on October 11 with 4th Canadian Infantry Division fed into the line on October 11 under command of Reserve Army's II Corps. This Canadian division would be bloodied in successive attempts to seize Regina Trench, a goal that would not be won until November 11. Seventeen days later the last Canadian division on the Somme would depart for integration into Canadian Corps. By then the Battle of the Somme, after five devastatingly bloody months, was considered closed.

Canadian battle casualties totalled 24,029—a mere fraction of the 623,907 Allied dead and wounded. The Germans reported 465,525 casualties, but this figure did not take into account a quarter of their wounded who were treated just back of the front and returned to duty. British statisticians reworked the German numbers for a tally of about 670,000. Tellingly, Gen. Erich Ludendorff, commander of the German 8th Army engaged on the Somme, considered it "had been fought to a standstill and was now utterly worn out."[2] He was determined to "save the men from a second Somme battle."[3]

Field Marshal Douglas Haig declared his objectives won and that therefore the Somme was a victory. Verdun had been relieved, the Germans subjected to heavy attrition. But if the German Army could ill afford the losses of another Somme, neither could the Allies. Attrition rates equal to those inflicted on the Germans would leave France and the British Empire so weakened of troop strength that neither would ever recover. Haig's tactics had raised war's horror and butchery to new heights, but the Germans struck back with equal ferocity and endured.

There had been no seminal change. The long, winding trenches of the Western Front divided by the killing ground of No Man's Land remained. Nobody knew how to break the stalemate. The Western Front, as Captain Hugh Urquhart wrote, had become the "Sphinx with the unsolved riddles. Each attempt to untie the Gordian knot met with further problems." While the "violence of the Somme had shaken the enemy, it was equally true" that it had traumatized the British Empire. "Thereafter there was a gradual weakening of the will to conquer. The drain of blood, the disappointment at the lack of definite results had imposed too great a strain on the vitality of the nation; its main line of resistance had been broken into. For German and British Empires alike, the winter and spring of 1916–17 was a turning point of the war."[4]

As winter descended, the weather only imposed greater misery on the weary troops. Each return to trench duty plunged them back into a place that seemed a portent of what hell must be like. In this cold hell, the mud, noise, and putrid stench of death and decay were always present. Unnaturally engorged rats were everywhere, often seen feeding openly on unburied corpses. A sleeping man might well awake to find one beginning to nibble on his finger or staring directly into his eyes. Rations were never sufficient. The persistent diet of corned beef, hardtack, tea, and watery jam was both monotonous and nutrient-deficient. Water was often polluted and stale by the time it was brought up from the rear.

New diseases thrived in this unsanitary and cruel environment. In 1915, doctors identified a new disease transmitted by the body lice that afflicted everyone. Soldiers afflicted with trench fever, as the disease was called, were left exhausted by fever, chronic headaches, and sore muscles, bones, and joints. Outbreaks of skin lesions on the chest and back worsened the condition. Recovery took about two months, but, as those suffering the disease were seldom evacuated to rear area hospitals; the majority were forced to just soldier on despite their symptoms. Trench foot—a literal rotting away of feet that could never be properly cleaned or dried—was a constant hazard, and sergeants routinely inspected men in an attempt to detect its onset at the earliest stages when it would be arrested by a proper cleaning and a fresh pair of socks. Trench mouth was a particularly disgusting malady caused by the difficulty of practising good oral hygiene, lack of fresh fruit, overuse of tobacco, and stress. It left a mouthful of bacteria called "acute necrotizing ulcerative gingivitis" that caused bleeding gums and rank breath. Men suffering an acute case often had all their teeth pulled after the gums turned grey and rotted. Highly infectious, it could be transmitted by sharing cups and gas respirators.[5] Not all diseases were new. Pneumonia, diphtheria, typhus, tetanus, dysentery, and scabies were all prevalent.

Battle fatigue was equally prevalent and paid little official attention, being often equated with cowardice. "He's got the jitters," men would say of a mate suffering it. Among the symptoms were inordinate irritability, insomnia, and responding to the slightest noise with body jerks and other startled gestures.

Even when a man was not suffering some psychological or physical malady, there was the constant cold and wetness during the winter. Sheepskin coats and wool uniforms were hard to keep dry. Poorly made leather boots were equally so. With spring came warm temperatures, but these meant sweat that soaked uniforms and made them stink. Heat also bred lice and no amount of scratching provided more than a second's relief.

Always there was the tiredness. When not fighting or standing sentry duty, there were innumerable fatigues—the aptly named work parties that kept the trench systems functioning. Men dug and repaired trenches, carried wounded to the rear and brought supplies forward, buried their dead, and performed countless other tedious, menial tasks.

Boredom was also a curse of trench life. Long lulls of quiet stretched between the terrifying times of battle and there was little to break the monotony. Men could only gamble, talk, work, and sleep so much of a day. Some men whittled or did other crafts that were possible in the trenches. Books were passed about until they fell apart. Singing was popular. But still the hours dragged.

* * *

The winter of 1916–1917 also brought a period of intense reorganization of the Canadian army, as it recovered from the losses suffered that fall and began rebuilding for the new spring offensives. Prime Minister

Robert Borden fired Sam Hughes on November 9 and appointed George Perley as Minister of the Overseas Military Forces. Perley possessed greater authority than the former Minister of Militia and Defence had enjoyed. From London, Perley concentrated on instilling a professional management style on an army that, under Hughes, had operated in an ad hoc, all too often chaotic, manner. Perley replaced Maj.-Gen. Henry Burstall with Maj.-Gen. Richard Turner and charged the former 2nd Canadian Infantry Division commander with running the Overseas Ministry. The Canadian Expeditionary Force had seventy battalions in England without plans for their posting to Canadian Corps or combat service. Turner amalgamated them into twenty-four reserve battalions and organized the battalions according to the soldiers' Canadian region or province, thus reinstituting the territorial regimental system Hughes had so despised.[6]

On the mainland, meanwhile, Canadian Corps had moved to a relatively quiet sector in the area of Lens and Vimy to rebuild. Each division now wore "Somme Patches"—coloured flannel rectangles sewn on the shoulders that provided recognition at a glance. In sequence from 1st Division to 4th Division, the colours were red, blue, grey, and green. Below the divisional marker another identified the soldier's battalion.

While unit flashes reinforced esprit de corps they also contributed to the growing friction between the divisions. In the winter of 1916–17, Canadian Corps was not a cohesive fighting force, but rather a grouping of four divisions whose men gave more allegiance to their division and battalion than the corps. A lingering animosity persisted between 1st and 2nd Divisions that had its roots on the 1914 Salisbury Plain training grounds. When in reserve, the two divisions maintained a wary distance. Third Division, having been shredded almost immediately after it deployed to the Ypres Salient and then mauled in the Somme, had suffered such casualties that it had lost all semblance of an identity. Its officers concentrated on building a sense of divisional esprit and cared less about how it fit within the Canadian Corps. Having just arrived on the scene, 4th Division was a stranger and the others had yet to decide if its officers and men could be trusted.[7]

Lt.-Gen. Julian Byng tackled the problem head on by forcing small groups of battalion commanders from each division to work through various tactical schemes at Corps headquarters. Byng was no stereotypical

British general. He cared little for spit and polish, concentrating instead on efficiency and results. Medical Officer Andrew Macphail described Byng as "large, strong, lithe, with worn boots and frayed puttees. He carried his hand in his pocket and returned a salute by lifting his hand as far as the pocket will allow."[8] Each group worked for about a week together and, every evening, Byng and his staff discussed solutions over dinner and drinks. This forced the officers to socialize. Drafts of more junior officers and non-commissioned officers were also sent to a corps school where exercises ensured they were mixed with counterparts from the other divisions.

Byng also deliberately shuffled officers and personnel from one division to another, ignoring the complaints this engendered. This British general, who had originally bemoaned having to command Canadians, now championed national identity over all other considerations. Loyalty to battalion and division were admirable, he repeatedly told the troops, but "above all things they were Canadians, and, accordingly, must devote themselves to the interests of that body which in the eyes of the world stood for Canada, namely, the Canadian Corps."[9]

It was a compelling argument and, as the winter wore on, a sense of corps identity took root and slowly began to blossom. Ever pragmatic, Byng knew a Canadian Corps identity would be greatly fostered by having himself and the other British corps officers replaced by Canadians. To this end he was already quietly mentoring Maj.-Gen. Arthur Currie to be his successor.[10]

* * *

Meanwhile, the Canadian Corps was struggling to absorb hundreds of reinforcements and still remain an efficient fighting unit. As was true for most battalions, many of 16th Battalion's wounded during the Somme were being invalided out of active service. This meant the majority of replacements were "strangers to the unit," being supplied from England in "haphazard fashion." Happily, the Canadian Scottish officers observed, these new soldiers "could not have been improved had the unit had a choice in the selection of reinforcement. They quickly imbibed the spirit of the Battalion; they were loyal to its traditions; they made it their own, just as if they had served in its ranks from the beginning of the war."[11]

Credit for how quickly the new men identified with the battalion went in large measure to its new commander, Lt.-Col. Cyrus Peck. On November 3, Lt.-Col. Jack Leckie had been promoted to command of the 2nd Canadian Reserve Brigade in England. While both Leckie brothers had maintained some degree of studied distance from everyone under their command, Peck was eminently approachable. Imaginative, thoughtful, and able to infuse humour into most situations, Peck's manner was such that people sought his approval. No crisis seemed to dent his confidence. He charmed the officers' mess with recitations from Shelley and Keats— poets Peck revered—and could draw upon a vast knowledge of the works of history and philosophy that he devoured at a prodigious rate. His wit was keen, but never used to diminish others. Although he was intellectually inclined, Peck's years on the British Columbian frontier set him at ease talking with the roughest soldier. Peck talked down to nobody and he made known his fierce pride in the battalion's troops. Repeatedly, he told visitors: "No such men as his own had ever lived before."

Peck also spent only as much time in battalion headquarters as necessary to ensure its smooth running. During combat operations, he was to be seen striding along the front—personal piper at his side. And when the signal to go over the top came, Peck normally "went forward with the Battalion in the attack; and sometimes, contrary to orders ... ahead of it." Cautioned repeatedly—given his ample proportions—against presenting such a conspicuous target, Peck countered that as "an aid to morale and comradeship, nothing ... could take the place of the personal example where officer and men took equal chances with death."

One thing Peck was adamant about. The Canadian Scottish was a Highland regiment and he recognized that heritage at every turn. Never was the skirl of pipes heard more often within a Canadian battalion's lines. Peck insisted on five pipers, one each for the companies and a fifth personal piper, accompanying the troops into battle. Each piper was allowed to play just two tunes, one to identify the position of his assigned company and the other to rally the troops he served and guide them to their objective.

"When I first proposed to take pipers into action," Peck later wrote, "I met with a great deal of criticism. I persisted, and as I have no Scottish blood in my veins, no one had reason to accuse me of acting from racial prejudices. I believe that the purpose of war is to win victories, and if one can do this better by encouraging certain sentiments and traditions, why shouldn't it be done? The heroic and dramatic effect of a piper stoically playing his way across the modern battlefield, altogether oblivious of danger, has an extraordinary effect on the spirit of his comrades."

Too much noise on the modern battlefield to hear pipers, skeptics countered. Peck volleyed back that the overwhelming din of combat seldom was continuous or long-lasting. "When you got under the enemy's barrage, which was only the work of a few moments, and when your own barrage got ahead of the advance, which generally happened, after the first one or two 'lifts' of the artillery, the skirl of the pipes could be heard for a considerable distance."

Another objection was that pipers presented easy targets. "Well," Peck replied, "that is part of the game. Officers, machine gunners and runners are conspicuous. People get killed in war because they are conspicuous; many get killed when they are not, and that's part of the game, too."[12]

War was a game with ever-changing rules. Verdun and the Somme had proven that, to avoid futile slaughter, new offensive tactics were required. Field Marshal Douglas Haig had sought to loosen the deadlock with the creeping barrage and tanks, but these had proved insufficient. Artillery could inflict massive damage, but it was unlikely to decide the battle and the tanks were still too crude and unreliable to carry the day.

Seeking new innovations, Byng had dispatched Currie to study French tactics. Currie came back impressed with the importance they placed on detailed reconnaissance, particularly the basic principle that every man spend time in the front trenches being thoroughly briefed on the ground to be covered, the location and nature of objectives, and the likely resistance. The French used aerial reconnaissance more than the British, providing even junior officers with aerial photos they could use to brief their men. Instead of designating trenches or numbered reference points marked on a topographic map as objectives, the French now selected recognizable geographical features—a summit, wood, or river—that would serve as highly defensible ground for repelling the inevitable German counterattack. Making a defensive stand in a just captured German trench, the French had concluded, was a mug's game—for these were designed to be defended against Allied attacks from the opposite direction.

Not only had the French revamped platoon tactics, but they also had begun conducting elaborate dress rehearsals on ground as similar to the real terrain as possible. At the company and platoon level, the *poilus* drilled in new fire and movement tactics that enabled each platoon to fight independently.

Some of this was not new. British training manuals pre-dating the war emphasized the need to adapt infantry tactics to the situation faced. But the French not only stressed fluidity and adaptability. They armed the platoon to ensure it possessed innately formidable prowess. Infantry, the French officers told Currie, must be the masters of the battlefield rather than artillery. In keeping with this dictum, French tactics insisted that the leading wave of an attack press through to the objective by flowing around strongly defended German positions, leaving them to follow-on forces.[13]

Infantry either prevailed or failed. And the platoon was the unit at the heart of infantry. Currie advocated adopting the French system by rote, an opinion also soon championed by the British War Office itself. The "efficiency of its platoon commanders will often be the measure of an army's success," declared one War Office memo. Remodelling of the platoon began.[14]

Suddenly, B.E.F. platoons were being given the weapons and organization to survive and dominate the battlefield. Canadian Scottish platoons were first equipped with one Lewis gun and then two to supplement the rifle, bayonet, rifle grenades, and bombs already employed. Each weapon had its special purpose. The "Lewis gun—a weapon of opportunity—and the rifle to deal with the enemy in the open, the rifle grenade and bomb to get at those behind cover, and the bayonet for hand-to-hand fighting. With the combination of these weapons, each supporting the advance as the need arose, it was possible for the commander and his men to initiate tactics suitable for a variety of conditions and ground … the purpose behind this grouping was to create a balanced, self-sufficient fighting body which could act as the spearhead of the attack, ready at a moment's notice to exploit the advantage of battle. Towards the attainment of this end all existing battalion organization was adjusted."[15]

Individual initiative was nurtured. Everyone was to know how to operate all the weapons. Should the platoon leader fall, the non-commissioned officer must be ready to take over. Command would keep devolving

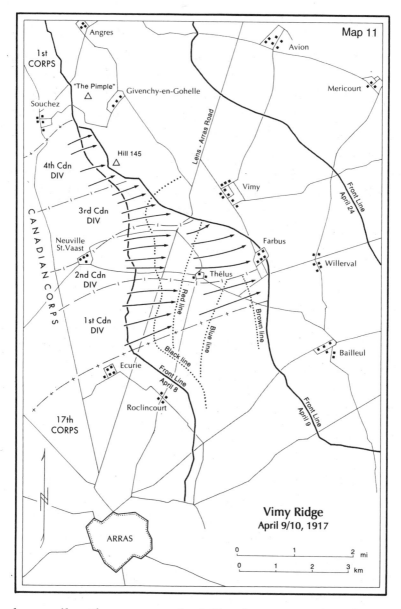

Vimy Ridge
April 9/10, 1917

downward until no man remained. The platoon was to be a dynam-
ic organism able to adapt to circumstances rapidly rather than adher-
ing rigidly to a prescribed plan. Horrific losses were still expected, but
the survivors should be able to fight through to the objective and hold
it until reinforced.

Chapter Eight

* * *

As 1916 gave way to 1917, Byng maintained a grinding training pace, for he knew that come the spring Canadian Corps would face its greatest challenge—the capture of Vimy Ridge. Situated north of Arras, this five-mile-long ridge stood just 457 feet at its highest point, but in a country of open plains Vimy Ridge dominated the surrounding terrain. After its capture in 1914, the Germans had transformed it into their most heavily fortified area in France. Its western slope and the crest line were honeycombed with deep underground caverns capable of housing entire battalions. A formidable trench system provided three lines of defence intended to hold the heaviest Allied assault until reinforcements could arrive to erase any gains won. Placed at regular intervals along the advanced trench line were concrete machine-gun emplacements. Completely surrounded by barbed wire, these bunkers served as independent fortresses. But their fields of fire also overlapped, so that the well-protected gunners jointly could cover the entire front. Because the Germans possessed the heights, it was impossible for the Allies to pull off a surprise attack, for their lines were completely exposed to observation. Unlike the slope facing the Allies, which rose gradually to the crest, Vimy Ridge's reverse slope fell away steeply to the Douai plain where thick woods provided excellent concealment for German artillery. With good reason the Germans had declared Vimy Ridge impregnable.

Byng knew his Canadians must prove them wrong or die trying, for Vimy Ridge was considered an essential objective in the forthcoming Allied offensive. The brainchild of Gen. Robert Nivelle, general-in-chief of the French Armies of the North and North-East, the offensive entailed a combined British and French attack from the Oise River to Lens intended to pin the opposing Germans in place while a second French attack along the Aisne River between Reims and Soissons achieved a breakthrough. With three great armies consisting of twenty-seven divisions striking across a vast front, Nivelle predicted that the Germans, unable to reinforce one sector by drawing troops from another, would be unable to prevent the long-sought breakout. Once the war became one of manoeuvre, the massed Allied force would be unstoppable.[16]

What made Vimy Ridge important was that its seizure would enable Canadian Corps to establish a blocking position that would secure not only the British left flank during the offensive but also that of the entire Allied forces. Because the B.E.F. would be fully engaged, Byng had been warned the Canadians must win Vimy Ridge alone.

It was a daunting, seemingly impossible task. The only thing working in their favour, Byng knew, was time. Arriving on the front in the late fall of 1916, they had ample opportunity to prepare and gain familiarity with the ground. Half of the Canadian Corps front faced Vimy Ridge's western slope. Because the Germans held the heights, the Allies considered their completely exposed front in the open plain indefensible. Consequently, rather than constructing an extensive trench system, the front was marked only by a line of small, isolated outposts. These were intended to serve no more than a short delaying function should the Germans ever come down from the heights to fight in the open, but there was slight possibility of this happening because no worthwhile advantage would be gained.

When the Canadian Scottish were stationed in front of Vimy Ridge for the first time in late November, their officers had held a group discussion to ponder what the advantage of "observation possessed by the enemy, perched as he was on the Pimple, the pinnacle of the Ridge at this end of it" must look like. They noted how the ground "climbed abruptly" out of the Zouave Valley "to form the westerly slopes of the Vimy Ridge which rose to the skyline in massive shape broadside on and shut out further view to the east." The thought of going up that western slope into the face of German fire produced a collective shudder.[17]

Quickly enough, however, the Canadians all knew they would have to do precisely that because the work undertaken by their engineer and pioneering units was all focused precisely toward the ridge. Old roads running toward the front line were repaired and new ones constructed. A 20-mile-long light rail track was laid that terminated three miles back of the front in the woods of Bois de Bray. "To this spot the transport sections of the various battalions repaired on the afternoon of each day, and on to trucks previously allotted to them, loaded up the rations, ammunition and the sundry other requirements of the men in the line. When darkness fell, off went the train, pulled by the tiny engine across the devastated area," while the trucks trundled the supplies to the front lines. This greatly reduced the normal expenditure of energy each battalion had to make carrying supplies up by mule or on the backs of men.[18]

Through the fall and winter the Canadians beavered away. To prevent having their signal lines severed by German artillery, they buried, seven feet underground, a "laddered" system of 21 miles of signal cable and 66 miles of telephone wire that created a multiplicity of links that could not be knocked out by one shell or even a series of direct hits.

Canadian Corps had 50,000 horses and inadequate water supply, so reservoirs were dug and 600,000 gallons a day was pumped to the Corps along channels running 45 miles long.

The Canadian *pièce de résistance*, what the Canadian official historian later declared "one of the great engineering achievements of the war," was created by the tunnelling companies: eleven underground galleries running almost four miles to the front lines. These electrically lit subways were 25 feet or more underground and through them ran the vital telephone cables and water mains. They also provided a protected route for moving assault troops forward and the wounded back. Huge chambers cut into the flanks of the tunnel throughways housed brigade and battalion headquarters, ammunition magazines, and medical dressing stations. By tapping into existing underground chalk-quarries, such as Zivy cave, room was created below ground to accommodate several complete battalions.[19]

Such marvels of engineering did not decide a battle's outcome. Byng and his protégé Arthur Currie believed victory would be won by the new infantry tactics being applied in combination with innovations in the use of artillery. In October 1916, a thirty-year-old McGill University engineer turned gunner had been appointed to command of Canadian Corps's heavy artillery. Considering artillery a science, Lt.-Col. Andrew McNaughton began developing the means to eliminate the German artillery—well hidden behind Vimy Ridge—with accurate counterbattery fire. Meticulously, McNaughton and his staff carefully detected the position of individual guns by studying photographs provided by aerial observation. They then had survey and sound ranging sections deduce the precise distance and positioning of the guns. "Wireless interceptions, captured documents and the interrogation of prisoners of war made an important contribution. Information from all these sources was rapidly collated and quickly transferred to the gun positions by an elaborate communication system."[20] By the spring, eighty-three percent of all the German guns hidden behind Vimy Ridge's eastern slope had been situated with pinpoint accuracy and assigned as a target to three batteries of heavy guns delegated to counterbattery work.

Destroying the German artillery was but one component of the complex artillery plan McNaughton and his staff developed. Byng and Currie insisted that all the German defensive works must be destroyed by artillery fire before the infantry assault. To achieve this required a massive artillery array, and British First Army provided 245 heavy guns and howitzers. Supporting field artillery numbered 480 eighteen-pounders and one hundred and thirty-eight 4.5-inch howitzers. From I British Corps came another 132 heavies and 102 field pieces. The density of firepower allowed one heavy gun for every 20 yards of frontage and one field gun for every ten. At the Somme the proportion had been one heavy every 57 yards and one field every 20 yards.[21]

The British high command predicted that a two-day bombardment would crush Vimy Ridge's defences, but Canadian Corps insisted on two weeks with the rate of fire doubling in the last week. This bombardment would target German trenches, dugouts, concrete machine-gun nests, and other strongpoints. Every detected ammunition and other supply dump, road junction, and communication node would also be pounded. To prevent repairs, the shelling would continue round the clock. A new fuse— No. 106—designed to trigger high-explosive shells and generate a splinter effect that sheared through wire had been extensively tested and would be utilized to break the wire fronting the German trenches. On the day of the attack the field artillery's bombardment would seamlessly transform into a rolling barrage of 100-yard lifts that would walk ahead of the artillery to the objectives. Meanwhile, the heavies, howitzers, and other field guns would subject known defensive systems to standing barrages. In all, 42,500 tons in "bulk" ammunition was added to a daily quota of 2,500 tons to enable the guns to fire whenever and at whatever rate was required.

In the weeks before the offensive, the Royal Flying Corps set about mastering the sky over Vimy Ridge. An extended mêlée ensued that pitted 400 Allied fighters almost every day against 150 German planes. While outnumbered, the Germans had superior planes and more experienced flyers. But numbers prevailed and, as the date of the offensive neared, the German flyers seldom ventured near the ridge.

On March 20, the artillery bombardment began, but half the available batteries stayed silent at any given time to prevent the Germans from determining the true weight of guns deployed. Then, on April 2, the intensive artillery phase opened as the heavies positioned in a great arc along a 22,000-yard front spoke with full fury. Thousands of shells crashed into the enemy lines in what the Germans later called "the week of suffering." More than a million rounds—a combined total weight of 50,000 tons—were fired by the heavy and field artillery during these days. The villages of Thélus, Givenchy, and Farbus were systematical-ly reduced to dust to deny their buildings to the enemy, the ridge and ground before it was transformed into a "pock-marked wilderness of mud-filled craters." Long stretches of the German trenches were obliter-ated and movement from the rear became laboriously time-consuming or even impossible. Many of the forward companies received no rations for two to three days, a fact that left them greatly weakened on the day of the attack.[22]

* * *

It was Easter Monday—April 9, 1917—when the Canadians went over the top. Byng's plan, presented to his divisional commanders on March 5, had seemed deceptively simple. It entailed an advance in four stages, with each piercing one layer of the German defences. Byng had marked each stage's objective on the map with a differently coloured line. The first, Black Line, was about 750 yards from the Canadian trenches and marked the forward German defensive positions. Red Line denoted the second objective—Zwischen-Stellung—a trench that ran from Thélus past the village of Vimy, which stood in the centre of the ridge, north-westward to La Folie Farm and Hill 145. Zwischen-Stellung was the fi-nal objective for the troops advancing on the left flank. Over on the right flank the map had two more lines with the first being Blue Line. This line passed through Thélus, Hill 35, and the woods of Bois de Bonval and Count's Wood. These woods overlooked the village of Vimy. Brown Line indicated the assault's final intent, which was to sever the German Second defensive front. It passed through Farbus Wood, Bois de la Ville and the southern part of the Bois de Bonval.[23]

In numerical order from right to left, the four Canadian divisions would advance simultaneously. Each would have two brigades forward and adhere to a strict timetable. Black Line would fall thirty-five minutes

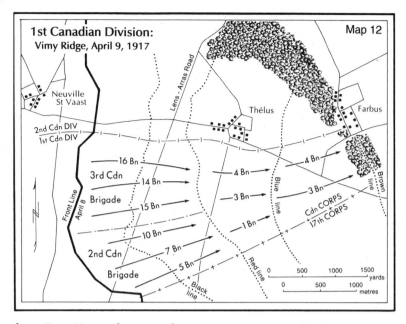

1st Canadian Division:
Vimy Ridge, April 9, 1917

Map 12

Neuville
St Vaast

Lens - Arras Road

Thélus

Farbus

2nd Cdn DIV
1st Cdn DIV

16 Bn

3rd Cdn

14 Bn

4 Bn

4 Bn

Brigade

15 Bn

3 Bn

3 Bn

Blue line

Brown line

Cdn CORPS
17th CORPS

Front Line

April 8

10 Bn

1 Bn

2nd Cdn

7 Bn

5 Bn

Red line

0   500   1000   1500
                              yards

Brigade

Black line

0   500   1000
                         metres

from Zero Hour of 0530. A forty-minute pause would allow the artillery to reorganize, and then twenty minutes' marching would carry Red Line—final objective for 3rd and 4th Divisions. Over the next two-and-a-half hours the two divisions that were carrying on to the right would pass their reserve brigades through to the front and advance 1,200 yards to Blue Line. Here the troops would pause another ninety-six minutes for realignment of the artillery and then push through to Brown Line. The deepest part of the Canadian penetration would total 4,000 yards. By 1318 hours Byng intended Vimy Ridge to be taken.

On the extreme right 1st Division would advance with its 2nd and 3rd Brigades forward. Brig. George Tuxford had elected to have three of his 3rd Brigade battalions up front. The 16th Battalion would be on the left, the 14th Battalion in the centre, and the 15th Battalion to the right. For 1st Division, Black Line coincided with a major German trench, Zwölfer-Stellung, which roughly paralleled Zwischen-Stellung at a distance of about 250 yards and lay about 700 yards from the brigade's starting position.

Shortly after dark on April 8, the Canadian Scottish had moved quickly and safely to their start point by way of Bentata Tunnel, one of the eleven underground galleries. By midnight the troops were in their positions, making themselves as comfortable as possible in the icy cold. Meanwhile, Lt.-Col. Cyrus Peck, Adjutant Lt. Sydney Douglas

Johnston, the battalion's artillery liaison officer, and three runners were still on the move to where the battalion commander intended to set up his Battle Headquarters. Finding Bentata Tunnel so crowded with troops the party could make little forward headway, Peck located an exit and the men started following a sunken road that led to the front. Within minutes they understood the advantage presented to the Canadians by the tunnel system as they were forced to dodge German artillery while slipping and sliding through mud. "Going forward the mud was terrible," Peck later wrote. "In one place I had to get out of my boots, climb on the bank of the sunken road and then pull out my boots after me." They had covered only a short distance when a shell landed in their midst. The artillery officer and two runners were killed by the explosion, which also wounded the other runner and threw Johnston into the air, leaving him badly injured. The still-conscious Johnston insisted on accompanying Peck only to collapse a few minutes later from loss of blood. Peck turned him over to stretcher-bearers and proceeded on alone.[24]

With his Battle Headquarters section shredded, Peck sent word that Captain Gordon Tupper of No. 3 Company was to report to him and become the battalion second-in-command. This was insurance in case Peck became incapable of command, for during the past few days he had been increasingly weakened by an undiagnosed sickness that by the night of April 8 forced his admission in a brief diary notation that he was "very ill" with stomach cramps and occasional bouts of vomiting.[25]

Tupper was ill-pleased by Peck's summons and pleaded to remain with his company, which along with No. 4 Company was to lead the attack. The two men were locked in an intense, but polite debate, when Major John Hope solved the problem with his timely arrival. Having been wounded the previous day, Hope had been evacuated to the rear. Knowing the battalion was short officers and not wanting to miss the offensive, Hope had checked himself out of hospital and a much-relieved Peck quickly gave him the battalion's second-in-command assignment while Tupper returned to his men.

Tupper came from a stalwart Conservative family. His father, Sir Charles Hibbert Tupper, and grandfather, Sir Charles Tupper, had both held important federal cabinet postings. Tupper's grandfather had even served briefly as the country's prime minister, assuming the position on May 1, 1896, only to be voted out of office in a resounding defeat ten weeks later. Major Reginald Tupper, who had been wounded during the April 22, 1915, charge on the woods, was George Tupper's older brother. Young George had enlisted when he turned eighteen and received an officer's commission in late 1915. Taking over No. 3 Company during the Somme fighting, he had established a reputation as a strict but fair disciplinarian. "Slim, supple, with a light moustache, carrying himself well, he looked little more than the mere lad he was; yet he had the poise and judgement of maturer years without losing the winsomeness of youth," Captain Hugh Urquhart observed.[26]

A few minutes before Zero Hour, Tupper sat in the dimly lit tunnel, jotting a note to his father:

> I am writing one of these "in case" letters for the third time, and, of course, I hope you will never have to read it. If you are reading it now you will know that your youngest son "went under" as proud as Punch on the most glorious day of his life. I am taking my company "over the top" for a mile in the biggest push that has ever been launched in the world, and I trust that it is going to be the greatest factor towards peace.
>
> Dad, you can't imagine the wonderful feeling; a man thinks something like this: Well, if I am going to die, this is worth it a thousand times. I have "been over" two or three times before, but never with a company of my own. Think of it—one hundred and fifty officers and men who will follow you to hell, if need be!
>
> I don't want any of you dear people to be sorry for me, although, of course, you will be in a way. You will miss me, but you will be proud of me. Mind you, I know what I am up against, and that the odds are against me, I am not going in the way I did the first time, just for sheer devilment and curiosity. I have seen this game for two years, and I still like it and feel that my place is here.... Good-bye, dear Father and Mother, and all of you. Again I say that I am proud to be where I am now.[27]

Not far from Tupper, Pte. Percy Twidale of No. 4 Company anxiously remembered a dream he had one night days before he enlisted in March 1916. In his dream, Twidale had been advancing through No Man's Land when a large chunk of shell casing slammed into his body and cut it in two at the waist. The two halves had been cast two to three feet apart and Twidale had sadly "wondered how I could get joined together again." This attack was the battlefield christening for the twenty-four-year-old farmer from the Calgary area. Although assigned some weeks earlier to the 16th Battalion, Twidale had been immediately seconded to the 1st Entrenching Battalion to work on road and rail construction behind the lines. Sent to the Canadian Scottish only a few days earlier, the young soldier barely knew the men in his platoon and was a stranger to them.[28]

In the early morning hours, the order came to leave the tunnel for the forward trenches. Weather was bitter—"squally showers of hail and sleet which chilled the bone; through this gloom the light of dawn was faintly struggling in." On the right, Tupper stood with his men while Twidale shivered over on the left as part of Captain James Scroggie's No. 4 Company. Lt. Charles Stanley Bevan's No. 1 Company was in the secondary trench and would come up behind on the right, while No. 2 Company under Lt. Morton Joseph Mason would follow on the left.

At 0500 hours, the great bombardment that had been raging suddenly shifted gears and the rolling barrage began with the sky to the rear flashing with flame and streaks of fire hissed overhead that threw "a weird gleam over the wet ground and the slimy sides and stagnant water of the crater depths." Some men prayed out loud; others jostled each other good-naturedly and cracked jokes; many stared quietly ahead with unreadable faces. Weapons were checked and rechecked. Tupper and Scroggie each had a company piper at his side.[29]

Seconds before the whistles blew, Twidale had a waking vision. "In front of me there was a bed with white sheets on it and my sister was kneeling by this bed with a white night dress on, praying for me." Suddenly Twidale shed his fear. No matter what happened he was ready. Then, "somebody yelled, 'We're away!' and we went over the top." Despite the eerie realization that everything before him precisely mirrored his pre-enlistment dream, Twidale never faltered. He strode toward his fate into No Man's Land.[30]

* * *

Fifteen thousand men formed the leading companies of the twenty-one battalions that charged through gaps opened in the Canadian wire and entered a maze of water-filled craters and destroyed trenches left over from past battles. Scattered across No Man's Land were pockets of rusting wire entanglements the men had to pick a way through. Mud sucked at their boots and, at times, they waded through mucky swamps of brown water thick as gumbo.

The German response was immediate—a heavy counter-barrage that sent shells shrieking over the heads of the Canadian Scottish but did little other damage because across the front their fire was mostly long. Well before Zwölfer-Stellung—the trench that marked 1ˢᵗ Division's Black Line—the Can Scots came under fire from German machine guns hidden in a string of craters. Men started to fall, but the platoons had trained precisely for this kind of moment. While one section slipped sideways and started throwing out covering fire, the other sections charged the guns, killing the crews with bombs and bayonets. The Canadian Scottish losses were heavy, but the new platoon tactics prevented the advance from stalling despite the unrelenting fire coming at them from both their front and flanks. "It was evident that these weapons were scattered everywhere in an irregular pattern on the shell-pitted ground over which the Battalion had to go forward. Men began to drop singly, others fell in huddled groups." The action became "a running fight, men rushing from shell-hole to shell-hole, the bodies of the fallen, indicating by their position the locations of the enemy's guns towards which this fighting was directed." One by one the machine-gun nests were silenced. Then, about 30 yards short of the sunken Arras-Lens road that passed within a few yards of the Zwölfer-Stellung trench, a line of German infantry opened fire from a deep ditch in front of the road. The men of Nos. 3 and 4 Companies ran straight into this devastating fire, gained the ditch, and then cleared it after a fierce mêlée of bayonet fighting. Many men were killed, their bodies left sprawled in the ditch. Among them was Major Gordon Tupper.[31]

Private Twidale came out of the ditch and stepped out on the road just as a shell exploded in front of him. A large piece of shell casing spun toward him, sickeningly mirroring the dream, only to strike his rifle and bend it "almost double. Instead of being cut in two, I threw the rifle down and picked up another rifle" from a fallen comrade. In that moment a piece of shrapnel pierced his leg, cutting clean to the shinbone. Twidale hobbled forward, but the rest of No. 4 Company quickly pulled far ahead.

To the left, No. 3 Company gained Zwölfer-Stellung with little further difficulty, but No. 4 was struck by machine-gun fire coming from a gap that had developed between the two companies. Breaking quickly into platoon formation to assault the gun from three sides, the men went forward only to be thrown back. Around the gun emplacement, the bodies of those killed lay in a fan-shaped configuration. The survivors dived into the cover of shell holes. No. 4 Company was pinned down. One of the men, twenty-four-year-old William Johnstone Milne, could see the gun position clearly. Slinging a bag of Mills bombs over one shoulder, Milne crawled under fire through the mud to within throwing range and chucked several bombs into the position. Milne managed to either kill or wound the gun crew and gain control of it. His action enabled the Canadian Scottish to secure Black Line and prepare to move on Red Line as scheduled.[32]

Private Twidale did not join the next phase of the attack. He hobbled instead toward the rear with six German prisoners. Once they were handed into the waiting cage, Twidale carried on to the battalion dressing station. He sat down outside, but when his turn came was unable to stand. Twidale's leg was broken, his combat experience destined to last just twenty minutes because the war would end before his injuries healed.[33]

Meanwhile the battle raged on. No. 4 Company again met trouble, this time as it closed on Zwischen-Stellung and was struck by fire from two entrenched machine guns. A rifle grenadier knocked one gun out, but the other was protected within a concrete bunker concealed behind a large haystack. Once again, Milne crawled to within a few yards of the position, jumped up, and threw several Mills bombs into the gun aperture. The gun crew was killed and other Germans holding the trench fled, presenting perfect targets to the Canadian Scottish, who cut many of them down with rifle and Lewis machine-gun fire. In the midst of this confusion, Milne was seen moving behind a small knoll that was suddenly struck by German artillery fire. His body was never found. On June 8, 1917, the young Scot, who had immigrated to Canada to take up farming near Moose Jaw, was posthumously awarded the Victoria Cross.[34]

When they paused at Red Line the Canadian Scottish "could see that the success which had been theirs had also come to the assaulting troops everywhere in sight. On the high ground to the left, the 2nd

Canadian Division men, easily distinguishable by the dark patches on the point of the shoulder, were busily digging in or moving about from place to place; similarly engaged down the slope to the right as far as … nine tall elms—the landmark which so clearly defined the junction of the Canadian Corps and the Third Army—was a long line of Highlanders and infantry wearing on the arm the bright red patches of the 1st Canadian Division. From north to south, behind the entire length of this ragged line of forward troops, advanced groups of men … all … moving at a deliberate pace, maintaining excellent intervals just as on the manoeuvre area."

At the head of one small group approaching Red Line trench were two Canadian Scottish pipers, Pipe Major James Groat and Piper Allan McNab, both "playing lustily." Right behind the pipers was Lt.-Col. Peck and RSM James Kay. Peck's personal servant and Kay's batman were a few steps back, the latter carrying a large crock of rum under each arm—a sight that elicited a hearty cheer from the ranks.[35]

Peck's servant hovered close, fearful the battalion commander might collapse at any moment. As Peck looked along the trench his physical illness was matched by a sickness of the heart. He estimated that between 350 and 500 men had fallen and as many as seventeen officers had been either killed or wounded. Lt. Bevan was among the dead and Captain Scroggie had been wounded. That left only one company commander unscathed. Despite these losses, Peck judged "the whole action magnificent." Officer casualties were later found to number twenty of the twenty-one who entered battle. This figure included Peck, ordered to hospital by the Medical Officer. Seven officers had been killed. As Major Hope came forward to assume command of the battalion, Peck started for the rear accompanied by two runners. A blinding snowstorm had descended on the battleground and Peck's party were lost for two hours before chancing upon an entrance to Bentata Tunnel.[36]

In less than ninety minutes the Canadian Scottish had lost almost as many men as the October 7–9 battle in the Somme had claimed, but this time fewer other ranks had died. Of the total 321 other rank casualties 99 perished, as opposed to 131 of 331 at the Somme.[37]

After seizing the Red Line, the 2nd and 3rd Brigade battalions became "spectators" for the rest of the April 9 battle. At 0940 the creeping barrage had pushed beyond the Red Line and 1st Canadian Infantry Brigade passed through to carry 1ˢᵗ Division's next objectives. Blue Line duly fell, as did Brown Line. The latter objective was indeed not protected by the trench that had been reported and so was taken without any resistance. From here, 1ˢᵗ Brigade pushed onto the crest of Vimy Ridge and captured German artillery in Farbus Wood and Station Wood. "Between two and three o'clock the same afternoon, standing on the crest of the Ridge between Farbus Wood and Station Wood looking eastward, it was possible to realize fully the meaning of the victory of the morning."

Major Hugh Urquhart, now serving as 1ˢᵗ Brigade's Brigade Major, could see the next German trench line far beyond Vimy Ridge and realized it was there for the taking. But the "prize, however, could not be grasped. The troops had reached the final objectives as outlined in operation orders; the impetus of the attack was spent: the right flank was swung back over a mile; the guns could not be moved over the shelltorn ground. For the time being it was impossible to carry out any appreciable exploitation." [38]

* * *

At corps headquarters, Byng had realized the opportunity and appealed for cavalry to take over the advance only to be told none was available. There was little time to worry about the potential opportunity lost, for on the left flank the fighting still raged as 4ᵗʰ Division struggled to fight its way through to Vimy Ridge's highest point, Hill 145, and the knoll to its left nicknamed "the Pimple." A storm of machine-gun fire had shredded the assault battalions and then chewed up the reserve forces until only the 85ᵗʰ Nova Scotia Battalion, a work battalion virtually untrained for combat, remained. At 1745 hours this battalion attacked and, in an hour's fighting on a night rendered pitch black by the blinding snowstorm, cleared the Germans off Hill 145. But the Pimple remained in German hands for three more days until 10ᵗʰ Infantry Brigade stormed through a heavy fall of sleet mixed with snow and cleared it on April 12 at a cost of half its men either killed or wounded.

Not until the Pimple fell was the Battle of Vimy Ridge concluded. In all, 40,000 Canadians had been directly involved in the fighting, and of these 3,598 died and 7,004 were wounded. One of the most impregnable sectors of the German front had been breached and the Canadians had taken 4,000 prisoners and overrun 54 guns, 104 trench-mortars, and 124 machine guns. Canadian Corps dug in 4,500 yards beyond its start line astride the Lens-Arras railway.[39]

Vimy Ridge was indisputably a great Allied victory, for it yielded the capture of more ground, prisoners, and guns than any previous British offensive. For Canada the battle was also a defining moment. For the first time all four Canadian Corps divisions had attacked as one and their determination and skill carried the day. It was Canada's proudest moment of the war and one that came to symbolize its emergence from colony to nation.

The assault on Vimy Ridge was but a small part of a far larger offensive. To the immediate right, the British Third Army had also won considerable ground while the British Fourth and Fifth Armies had also achieved major gains to the left. Nor did the offensive end with Vimy Ridge's capture, but the role Canadian Corps played in the later fighting was limited. On April 28, 1st Division's 2nd Infantry Brigade struck a bulge in the German line called the Arleux Loop to support an adjoining British assault. While the British offensive collapsed, 2nd Brigade achieved "the only tangible success of the whole operation" by pinching off the loop. But the cost was nearly 1,000 casualties. Following this operation 1st Canadian Infantry Brigade teamed up with 2nd Division's 6th Infantry Brigade in a joint drive on May 2 from Arleux to Fresnoy-en-Gohelle. Although initially successful, German counterattacks soon pushed the Canadians back to their start line.

Meanwhile, the great French offensive intended to break through the German lines into the open country behind had yielded a massacre that cost 200,000 French casualties for a gain of a few miles and about 28,000 prisoners. Gen. Nivelle was sacked and replaced by "the hero of Verdun," Gen. Philippe Pétain. He inherited an army on the verge of open mutiny with one division refusing orders to return to the line. Some mutineers were executed, many more exiled to Devil's Island and other French penal colonies, and the mutiny broken. But dissent and resentment lingered in the ranks. Pétain personally inspected the majority of the French units and came away convinced the *poilus* were determined not to surrender an inch of ground, but they would bluntly refuse more meaningless attacks. Better living conditions were also demanded and longer periods of leave. Pétain promised to do what he could for them.

One thing was clear, though—the French Army was spent and it would take months to return it to being capable of offensive action.

Yet for the Allies to assume a completely defensive posture on the Western Front was anathema to generals and politicians alike. If the Germans realized how far French morale had fallen, surely they would capitalize on it with a major counterstrike. Despite public sentiment throughout the Empire that there must be "no more Battles of the Somme," Field Marshal Douglas Haig decided the B.E.F. had no choice but to launch a new offensive to again try breaking the stalemate. He would strike near the end of July in the blood-soaked Ypres Salient.[40]

It Isn't Worth a Drop of Blood!

- JUNE 7, 1917–AUGUST 4, 1918 -

On June 8, Canadian Corps deployed to a new front near the French coal-mining town of Lens. Just two days earlier, Arthur Currie had been knighted, promoted to lieutenant general, and succeeded Gen. Julian Byng as corps commander. Byng's long intention to see Canadian officers at the helm of the corps was finally realized and he departed on good terms with everyone to command the Third Army. One of Currie's first acts was to promote Brig. Archibald Cameron Macdonell to command 1st Division. "Archie" to his friends, the silver-haired, Windsor-born, fifty-three-year-old was Currie's physical opposite, a straight-backed man who looked born to wear a general's uniform. Macdonell had gone from being a North-West Mounted Police officer to command the Lord Strathcona's Horse cavalry regiment in South Africa. At the head of 7th Infantry Brigade, he had been twice wounded in 1916 and was one of Currie's closest friends. "Old Mac," Currie called him, while the other ranks affectionately referred to Macdonell as "Batty Mac."

Currie's giving 1st Division to Macdonell angered Prime Minister Robert Borden, who had favoured Maj.-Gen. Garnet Hughes for the position. The son of Sam Hughes currently commanded 5th Canadian Division, was permanently consigned to home defence duties in Britain, and had been clamouring incessantly to lead a fighting division. But Currie had no use for either Garnet Hughes or his father. "I'll get even with you before I'm finished," Garnet Hughes shouted during a three-hour argument in London where he had demanded that Currie reverse his decision.

Sam and Garnet Hughes were soon presented with a gilded opportunity for revenge when it was discovered that, in 1914, Currie had purloined $8,300 intended for the purchase of uniforms for the Victoria 50th Gordon Highlanders to pay off business debts. Currie had nursed this guilt while the regiment's creditors, who had provided the uniforms and gone unpaid, patiently compiled evidence that proved Currie's duplicity. In June 1917, they submitted to the government sufficient evidence to paint the new corps commander a thief. Only the intervention of two Canadian generals—Maj.-Gen. David Watson and Brig. Victor Odlum—with a $10,883.34 loan to repay the missing funds with interest prevented his being sacked in disgrace. Scandal notwithstanding, Currie's promotion stood and so did Macdonell's.

Currie had spent most of June in London as these proceedings ran their course. Upon his return to corps headquarters, Currie met with the First British Army's commander. Gen. Henry Horne told him the Canadian's current assignment was to pin German divisions in front of its line to prevent their being sent to meet Field Marshal Douglas Haig's July offensive. But the mission was not to be passive. Instead, Horne wanted an attack astride the Souchez River to eliminate a small salient between Avion and Lens's western outskirts. Two previous attempts by 4th Canadian Division's 10th Brigade to carry the salient had achieved little but had resulted in 550 casualties.

Wresting the salient from German hands, Currie decided, would cost more in casualties than was warranted. Instead he ordered a series of hit-and-run raids by 3rd and 4th Divisions that convinced the Germans to collapse the salient at the end of June and establish a more defensible line running in front of Avion. This left Lens almost encircled by the British.

On July 7, the Canadians assumed responsibility for a three-mile length of front facing Lens. Years of shelling had reduced the town to rubble "encircled by a wreath of shattered pithead installations."

Currie climbed a hill behind the lines and spent the day examining the ground. Hill 70 stood on one side of Lens and Sallumines Hill on the other. Hill 70 was an uninspiring barren limestone dome with clusters of brick company-owned miners' cottages scattered across its slopes. The cellars of these shelled-out ruins had been transformed into protected fighting positions linked together by a spider web of trenches and tunnels. Simple enough to take the town, he realized, but the Germans on the hills would then hit the Canadians with murderous fire. There was also nowhere behind the lines to hide artillery within range of Lens. The guns would have to set up on the open plain.[1]

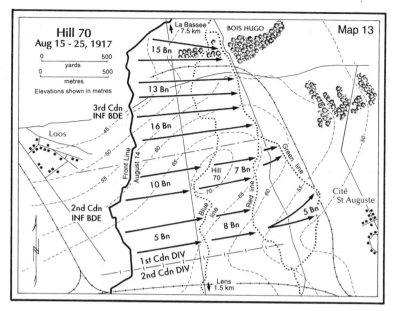

"If we are to fight," Currie told Horne the next day, "let us fight for something worth having." That something was Hill 70. Take it, dig in, and bleed the Germans when they counterattacked. Horne deferred the decision to Haig, who came to Canadian Corp headquarters on July 23 to hear Currie's plan. The Canadian general had spent the intervening time well and presented a full operational plan that proposed blasting the Germans off Hill 70 with a massive artillery program—for which he would need more guns. Although Haig's artillery chief chided that the Canadians had sufficient firepower, the field marshal curtly intervened, saying: "See that General Currie gets the extra guns he wants."[2]

Sour weather forced a delay from August 4 to August 15, which suited Currie fine as it gave more time for the meticulous planning and preparations that he favoured. Although Hill 70 was the primary objective, the Canadian offensive would span two miles of front from Bois Hugo on the left to Cité Ste. Elisabeth on the right. Hill 70 lay about 750 yards south of Bois Hugo. From Hill 70's summit to Cité Ste. Elisabeth the ground was cluttered with wrecked mine works and buildings the Germans had transformed into fighting positions. Responsibility for taking Hill 70 went to 1st Division with 2nd Division given the job of clearing the ground south of it. In 1st Division's sector, 3rd Brigade would be on the left and 2nd Brigade the right. Three 3rd Brigade battalions would advance on narrow lines to clear the area north of Hill 70 with 16th Battalion brushing past the flank of its northern slope, while the 13th Battalion advanced to its left with 15th Battalion directed against Bois Hugo. The 10th Battalion from 2nd Brigade with 7th Battalion in trail would seize Hill 70 itself, and the 5th Battalion followed by 8th Battalion would clear the southern slope. In all, the two divisions would deploy ten battalions. The attack closely mirrored that on Vimy Ridge with an advance divided into three stages of which the German front line would be the destination for the first bound. Thereafter the German second position running across Hill 70's crest, designated Blue Line, would be the next objective. The final stage would end at Green Line, a section of frontage running behind the eastern or backslope of Hill 70 that lay 1,500 yards from the start point. Zero Hour was set for 0425 hours.[3]

* * *

The Canadian Scottish had formed up in trenches on the front during the night of August 13–14. No. 2 Company, under Major Edward Gilliat, would lead the attack on the right. Gilliat was a hardened veteran, who had been with the battalion since 1914. On his left was Lt. Bill Petrie's No. 1 Company. Petrie had joined the Canadian Scottish in March 1916. Each company was to advance to Blue Line with two platoons forward and two following in another wave. Major James Murphy's No. 4 Company with its four platoons formed line abreast would follow directly behind the leading companies while Lt. George Francis Mason's No. 3 Company provided the mopping-up force for bypassed German strongpoints. The fact that relatively new and inexperienced lieutenants commanded two of the companies reflected the shortage of officers that still plagued Canadian Corps.[4]

Piper Alexander "Alec" McGillivray stood fretting in the trench as the countdown to Zero Hour began. Finally turning to CSM Frank Macdonald of No. 2 Company, the twenty-nine-year-old lance corporal, who hailed originally from Acraracle in the Argyllshire region of Scotland, quietly whispered that he felt "anxious," afraid that because he was so slight the weight of the pipes and other equipment might leave him scrambling behind the men—which would "bring disgrace on a Highland piper."

Macdonald pondered the matter for a moment. "Well, if you think that way, ask the company commander to allow you to climb out before us," he suggested. McGillivray quickly secured Major Gilliat's permission and as the barrage opened "he led off the advance, well ahead of the attacking wave, playing his pipes."[5]

CSM Macdonald set off hot on the piper's heels as soon as the whistle sounded only to snag his kilt in a tangle of wire and pitch onto his face in the mud. As he struggled to free himself from the wire, Macdonald found himself shoulder to shoulder with a private who had suffered the same head-first plunge. As the two wiped the muck off their faces the private quipped, "Well, Mac, I guess if you and I were hung for beauty now, we would be innocent men."[6]

It was a clockwork advance, for the bombardment shattered the will of the Germans in the front line. Those not killed or wounded either surrendered or fled. The leading companies hurdled the German front trenches and pressed on across ground badly cratered by the bombardment for Blue Line about 500 yards distant. In negotiating around a concentration of craters, Lt. Petrie strayed far to the left and a dangerous gap opened between his company and Gilliat's. From his rear position, Lt. James McIvor, leading a No. 3 Company platoon acting as a wiring party, assessed the problem and rushed his men forward and plugged the hole between the two companies. Twenty-five minutes after Zero Hour the battalion sent back a signal that it was on Blue Line.

A forty-minute planned pause followed to let the artillery work over the ground about 200 yards to their front. While the Canadians waited, two German machine-gun crews slithered up intervening communication trenches to bring them into range. From the cover of a crater, Lewis gunner Cpl. Harry Gracie spotted one of the crews "groping around under cover trying to place the gun; he waited until the Germans fully exposed themselves and then, opening fire, killed the whole of the crew." This action earned Gracie a Military Medal. Meanwhile, the moment the other gun crew opened fire its position was detected by CSM Macdonald and one of No. 2 Company's other sergeants destroyed it with a few well-placed bombs.[7]

Throughout this action, Piper McGillivray had played without pause, marching up and down in front of the Blue Line trench. Then, seeing that 13th Battalion on the left was having a bad time because the trench where they were forming up was being subjected to intense German artillery fire, McGillivray paraded over to rally the beleaguered Royal Highlanders.

"Just at this time," wrote the 13th Battalion's regimental historian, "when all ranks were feeling the strain of remaining inactive under galling fire, and when the casualties had mounted to over 100, a skirl of bagpipes was heard and along the 13th front came a piper of the 16th Canadian Scottish. This inspired individual, eyes blazing with excitement, and kilt proudly swinging to his measured tread, made his way along the line, piping as only a true Highlander can when men are dying, or facing death, all around him.

"Shell fire seemed to increase as the piper progressed and more than once it appeared that he was down, but the god of brave men was with him in that hour, and he disappeared unharmed, to the flank whence he had come."

As McGillivray rejoined the battalion, No. 2 Company and No. 4 Company headed for the Green Line. Resistance was slight and the objective fell in short order, but the trench proved so badly damaged as to be unrecognizable as a defensive work. McGillivray strode right over it without pausing and a good number of No. 2 Company followed. Suddenly a German soldier rushed McGillivray, who dropped his instrument and engaged the man in hand-to-hand combat. For several minutes the two men rolled back and forth in the mud until McGillivray managed to kill the German with his bare hands. Stumbling to his feet, the piper cast about in vain for his pipes. CSM Macdonald came over to McGillivray and said headquarters had sent orders for the pipers to go to the rear. With the advance over, their job was done and they posed too conspicuous a target for the snipers who would soon be harrying the battalion front lines.

McGillivray pleaded not to have to go back until his pipes were found, but Macdonald promised he would see to the job personally. Reluctantly McGillivray departed. The next morning Macdonald found the pipes 40 yards in front of the Green Line and took them back to give to McGillivray. But the piper was not to be found at headquarters and nobody there had seen him. After a lengthy search it was concluded McGillivray must have been blown to pieces by a German shell and disappeared into the mud without a trace. His courage on August 15 ultimately led to a posthumous Military Medal.[8]

To the right of the Canadian Scottish line, Hill 70 had fallen. So too had all the other Canadian objectives. In the early afternoon a desperate counterattack struck the southern front held by 2nd Division, but it was shattered by Canadian artillery and the new line held firm. Finally the Germans confined themselves to subjecting the Green Line to a sustained artillery pounding that went on long into the night.[9] For the Canadian Scottish, the shelling and counterattacks that developed the next morning and continued until they were relieved on August 17 took a heavier toll than the actual advance.

The casualty toll could have been even higher had it not been for the sharp eyes of a No. 2 Company sentry who at daybreak on August 16 told CSM Macdonald that he suspected shell-holes to their front actually concealed an underground fortification still held by the Germans. He had noted the position of an abandoned Maxim machine gun lying in No Man's Land about 50 yards from his station, only to realize a little later the gun had mysteriously moved several yards. The sentry was convinced the Germans were covertly retrieving the big gun which, unloaded, weighed forty pounds.

Macdonald and a couple of men went out to investigate and found the machine gun lying on the edge of a fortified shell-hole covered with chicken wire. Three wooden steps led to the entrance of a well-concealed dugout inside the crater. Macdonald could hear voices muttering in German down in the dugout's darkness, but when he called to them to surrender the voices abruptly ceased.

Tearing away the chicken wire, Macdonald and his men threw a couple of Mills bombs down the steps. Then they rushed in, coming face to face with three terrified lads who appeared younger than eighteen and had been wounded by shrapnel from the bombs. Macdonald made the prisoners carry the Maxim back to the Canadian lines.[10]

In the early morning hours of August 17, the Canadian Scottish began pulling out of the line in a relief so hampered by heavy shelling that Lt.-Col. Peck and his battalion headquarters staff had to personally oversee the process by extracting the men in groups and then feeding the same number of relieving troops through to the front. It was a process that took hours and at its end Peck and his staff were "a group of tired looking, mud-stained men, headed by the pipe major." To buoy their spirits, Pipe Major James Groat insisted on playing ceaselessly as the weary party walked in the pre-dawn light toward the rear-area village where the Canadian Scottish had been billeted. The skirl of Groat's bagpipes warned the battalion of Peck's approach and it was to his surprise that, as the headquarters party came along the main street, a large group of soldiers "rushed out into the street, many of them without boots or puttees and some without kilts. They greeted the party with cheer upon cheer and, in a band, escorted the procession to Battalion headquarters."[11]

Although the men's enthusiasm was in large part due to their belief that, despite a hard fight, they had suffered few casualties, the battalion had not got off that lightly—257 being killed or wounded. Two officers had died—including Major James Murphy—and five were wounded. In the ranks, 61 men died and 189 suffered wounds.[12] But still they had tasted a second victory and morale soared with some prognostications that the war would be over before year's end.

* * *

On August 19, Currie decided Hill 70 was secure enough to begin the job of capturing Lens. Two days later 4th Division struck and a bitter fight ensued with possession of the town contested until 3rd Division took over and, two days later, the Germans fell back. Canadian Corps tallied its casualties for the full ten-day operation at 9,198. But against this was an intelligence estimate of 30,000 German casualties, mostly inflicted by artillery. The gunners reported that they had never before been presented with so many German troops concentrated in the open and presenting perfect targets. Currie's intention to seize Hill 70 and bleed the Germans by smashing their counterattacks had worked. Thirty-five counterattacks entailing troops from no less than sixty-nine battalions had been repelled by the Canadians.[13]

The "Canadians had attained their ends," read one German report. "The fighting at Lens had cost us a considerable number of troops which had to be replaced. The entire preconceived plan for relieving the troops in Flanders had been upset. One had to reckon with a continuation of the attack by the Canadian divisions. Crown Prince Rupprecht therefore refrained from attempting immediately to recapture the lost ground at Lens, which would have required strong new forces and promoted the very intentions of the opponent."[14] Belatedly the German Sixth Army commander had twigged to Currie's intention, but it was clear the Germans were done offering themselves up for slaughter by massed artillery.

First British Army's Gen. Henry Horne and Currie both wanted to ensure Lens was secure with a two-pronged offensive, with one advancing southeastward from Hill 70 while the other drove northeastward from Eleu to gain the Sallumines Hills. Such an operation would force the Germans to continue committing men to this front who otherwise could be sent to the aid of those divisions heavily engaged in the Ypres Salient. But it soon became clear that Haig was directing so many British troops and supplies to his operations in the salient that First Army could not remain on the offensive.

This left Canadian Corps with little to do but stand in place, which was fine as far as most of the troops were concerned. Trench watch was considered better than battle because every stretch spent on the front earned equal time in a rest camp. Not that trench duty was without its hazards. During this period, which ended on October 14, 16th Battalion suffered ninety-seven casualties of which twenty-three were fatal. But that was a far cry from the butcher's bills of battle, especially as it represented the passing of forty days.[15]

Such periods of relative calm never lasted. On October 3, Currie was warned that Canadian Corps would go north to Ypres Salient. Passchendaele was now a household word in Britain and it would soon resonate in Canada. "Passchendaele," Currie bellowed on receiving the news. "What's the good of it? Let the Germans have it—keep it—rot in it! Rot in the mud! There is a mistake somewhere. It must be a mistake! It isn't worth a drop of blood."[16]

For three long months, Passchendaele had thirstily soaked up all the blood British and Anzac troops could spill. On July 31, the Third Battle of Ypres had begun and before the day was out 30,000 Commonwealth troops had fallen dead or wounded. Since then, the toll had risen steadily, surpassing 100,000 by mid-October. German casualties were little less. By early October, Haig was convinced the Germans were all but used up and one more push would collapse their front. When four Australian and four British divisions won significant gains at a cost of about 20,000 casualties, but inflicted equal losses on the Germans and took 5,000 prisoners, Haig was certain he was right.

Haig was not far off the mark. A later German history described October 4 as "the black day." Gen. Erich Ludendorff made special mention of the "enormous losses" his army had suffered and Crown Prince Rupprecht began considering what had hitherto been unthinkable— abandoning the ridges that hemmed the British inside the salient and falling back to a new defensive line.[17]

One more push, Haig decided, even as the weather deteriorated on October 7 with a gale of "cold, drenching rain" transforming the battlefield into a freezing hellhole. Passchendaele Ridge would fall, the Field Marshal declared, and the troops would be spared another mud-drenched winter in the bogs below. His Australian and British generals thought a winter in the bogs preferable to attacking the ridges in the rapidly deteriorating weather, but ultimately they conceded to try. And try they did on October 9 at a cost of 10,000 casualties and then again on October 13 for a loss of 13,000 more. That finished the Australian and British divisions.[18] So Haig sent for the Canadians.

Currie had prayed these attacks would succeed and spare his men from the grinder. He arrived at British Second Army headquarters despondent but determined to argue against madness. Taking army commander Gen. Sir Herbert Plumer aside, Currie said the Canadian casualties in a Passchendaele operation would number 16,000. Even were they to succeed would such a sacrifice be worthwhile? Plumer said Currie had no choice. The orders were plain.

Haig and Currie met later at Canadian Corps Headquarters. What words passed between them went unrecorded, but observers noted Haig's body language seemed to indicate coaxing, Currie's resistance. Then Currie nodded, as if in agreement.

Thereafter Haig spoke to the Canadian officers. Passchendaele, he declared, "must be taken, and I have come to ask the Canadian Corps to do it." Currie, he acknowledged, "is strongly opposed to doing so. But I have succeeded in overcoming his scruples. Some day I hope to tell you why this must be done, but in the mean time I ask you to take my word for it.... I may say General [Currie] has demanded an unprecedented amount of artillery and I have been forced to acquiesce."[19]

Currie made no bones of the fact that he thought Canadian Corps was being put at risk to "resuscitate a campaign that was already played out." But Haig continued to pound the drum of the British need to support the French by pinning down German divisions, doing the same to divert attention from a planned offensive by British Fourth and Fifth armies near Cambrai, and to secure a winter line on Passchendaele Ridge above the miasma of mud.[20]

Canadian Corps relieved the 2nd Anzac Corps on October 18, moving into a front that ran along the Stroombeek Valley between Gravenstafel Ridge and the heights of Passchendaele. The Canadians had known this ground during previous deployments, but they barely recognized it now. The villages of St. Jean, Wieltje, and Fortuin had disappeared without a trace. So had the woods that had been green in 1915 and the farms that had still looked prosperous. In their place was a wasteland.

The shelling that destroyed all the natural drainage had combined with relentless rains to transform the low ground facing the ridge into a deep bog of yellow mud. The countless shell-holes were brimming with brackish water. Oozing mud had swallowed the roads and foot-paths whole. Duckboard pathways built over the mud were perilous, and soldiers could conceivably drown with a misstep. Strewn everywhere were corpses, entangled in the wire on the slopes of the ridges, floating in the shell-holes, and laying half-buried in the mud. There had been no ceasefires and the removal of wounded alone was almost beyond the resources of the stretcher-bearers. It was not uncommon for sixteen men to be required to carry out a single wounded soldier and inevitably some members of a stretcher-bearer party would be shot down by the machine guns on the ridge. Rats picked through the mud for their next meal and, more boldly—chattering and flapping—did thousands of crows. Until temperatures dropped to freezing, flies continued to swarm by the millions, combining with the omnipresent lice and fleas to constantly crawl upon the men's skin and uniforms. The stench of rotting meat mixed with human and animal waste was appalling.

Currie, who "consistently sought to pay the price of victory in shells and not the lives of his men," concentrated on getting the guns needed before Haig forced an attack upon him. Inherent to the Canadian Corps were 350 field and heavy guns manned by 20,000 men, but he had been forced to leave some of these behind in the Lens area. Promised that 250 heavies had been left by the Australians for Canadian use, Currie's gunners found only 227 and 89 of these were non-operational. Of 306 18-pounder field guns, only half were serviceable and many were "dotted about in the mud wherever they happened to get bogged." Because of the mud, most of the guns were closely and dangerously bunched together.

The gunners and engineers set about putting things to rights with construction. Between mid-October and mid-November they constructed two miles of double plank road and more than 4,000 yards of heavy tramlines that enabled the movement of guns, ammunition, and men. Entire brigades were put to carrying and building.[21] 1st Division's 3rd Brigade drew the lot of serving as a workforce and so the Canadian Scottish "for miles ... trudged under the shell fire, up the roads and narrow board walks to Passchendaele, at the apex of the salient; they supplied work parties and carrying parties; they held the scratches and shell-holes dignified with the name of front line; No. 16 Platoon, by means of a minor operation, captured a ruined house on the left of the Battalion front; but neither the 16th nor any other unit of the 3rd Brigade took part in a major attack."[22] Meanwhile, the corps paid the cost of the construction work with 1,500 casualties.[23]

Currie kept negotiating postponements. Haig insisted he must gain possession of Passchendaele, the little Flanders crossroads village that stood on the centre of the ridge's crest. Currie decided the only way to get there was by three limited advances with each phase remaining well inside the range of his artillery. Once on the objective, the infantry would dig in and pause for about three days while the gunners dragged their artillery forward to establish a new firing line. Because conditions were so vile and dangerous—every square inch being subject to German fire—Currie decided it was too obvious a signal that an attack was coming to assemble the assaulting brigades in the front lines only a short time before Zero Hour. Instead, they would occupy the front lines two days before the attack, even though this meant they would be exposed to all the normal stress of front-line duty during this period.

Finally, Currie declared he was ready to attack on October 26. Third and Fourth Divisions would lead with their axis centred on the village but separated by the impassably flooded Ravebeek swamp. They would go up against German positions tied together by an array of concrete pillboxes concealing any number of machine guns and thickly protected by belts of wire. There would be two keys to victory: the firepower of the gunners—and the sheer guts of the infantry. If either failed the Canadians would be slaughtered to no avail.

On October 25, the already cheerless weather broke with a heavy rainfall. At dawn the following morning the assault battalions picked their way forward behind a rolling barrage, trying to circumvent the shell-holes. Still, several men lost their footing and drowned as their heavy equipment pulled them under. Yellow mud clung to their gear and clothing. Soon each man dragged along an extra twenty to thirty pounds of muck in addition to their fighting kit.

The platoon tactics practised so assiduously before Vimy Ridge served the Canadians well as they closed on the pillboxes, whose inherent strength also proved their weakness. Able to see only what lay in view through the narrow apertures, the German gunners depended on infantry in the trenches behind them to protect them from being attacked from blind sides. Recognizing this vulnerability, one platoon section would hit the rear trenches with withering fire from a flank while the rest rushed forward and eliminated the gunners with Mill bombs. German prisoners could be left there by the assault troops and mopped up later by follow-on forces. This was a deadly game, however, because the Canadians were exposed and under constant fire from German positions farther up the slope as they clawed their way toward the summit.

The two divisions took three days to gain their first objective at a cost of 2,481 men. But they were still well short of the prize—Passchendaele. On October 30, the reserve battalions renewed the drive, gaining 1,000 yards across a 2,800-yard-wide front for 2,321 casualties. That left 3rd and 4th divisions spent, so Currie fed the 1st brigades of both 1st and 2nd divisions forward on November 6. The fresh troops succeeded with 2nd Division's 27th Battalion, claiming the honour of eliminating the pillboxes where the village had once stood. Victory came at a terrible cost, with 734 men killed out of a total casualty toll of 2,238. There remained the ridge's summit and Haig demanded its possession. On November 10, 1st Division's 7th and 8th Battalions seized it and then desperately repelled a succession of counterattacks. At nightfall the Germans slunk back and the Canadians established a series of outposts in shell-holes and dugouts on Passchendaele's east slope. Losses this day numbered 1,094 casualties of which 420 died. But the day's action concluded the Third Battle of Ypres, also known as Second Passchendaele. Four days later the Canadians started handing off the front and by the 20th had departed the godforsaken salient for good. Passchendaele had cost the corps 15,654 casualties, just a few hundred less than Currie's prediction.[24]

"I look back on the Passchendaele show as a nightmare," one Canadian Scottish soldier wrote. "The ground was strewn with our dead. I have never seen anything to compare with the holocaust. When I think of shell-holes filled with water; the road leading up to the ridge heavily shelled day and night; wading through water, mud up to the knees; the stretcher-bearers carrying the wounded, eight men to a stretcher, and sometimes the whole party would be smashed up before they reached the dressing station, it makes me wonder how the troops stood it all."[25]

The Canadian Scottish thanked their luck to have been spared an offensive role. But they could never forget the Ypres Salient or the fact that more than half their total casualties during the course of the war occurred inside its maw.

* * *

While Canadian Corps was granted a long-deserved break, the British launched a new major offensive at Cambrai. Passchendaele had still raged as Lt.-Gen. Julian Byng and his Third Army put final touches to an audacious plan that, in one bold move, sought to "rupture...the German front from St. Quentin, seventeen miles south of Cambrai, to the canalized River Sensée, five miles north of the city. It was Byng's intention to gain possession of the area lying between the Canal du Nord and the St. Quentin Canal, bounded to the north by the Sensée.... With this accomplished the whole German line west of the Canal du Nord would be endangered."[26]

Before being ordered to Passchendaele, Currie had hoped the Canadians would be part of this operation—recognizing that its execution might revolutionize the art of warfare. But Passchendaele left it too spent to participate.

Third Army intended to unleash the war's first truly mechanized and combined arms offensive, which the Cambrai front ideally suited. Low, gently rolling ground little pocked by the shelling that had chewed up most of the Western Front rendered it ideal tank country, and the British planned to employ 378 in support of five infantry divisions. Together this combined force would smash the Hindenburg Line. Once this formidable German defensive line was breached the Cavalry Corps astride their chargers would sweep across the open plain to isolate Cambrai and win a crossing over the Sensée while the infantry cleared the city and Bourlon Wood to the northwest. When the infantry and tanks caught up to the cavalry at the Sensée, the British would cut off any German forces still holding the front lines to the west by attacking their rear.

Ahead of the army advance, hundreds of Royal Flying Corps aircraft would swoop down to plaster the German forward trenches with bombs, while 1,000 artillery pieces lay down a massive barrage. Coordinating the air strikes and artillery to occur in concert with the offensive represented another tactical innovation—employment of massed armour being the other. The commonplace protracted pre-assault bombardment was abandoned in order to gain surprise. The gunners would not even pre-register targets. Instead they would shoot from the map, relying on recent survey techniques and better calibration of guns.

Intelligence reports indicated the Germans were unconcerned about this sector of front. They rotated three divisions into the area at a time, using it as a rest stop for battle-weary troops from the Ypres Salient—gaining it the sobriquet "Flanders sanatorium." While German intelligence had noted that Third Army was more active here than normal, it had issued warnings only to expect more localized raiding.

At 0620 hours on November 20, when the RFC suddenly swarmed from the skies and the guns unleashed one massive volley of fire the Germans were caught entirely surprised. The front-line troops, taking the brunt of the artillery and aerial attacks, looked out at No Man's Land fearfully to witness "the unprecedented and awesome sight and sound of a long line of tanks rumbling forward" from a start line no more than 1,000 yards away. Behind came great waves of infantry. The tanks flattened the barbed wire. Then they released large clusters of wood called "fascines" that were attached to their front ends into the trenches and ground across these impromptu bridges.

Six thousand dazed and bloodied Germans surrendered without offering the slightest resistance and the mighty juggernaut continued to advance despite stiffening resistance as reinforcements frantically tried to plug the hole. By evening, the British had torn the Hindenburg Line open with gains of three to four miles in depth at a cost of 4,000 casualties. But the tanks had suffered badly, 65 being destroyed by German fire and another 114 breaking down or becoming stuck. The British had also failed to break the Masnières-Beaurevoir Line—the last major German trench—before it was heavily reinforced, which made it impossible to unleash the cavalry. A communication mix-up, however, had resulted in "B" Squadron of the Fort Garry Horse—part of the Canadian Cavalry Brigade serving in the British 5th Cavalry Division—believing the ground open. They rode instead into a slaughter from which only forty men returned.[27]

The impetus lost, British Third Army was forced onto the defensive and, over the next three days, lost virtually all the ground gained. Had they been reinforced, Byng's troops might have held, but Passchendaele had claimed all the British reserves. In the first week of December, a prolonged snowstorm ended the fighting. An attack for which expectations had run high cost 44,000 casualties with nothing to show but German losses of 41,000. The year ended with Allied morale at its lowest ebb. Not only had the costly offensives of 1917 largely ended in disaster, but Russia had surrendered, freeing up hundreds of German divisions for service on the Western Front. On October 24, the Allies had been given a foretaste of the import of Russia's surrender when Germany and Austria launched a massive offensive against Italy at Caporetto. In a matter of days, the Italians lost 80 miles and 265,000 men surrendered. Only the hurried reinforcement by five British and six French divisions prevented a complete collapse.

* * *

The Canadian Scottish closed the year facing Lens and Méricourt as part of a new Canadian Corps deployment. Despite the fact that both combatants practised active defence, which for the Germans entailed nightly raids while the Canadians concentrated on ambushing the raiders before they penetrated the outer defences, the sector was considered a quiet one. Since December the entire Western Front had shivered in the coldest temperatures so far recorded during the war. The Canadian Scottish rotated trench duty on a front running from immediately north of the Lens Canal on the left to a deep railway cutting south of the Lens-Béthune Road on the right. There was no contiguous trench. The front consisted instead of separated posts inside the ruins and cellars of houses that had once made up the village of Liévin.

As usual, the Germans held overlooking high ground, so the Canadians played a game of "hide and seek" to prevent them from identifying which posts were actively held. All movement was at night, which had worked well until the front became covered in "a mantle of snow." After that the Germans could clearly see the footprints leading to each post and were able to mark their positions before the snow melted. Then, on one of the "bright moonlight nights which prevailed, [the enemy] saw the relief parties moving out [and] opened on them with his large [trench mortars]. He could have employed no more effective weapons. The huge bombs burst amongst the houses and on the roadways, sending showers of bricks and stones in all directions and inflicting many casualties."

December 23, one Can Scot wrote in a letter, was "the coldest day I have seen out here." The battalion spent the day on the move back to corps reserve at Canada Camp in Château de la Haie. This, the soldier added, was "the rottenest, coldest bare camp we have ever seen." In these drab surroundings, in the midst of continuous cold and blustery weather, the battalion passed Christmas and New Years. "At midnight, 1917–18, Last Post was blown, 'Auld Lang Syne' sung, and immediately afterward the Pipe Band played in the New Year."[28]

A week later, the Canadian Scottish cheerfully marched away from the front lines entirely to the town of Bruay. They narrowly beat being caught in a blizzard en route that left behind three to four inches of snow quickly blown into high drifts by a sharp wind. Having come to Bruay for a three-week training period, the troops could do little but hole up and wait for the snow to abate. After several days the skies cleared but the snow melted so rapidly it flooded much of the town and adjacent training area. Abandoning the training plan, the men were instead given "freedom to enjoy the comfort of their billets and the social enjoyments of the town" until they left Bruay on January 28.

During this breathing space from front-line duty the complement of officers was brought to full strength. Major Roderick Bell-Irving became Lt.-Col. Peck's second-in-command and Captain John Paton, who had enlisted in the Seaforths as a private and earned a battlefield commission in 1916, was the adjutant. The company commanders, some of whom returned after recovering from earlier wounds, were all respected veterans. No. 1 Company's Captain Alan "Gus" Lyons had started out as a sergeant before a June 1916 commissioning. Major James Scroggie, wounded at Vimy Ridge, returned to command No. 2 Company. Fiercely ambitious, Scroggie was rumoured to have a Lt.-Col.'s star stowed in a pocket just in case fortune elevated him to battalion command. But Scroggie was also much respected, to the point that junior officers often asked during a crisis, "What would Scroggie do here?" Twenty-year-old Captain George Francis Mason retained No. 3 Company. He was another officer who had risen from the ranks. Mason had been present at every major engagement 1st Division fought and suffered a wound at the Somme. He was one of Peck's most valued officers and a man whose judgement the battalion commander trusted implicitly. Major Arnott Grier Mordy had assumed command of No. 4 Company upon Major James Murphy's death at Hill 70.

Of the forty-seven platoon commanders in the four companies, thirty had been commissioned from the ranks. Major Hugh Urquhart, who often visited his old battalion, believed that this gave the Canadian Scottish "a treasure of experience and ability. They had to bear a load of responsibility during critical times in the history of the Battalion, and they shouldered it with a competence and keen fighting spirit which proved them to be officers of a high calibre. It can be said of them, as a body, that at no time did the Battalion possess more efficient subalterns."[29]

Two of these officers demonstrated their ability clearly on February 13, when two raiding parties ventured into No Man's Land near Loos. Scroggie headed one team of raiders, but when his men ran afoul of heavy wire in front of the German trenches and could not get through he led them back home without contacting the enemy. The other party under Lt. Sydney Johnston, who had been commissioned in 1916, fared better. Accompanying Johnston was Lt. Ben W. Allen, commissioned almost precisely the year before the raid. Before the raiding party had set out Johnston split it into two groups so that twenty men were under his command and twelve Allen's.

Johnston also meticulously inspected the extra equipment the men carried. "Mills grenades; ammonal tubes; twenty pound ammonal charges, wire cutters, rolls of chicken wire with slats nailed across, Very pistol flares, and flash lamps. We are like a traveling circus," he wrote afterward. Two men led, tasked with laying white tape up to a gap found in the German wire during a previous reconnaissance. The two lieutenants had agreed on a simple anvil and hammer plan with Allen's party serving as the anvil. At Zero Hour, Allen would blow a captured German gas-alarm horn, rush a trench called Horse Alley, seize a good fighting position, and then intercept the Germans Johnston's "hammer" party drove their way during their push along the trench from the right.

Because of their heavy loads and a nerve-wracking few moments when the Germans shelled an approach trench with gas rounds that forced everyone to don their box respirators, the party finally caught up to the advance party by the wire only at 0250 hours. The two men reported they had been unable to find the gap and the wire seemed intact all along the line. Johnston was little surprised and had taken the precaution of having his men carry with them several large rubber bath mats. As a pre-planned artillery bombardment hit the German lines to cover their move, Johnston took one section of the party forward "and before the barrage lifted we had bath mats over the old trench and others across the first line of barbed wire. Someone in rear yelled to come back, that I was in the barrage. Second line of wire was on screw pickets—tore it off pickets and pulled it around the bottom of them—get over and barrage lifts just then. [Private] Tommy [Thompson] comes up to me, section following, and we scramble over the third row of wire. Tommy and I rush for the trench, bombing as we go, and I get in first, Tommy landing on the top of me. The section gets all in and to my joyful surprise the other sections also rush forward; machine guns are silent by this time."

The hammer and anvil plan, Johnston realized, was out the window because the party had been forced to go through the wire in a single group with no time to split up before the fighting began. So Johnston placed the men in line with Allen commanding the right-hand sections while he oversaw the left-hand group with the intention of just seeing how the Germans would respond to their incursion. Soon they heard tramping noises approaching and the men "crouched down at the corner of a traverse, all ready for them, and when we reckoned they were about on us I sprang out, revolver pointed ahead. Behold a solitary be-spectacled Hun, who when he saw us, threw down his rifle with a bang on the trench-board, off with his equipment like a flash, and up with his hands. 'Twas funny! He did it, as if he was doing rifle exercises to numbers. The corporal sprang on him and pummeled his face, but I hauled him off."

Johnston decided to lead a charge in the direction the prisoner had approached from. "Then followed a very busy, thrilling time—ammonal tubes in dug-outs and a good deal of wrecking and killing. It was hard work getting prisoners, but eventually we managed to preserve a few, for what good would it be if we don't bring back prisoners, the staff frown on us and doubt our stories. It was funny to see some of our fellows shove a mobile [ammonal] charge down a dug-out, then stand back to watch it go up—darned wonder they didn't go up too. We were absolutely at home and dominated the sector we occupied. A Hun kneeling at the bottom of a dug-out fired at me, striking me in the arm—put mobile charge down on him."

When the battalion recall rocket arced into the sky, Johnston's first thought was that he hated to leave. But he realized their luck would soon run out when the Germans rallied, as they surely would. Johnston and Cpl. Stuart Rankin hung back, ensuring all the party got safely away with the prisoners in tow. Then not wanting to carry back their remaining twenty-pound ammonal charge, the two men hunkered beside a dugout, yanked the gas curtain back and were just about to chuck it in when Johnston saw that the occupants were "two Huns, youngsters; badly scared and apparently wounded. As they were wounded we left them, but the corporal didn't like the idea of letting them be an excuse for not putting the mobile charge down, but I chased him along to the next dug-out.

"We are just preparing to leave the trench when a light and a moving figure appears in No Man's Land coming along above the trench. Windup; think it's a counter attack. We crouch down in the trench and against the sky-line see one man—very large. I yelled at him our half pass-word and to my surprise got the other half back. Then towards us stalked this figure, cursing to beat blazes—it's Gus Lyons, my company commander; and he came over by himself to see what the blankety blank, etc., was keeping us. He stood on the top of the trench and just gave us the very devil. So the three of us started back across No Man's Land walking, talking and using our flash lamps—no war at all. However, when we reach our line it isn't so pleasant, an awful strafe of minnies and funs is on, but we barge through the strafe with our six prisoners and a machine gun as jubilant and happy a crowd as could be imagined."[30]

* * *

Trench raids provided valuable intelligence and kept the opposing side on its guard, but they could not yield victory. Save a negotiated peace, victory would go to the side that succeeded in breaking free of the trench system and marched either to Paris or Berlin. On March 21, 1918, in a stunning reversal for the Allies, the Germans struck first along a 50-mile-long front between Arras and St. Quentin held by British Fifth Army. The offensive's mastermind, Gen. Erich Ludendorff, believed he could shatter the British before the French could rally to their aid. In an all-or-nothing effort, the Germans struck with their very best troops in the lead. After less than three days all the gains won during the Somme offensive were erased and entire British divisions annihilated as the Germans drove a wedge between the British and French forces. Ludendorff kept enlarging this hole, pushing the British toward the sea while the French contributed to its size by swinging to the east to protect Paris. Within a week, however, the offensive fell victim to the problem that had plagued everyone since the war began— Ludendorff's storm troops outran their supplies and reinforcement stream while suffering huge casualties for the ground won. On April 5, with British resistance stiffening, the offensive sputtered to a halt while the Germans were still short of their primary objective of Amiens, a town at the juncture of the Somme River and its major tributary, the Avre. The butcher's bill was 163,500 British and 77,000 French casualties compared to 238,000 German losses. But most of Germany's best troops were now dead or wounded.

Canadian Corps played no part in meeting the German offensive. But the crisis had almost precipitated its dissolution when Haig sought to send the Canadian divisions individually to plug holes in the shattered line. Only Lt.-Gen. Currie's vigorous objections saved the corps this fate. As it was, to enable First Army to send divisions to reinforce the beleaguered Fifth Army, the Canadian 1st and 2nd Divisions were allocated as a reserve to the former army. Currie was left with just two divisions holding a 10-mile front, which he charged was "altogether too much, but owing to lack of men in British Army it cannot be helped. I am told we have 430,000 men in Mesopotamia. What a splendid place for a reserve!"[31]

When the crisis passed, 1ˢᵗ Division returned, but the corps remained stretched thin and not until five British divisions relieved the Canadians in the first week of May was the situation corrected. The Canadian Corps went into a rest period that lasted until July 15. The interval was spent honing skills, with emphasis placed on "infiltration," where the "attacking troops were trained to work around strong points and machine-gun nests that were putting up stiff resistance; to find the line of least resistance, push in, and isolate garrisons still fighting. More distant objectives, involving the capture of ground from the enemy's outpost zones back to his gun lines and beyond, were also allotted to battalions.

"These were tactics which called for an exceptional degree of daring and resources in the infantry. Front-line men had not only to close with the enemy in circumstances of comparative isolation—that is, without the moral support of the old close order formation—but they had to think and co-operate skillfully with the other troops engaged alongside of them; there could be no more blind charging. 'Cannon fodder' had to give place to a high type of disciplined manhood, if attacks, under the new methods, were to carry the day in the face of a determined enemy."[32]

The Canadian Scottish diligently studied the new syllabus and then applied it for real in a front-line tour toward the end of July by conducting raids with ever greater numbers of men involved. On August 4, the battalion boarded a train and headed north. The men had no idea of their destination, but knew they must be headed again toward a great battle. It would come in just four days at a place called Amiens.

chapter ten

Decision at Amiens

- A U G U S T   8 – 2 0 ,   1 9 1 8 -

The failed March offensive did not deter the Germans from continuing to pursue a decisive victory over ensuing months. Gen. Erich Ludendorff recognized that Germany was running out of time, for soon the Allies would have thousands more troops available. Although the United States had declared war against Germany on April 6, 1917, its army had been too small, poorly trained, and ill-equipped to have any impact on the war. A year after the declaration the Americans had managed to deploy only nine divisions to Europe, but the pace of its military buildup was quickening and before 1918 was out a powerful expeditionary force would be ready for combat. The numerical superiority the Germans currently enjoyed on the Western Front would be reversed.

Ludendorff did not believe his armies could triumph once they were outnumbered. On April 9, therefore, he had ordered a new offensive in Flanders. By month's end the Allies had contained it, but Passchendaele, Messines, Ploegsteert, Wytschaete, Merville, and Mount Kemmel were all in Germans hands. Only Ypres and a fragment of the salient remained in Allied hands. At the end of May the Germans struck in the Champagne region north of Reims with an advance aimed at Paris that came within 30 miles—so close the Germans could see the Eiffel Tower—before being stopped by a French commitment of its entire reserve of twenty-seven divisions aided by two green American divisions.

"Again and again our thoughts returned to the idea of an offensive in Flanders," Ludendorff wrote, but clearly the Allies—there now being American divisions employed there alongside the British and French—were too strong. Hoping to leech off some of this strength, Ludendorff launched a two-pronged offensive from Reims on July 15. Prepared, the French Fourth Army dealt the eastern prong a sharp defeat. But the German Seventh Army, constituting the western prong, managed to get six divisions across the Marne between Château Thierry and Epernay, creating a salient eight miles wide by four miles deep. The French counterattacked in force on July 18, and by August 7, had driven the Germans back on the defensive behind the Vesle River to the west of Reims. Ludendorff's "great gamble" had ended with the loss of a million irreplaceable troops either killed, wounded, or lost as prisoners. Of Germany's 201 divisions on the Western Front, 106 were now unfit for battle. In the British sector were fifty-three British and Commonwealth divisions with thirty-six on the front lines. Also supporting the British as a reserve were four American divisions and one Portuguese. The French had eighty-four divisions up front—seven of these being American and three British. The French-sector reserve numbered thirty-nine divisions, of which seven were American, one British, and two Italian.[1]

On May 8, sixty-seven-year-old Gen. Ferdinand Foch had been appointed commander in chief of the Allied armies to ensure operations on the Western Front were fully co-ordinated. Credited with the French victories on the Marne in 1914 that had stemmed the initial invasion, the "Hero of the Marne" was offensively minded, but could only remain on the defensive until the German offensives ran their course. By July, however, Foch saw opportunity for a limited British offensive "astride the Somme, in an easterly direction, from the Luce and Ancre [rivers], with the object of disengaging Amiens."[2] The French would also undertake a series of small offensives. "How long these different operations will take and how far they will carry us cannot be determined now," Foch told Field Marshal Douglas Haig. "Nevertheless, if the results at which they aim are attained before too late in the year, we can from now onwards look forward to an offensive to be launched at the end of the summer or during the autumn of such importance as will increase our advantages and leave no respite to the enemy."[3]

Amiens was ideal for offensive operations, its rolling plateau hardened now by the summer's sun and unchurned by shelling. Already the Australian Corps had launched a limited attack at the beginning of July that utilized the tactics first employed at Cambrai of advancing a massed tank force in concert with a surprise artillery bombardment. The town of Hamel had been retaken and Lt.-Gen. John Monash, the Australian Corps commander, had since vocally advocated a larger-scale operation.

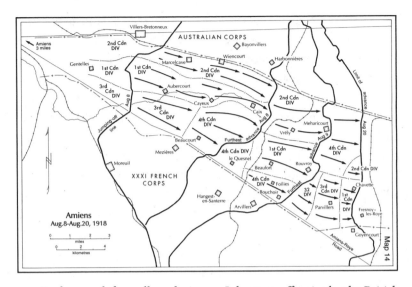

Amiens
Aug.8-Aug.20, 1918

Foch agreed, formally ordering on July 28 an offensive by the British
Fourth Army and French First Army that would advance "as far as possible in the direction of Roye," almost 15 miles behind German lines.
Gen. Henry Rawlinson's Fourth Army was really the British Fifth Army
rebuilt after its near destruction during the German March offensive.
Rawlinson had just two corps, the British III and the Australian Corps,
so Haig sent him the Canadian Corps. On July 30 the Canadians travelled in great secrecy by train and bus to a concentration area southwest
of Amiens. Without surprise the offensive would surely fail. Considering
the Canadians among B.E.F.'s best shock troops, the Germans carefully
tracked their whereabouts in expectation that wherever Canadian Corps
appeared an offensive might follow. To throw the Germans off the scent
Allied intelligence leaked falsified reports that placed Canadian Corps
near Ypres.[4]

   Dawn of August 7 found 100,000 Canadians with all their guns
and transport hidden in the cover of dense forests little more than three
miles from the German front lines. Overhead, Royal Air Force spotter
planes scanned the woods to make sure no sign of the troops could be
seen while bombers droned loudly over the German front to mask the
sounds of 604 massing tanks. Fourth Army's 1,386 field guns were each
assigned to cover a mere 29 yards of frontage, while each of the 684 heavies would concentrate on 59 yards. The French brought to the front another 780 field and 826 heavy or super-heavy guns.

Rawlinson followed the script devised at Cambrai. From left to right he lined up III Corps, the Australians, and then the Canadians, who rubbed shoulders with the French. The artillery barrage would begin twenty minutes before the troops went over the top. It would fall to the tanks to tear holes in the wire for the infantry to pass through, and tank fire would also have to suppress German machine guns. As the British III Corps had been badly mauled in the spring, Rawlinson was counting on the tenacity of the Australians and Canadians to carry the day. The plan called for an advance in two stages, with the final objective being a line running from Harbonnières on the left past Cayeux in the centre, to just north of Mézières on the right—distances ranging from 4 to 6 miles. Once the final objective was secured, the Cavalry Corps would plunge through to capture the old Outer Amiens Defence Line, 3 to 4 miles farther along. Zero Hour was set for 0420 on August 8.

Lt.-Gen. Arthur Currie put the 2nd Division on the left, the 1st in the centre, and the 3rd to the right. In 1st Division's sector, Maj.-Gen. Archie Macdonell had 3rd Brigade forward and its commander, Brig. George Tuxford, assigned the right flank to 16th Battalion, the centre to 13th, and the left to 14th.[5] Once 3rd Brigade reached the Green Line, as the objective for the first bound was designated, 1st Brigade would leapfrog forward and be passed in turn by 2nd Brigade. Everything, Tuxford told his battalion commanders, depended on speed.[6]

Although generally favourable ground for tanks, several tributaries of the Somme and Ancre rivers had cut narrow valleys in Fourth Army's sector. The Canadian Corps sector was particularly affected. Although the knee-deep Luce was only 30 feet wide, over the centuries it had carved out a 200-foot-deep by 200-foot-wide gully that was heavily wooded and wound in the direction of the advance while various little tributaries had created gullies that cut across the Canadian frontage.

Throughout the day preceding the attack, the Canadian Scottish lay hidden in wait. Lt.-Col. Cyrus Peck permitted only small reconnaissance parties sent forward one after the other to inspect the offensive terrain. To prevent the Germans from realizing a buildup of forces had taken place, the Australian Corps had extended its lines so that it occupied the frontage assigned to the Canadians. Come the evening the Australians would slip to the side as the Canadians moved up. The 16th Battalion would relieve 49th Australian Battalion. So shrouded in secrecy was the planned offensive that when officers from one Can Scot reconnaissance party quizzed the Australians they "knew nothing of the intended offensive, or the fact that tens of thousands of Canadians lay under cover a few hundred yards behind.... No direct questions affecting the operation could therefore be asked of its officers, a rather unsatisfactory state of affairs, as the jumping-off area bordered the outpost line, which was 800 yards ahead of the main trench and inaccessible by day."[7]

Just before midnight, the Canadian Scottish assembled by companies to receive battle supplies and rations. What would normally be a quickly executed process dragged on for hours. In order to prevent the noise of large parties coming forward from tipping the Germans to the fact something was up, the Canadian battalions were all supplied by small parties coming up one after the other. Zero Hour was almost upon them before the process was complete. Peck had anxiously watched the supplies being doled out and finally accepted that his troops would not be ready "until the last minute."[8]

Their kit, though, was lighter than ever before. To emphasize speed the heavy packs were left behind. Instead they slung small, light haversacks on their backs. But stuffed with 170 rounds, four grenades, forty-eight hours' worth of iron rations, water bottles, and a ground sheet, the haversacks bulged to capacity. The Lewis gun crews crammed fifty magazines into pouches and still worried about running dry.[9] But the troops were assured that the twenty-two tanks supporting the brigade, seven of which would advance with the Can Scots, would provide them with a mobile source of supply. Each tank was loaded with 21,000 bullets and an array of shovels, picks, water canisters, and grenades.

Peck told his officers that the Zero Hour barrage would "be laid down 200 yards in front of the jumping off position, remaining there three minutes. It will then lift 100 yards every two minutes for 2 lifts, 100 yards every three minutes for 8 lifts and then 100 yards every 4 minutes until the limit of the barrage is reached. M.Gs. will barrage after this. One mobile brigade of field artillery will move forward with the attack. A protective barrage of smoke will be placed on Green Line during the halt."[10]

After issuing these orders, Peck chanced into Padre Frederick Scott, who had come to join 16th Battalion in going over the top. "If anything happens to me don't make any fuss over me; just say a few words over me in a shell hole," Peck told his friend. "You will be all right, Colonel. There will be no shell hole for you," Scott replied firmly.[11]

As the battalion marched out of the woods and down a slope toward the battle front, the starlit night was silent except for an occasional gun and the explosion of the odd German shell directed at a nearby crossroad. By 0345 hours the men were in their jumping-off position. So quickly had the move to Amiens come about that some officers were missing because they had been away on leave. A few others were sick. This meant the roster in place through the spring had been modified for the attack. Major James Scroggie consequently served as battalion second-in-command, so Captain Cyril Jones led his No. 2 Company. No. 3 Company was commanded by Major Thomas Floyd and No. 4 by Major McKenzie Render, while Captain Gus Lyons, as he had for so long, led No. 1 Company. Nos. 3 and 4 Companies would lead with the other two following close behind.[12]

"Bronzed, fit, and confident, at the zenith of its power, [the corps] lay ready to give battle," Major Hugh Urquhart later wrote. "Nurtured by wise leadership, consummated by the long summer training of 1918, Corps unity and strength—terms which in the spring of 1917 had little meaning for Canadians—had become a reality, and had begotten by that morning of August 8th such a mighty instrument as should, for all generations, be the pride of Canada and the source of inspiration to every citizen within her borders."[13]

* * *

Shortly before Zero Hour, Peck walked to the front line "and found everything in readiness. Dense fog hung over the land."[14] The fog had risen out of the marshes bordering the Luce's northern bank just twenty minutes before the assault was to begin and had quickly enveloped the entire battle front. Caught in the middle of forming their assault lines, the Canadian Scottish were so blinded that they had difficulty getting properly positioned. At the last minute Peck was told the two leading companies were not brushing shoulders. Not knowing if this was true, Peck ordered Lt. Bill Mackie, recently promoted from the rank of CSM, to plug any gap with his No. 1 Company Platoon if he saw that one actually existed.

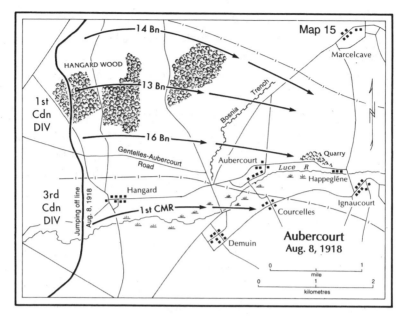

A single bomber could be heard droning back and forth over the German front lines and occasionally it dropped a bomb that exploded with a thump. But, as the mist thickened and gained in altitude, the plane flew off. A few minutes later the troops heard the tanks coming up. "The noise crept nearer. It grew louder and louder to a rumble, clatter and clank. It seemed as if it must surely reach the enemy and give him warning." But the Germans fired no flares and sounded no alarms.

Suddenly, at 0420, the barrage began and, as one, the Canadian Scottish surged out of the trenches toward the enemy. Peck watched with pride as his men, "who had been straining at the leash, sprang out of the trenches with the utmost eagerness. The ground mist was now greatly augmented by smoke, and the keeping of direction was very difficult."[15]

Peck was surprised when the Germans failed to respond to the creeping barrage with counter artillery. Nor at first were there any gunshots from their forward outposts. Most of the men manning these either fled or surrendered. Captain Jones of No. 2 Company had Piper Maclean at his side. Telling Maclean to play "The Drunken Piper" at quick time Jones led his men in a charge to an emplacement housing several large trench mortars. "Jumping into the trench we saw in front of us the entrances to two dugouts each guarded with a machine gun mounted and well camouflaged. We shouted down to the enemy and up they came—one officer and sixty men. They were taken completely by surprise; some of them were in their stocking feet and partly clad."

Lieutenant Mackie, meanwhile, had discovered a gap between the two leading companies and plugged it with his platoon. He and his men overwhelmed one machine-gun position only to find themselves raked by another behind them. "I placed the men in cover, took the Lewis gun corporal and two men and started back to investigate. On the rising ground on our right was a clump of trees and in them a machine gun nest. Just as we attacked it from one side, Sergeant Mowatt and men of No. 4 Company attacked it from the other and soon all was over," Mackie recounted.[16]

Gaining the northern slope of the Luce gully, the Can Scots advanced down a gentle grade that seemed little more than a dip. But the mist by the river was impenetrable. Suddenly there "loomed up directly ahead ... a high dark mass which at first hurried glance seemed like a strong fortification. The first part of the Battalion to see it was the centre, where, at the moment, the Commanding Officer was present. Colonel Peck gave the order to charge. The men at once rushed forward, some thirty yards or so, only to find themselves up against an almost perpendicular bank."

At first it seemed they would not be able to climb this southern slope and continue to follow their assigned line of advance. But scouts groped along the flanks and soon reported that, to the right, it ascended more gradually. Following behind the scouts, the battalion clawed its way up to gain the Gentelles-Aubercourt road along which the supporting tanks were slowly creeping. Piper George Firth Paul, accompanying Peck's command section, impulsively jumped on top of one bearing the name "Dominion" and skirled out the Canadian Scottish authorized march, "Blue Bonnets over the Border," as the mighty machine rumbled alongside the advancing infantry.

Both the fog and the rugged nature of the country made it difficult for Peck to keep track of his companies, but the assignments of pipers to each one quickly proved its worth. "Our pipers played with their accustomed steadiness and stolid courage. I found the pipers of the greatest usefulness, not only to encourage and inspire the men, but the keen ear of one Piper could detect the tones of the others through the dense fog and enabled us to identify the companies in the advance."[17]

As the sun broke through the mist, Peck saw scattered on the plain German antitank guns and mortars in the open with their covers still on. What few enemy soldiers were about "seemed utterly demoralized and surrendering with alacrity."[18] As the battalion's leading wave advanced up a "long grassy slope above the Aubercourt road north of Demuin, the mist cleared without a moment's notice."

Peck, having told Paul to get off the tank, hurried ahead of his men with the thirty-eight-year-old piper alongside to gain the crest in order to see what resistance lurked ahead. Just as the two men came up on it, a machine gun opened fire and Paul fell dead at Peck's side. Peck then heard several shots from a revolver, and Captain Alec MacLennan, the battalion intelligence officer, emerged with gun in hand and shouted that he had killed the gun crew. MacLennan, accompanied by scout Private Frank Durham, had been roving the battlefield independently. He was now "amazed to see Colonel Peck coming towards me only fifteen yards away" and seemingly alone.

German resistance suddenly stiffened. On the right the Germans had established a strongpoint in an old chalk-mining pit and behind this lay a heavily manned trench designated Bosnia. About 600 yards to the left the shoulder of a hill was defended by several machine guns and snipers, who caught the Canadian Scottish in a crossfire. The snipers targeted the commanders, shooting Major Render dead and wounding Major Floyd. CSM Frank Macdonald took effective control of both his No. 4 Company and No. 3, leading a charge on the chalk pit. After a fierce mêlée, the Germans were overcome. A battalion commander and his headquarters section along with a doctor and his dressing station staff were among the prisoners. The latter were put to immediate work treating the many Canadian wounded. Lt. Mackie added his platoon to the strength of the two companies under Macdonald. The advance continued toward Bosnia Trench, but machine-gun fire soon drove the men to ground.

Mackie ordered everyone to stay down while he and a corporal packing a Lewis gun crawled along a shallow ditch bordering the Demuin road to close on the trench. From the ditch, the two men located four machine-gun positions, and when one crew exposed itself to fire on the pinned-down Canadians the corporal killed all five of them with a long burst of fire. He then knocked out a second gun by killing two of its crew and wounding the others. Anytime one of the two remaining crews tried to bring their gun into action, the corporal forced them down with a well-aimed burst. Finally the officer commanding the machine-gun position stood up and waved Mackie and the corporal over. Not a chance, Mackie thought, as he signalled the German to approach him instead. Both stared long and hard at each other and then walked toward each other like gunfighters. They were 30 yards apart when the German went for his pistol, but Mackie was faster on the draw and shot him dead. Then the lieutenant and the Lewis gunner rushed the trench, taking the remaining Germans prisoner.

That ended the resistance at Bosnia Trench and enabled Mackie and his men to swing over to assist the rest of the battalion, which was engaging the Germans on the hill. Peck was here, personally directing the struggle to clear it of machine-gun positions and snipers. Finally, a Canadian Scottish sniper wriggled to an abandoned gun-pit within range of the Germans and drilled any who showed themselves in the head with a single shot. After a few of the enemy snipers were killed, the rest fled.

While the sniper was at work, Peck ordered one of the tanks to go forward with Mackie's No. 1 Company platoon in support to finish off the machine guns. Inside the tank, serving as an observer, Canadian Scottish Lt. James Rodgers felt like he was in a Turkish bath. The heat was fierce, everyone aboard was showered in sweat. Not only the heat made riding in the tank almost unbearable, the fuel stench was over-whelming and German bullets "striking the tank made a noise like riveters working in a shipyard…. We ran into a strong machine-gun post and the Germans kept firing at us until we were right on top of them. Their fire was so accurate that it put our six-pounder on the left side of the tank out of action.

"By the time we reached the cross roads near Aubercourt, I was feeling dizzy from the gas inside the tank as were the other members of the crew, and afterwards I fainted right away."[19]

The rest of the battalion bypassed the hill to clear the Germans positioned between Bosnia Trench and Aubercourt. Two No. 2 Company platoons headed straight for Aubercourt, but as they closed on the houses a machine gun hidden in one burned off a long burst that killed Lt. Archibald McConechy and Sgt. Mathew Barrett. Their commanders killed, the two platoons took cover. But Pte. Frederick Sumner, who had started stalking the machine gun in a flanking manoeuvre the moment it opened fire, broke the impasse by killing the crew with rifle fire.

From where he was, just west of Aubercourt, Peck had seen the platoons become stalled and ordered CSM Robert Kennedy to attack the village from the right. A member of the original contingent, Kennedy had fought in every major engagement, been twice wounded, and awarded a Military Medal in 1916. Kennedy performed as usual, leading his men into the village, knocking out the remaining machine guns and overrunning a battery of 5.9-millimetre guns abandoned by the Germans. His actions this day earned a Distinguished Conduct Medal and over the ensuing months he would add two bars for gallantry to the decoration before being fatally wounded on November 1, 1918.

Although Aubercourt had been taken, the hill where the battalion had originally been held up remained contested ground. Heavy volumes of machine-gun fire indicated that the tank and Mackie's men were meeting stiff resistance. Putting Captain Alexander MacLennan in charge of another ad-hoc unit, Peck sent it up the hill from the German's rear. MacLennan's party followed the Aubercourt-Happeglene road, and as they rounded a bend came under fire from a quarry 200 yards ahead. The party was bunched and fourteen men went down, killed or wounded. The two soldiers of a No. 1 Company Lewis gun crew threw themselves down in the middle of the road to the front of the stricken men and began firing at the Germans. Lying in the open right next to the equally exposed gunners, MacLennan directed their fire. The Lewis gunners kept the weapon hot until all their ammunition drums were spent. Then they scooped up two rifles and continued shooting until the German machine gun fell silent. "I never witnessed a braver deed," MacLennan later said of the gunners. "Their coolness, courage and marksmanship in the face of great danger was remarkable." MacLennan always regretted that, in the confusion of the battle, he never got the men's names. For his own courage under fire, MacLennan was awarded the Military Cross on September 16, 1918, and the bar on January 11, 1919.

With MacLennan's relief party held up, Peck sent a second tank up the hill supported by another Canadian Scottish platoon. When it came up alongside Mackie's men and the other tank, the Germans surrendered. The enemy at the quarry, including a regimental commander and his staff, also gave up. This ended the battalion's fight, as it now controlled all the assigned Green Line objectives. It was about 0715 hours.

As 1ˢᵗ Infantry Brigade passed through 16ᵗʰ Battalion, some of the Canadian Scottish shouted, "Fritz, beat it! Get a move on before the war, stops."[20] Move the Canadians did. By dusk the Germans had been thrown back eight miles on their front while the Australians gained seven miles. On the flanks the French had advanced five miles and III Corps two. Canadian losses were 1,036 dead, 2,803 wounded, and 29 men lost as prisoners. But German prisoners tallied 5,033 and 161 guns had been captured. Peck estimated that 16ᵗʰ Battalion had taken more than 900 prisoners and bagged 18 heavy guns, 17 trench mortars, and 30 machine guns for a surprisingly low casualty count of 144.[21]

The British Fourth Army counted its total casualties at approximately 8,800. The butcher's bill this time had been entirely weighted against the Germans. They admitted losses of up to 700 officers and 27,000 other ranks with more than two-thirds having surrendered. "August 8," Ludendorff wrote, "was the black day of the German army in the history of this war. Everything I had feared … had here, in one place, become a reality."[22] Two days later, as Ludendorff reported to the Kaiser, the German ruler interrupted. "We have reached the limits of our capacity. The war must be terminated." But this could only be achieved by opening peace negotiations, something the Kaiser refused to consider.[23]

* * *

Amiens had finally given the Allies a decisive triumph. "The surprise had been complete and overwhelming," Currie wrote. "The prisoners stated that they had no idea that an attack was impending … The noise of our tanks going to the final position of assembly had been heard by some men and reported, but no deduction appears to have been made regarding this. An officer stated that the Canadians were believed to be on the Kemmel front."[24]

Field Marshal Douglas Haig intended to keep driving the Germans. "Having secured the old Amiens defence line," he declared, "the Fourth Army will push forward to-morrow and establish itself on the general line of Roye–Chaulnes–Bray sur Somme–Dernancourt." To reach the new objectives the army's right flank—where the Canadians were—would have to gain nine miles while III Corps need win only a mile. To the right of the Canadians, the French would continue advancing toward Roye while simultaneously broadening their front by another 16 miles to stretch the Germans ever thinner.[25]

Haig recognized Canadian Corps faced the greatest challenge meeting its objectives. There would be no surprise. The Germans would be ready and waiting. In fact, by the evening of August 8, seven German reserve divisions had bolstered the front and three of these faced the Canadians. Each passing hour gave these fresh troops more time to prepare fighting positions.

Confusion at Fourth Army headquarters ensured the Germans had sufficient time to get ready. At 1630 hours on August 8, Gen. Rawlinson arrived at Currie's advanced headquarters in Gentelles. Currie was touring his various divisional headquarters so "Rawly the Fox" contented himself with discussing matters with Currie's general staff officer, Brig. N. W. Webber. Rawlinson was in fine fettle, proclaiming that much credit for the day's victory must go to the Canadian Corps. What did Currie need for the coming day? Rawlinson wondered. Webber knew exactly what the corps needed—a fresh division to relieve the badly worn 3rd Division. Rawlinson promised to release the 32nd Imperial Division from the army reserve and wired the required instructions to his headquarters. Webber and he then fleshed out a plan whereby 1st and 2nd Canadian Divisions would resume the advance at 0500 hours with the 32nd Division passing through 4th Canadian Division in the morning to come up alongside.[26] The 3rd and 4th Divisions would then move into reserve.

Shortly after Rawlinson's party drove off, a cable from Fourth Army headquarters was delivered to Webber. Rawlinson's chief executive officer, Maj.-Gen. A. A. Montgomery, had peremptorily cancelled the 32nd Division's movement orders and demanded that Webber proceed immediately to Drury—the closest telephone link from the Canadian front to Fourth Army—about eight miles west of Gentelles. Travelling upstream by car along roads clogged with supply transports and vehicles bearing the 32nd Division's battalions in the opposite direction, Webber was unable to reach the phone until two hours later. The moment he came on the line, Montgomery left Webber no doubt that he was "very irate with [Rawlinson] for daring to give away 32nd Div[ision] and with myself for aiding and abetting." The British division was immediately ordered to turn about and march back to whence it came. With 3rd Division having already moved to the rear, it was now instructed to get back to the front to resume the offensive in the morning. Montgomery was unconcerned that such a major regrouping of divisions would necessarily delay the Canadian resumption of operations.

Webber returned to corps headquarters and broke the news to Currie. Then the two officers and their staff worked through the night to issue fresh orders. Because telegraph communication with the forward divisions was unreliable these orders had to be delivered by dispatch riders. None of the divisional commanders received instructions before 0400 hours and some not until 0500 hours, so the advance was set back to 1000. Hours had been wasted.[27]

Even before Montgomery countermanded Rawlinson's orders, the divisional commanders had been hard pressed to be ready by early morning. In 1st Division's case it had to move to a new frontage, which required the brigades to sideslip 5,000 yards southward in order to face the villages of Beaufort and Warvillers. To the divison's left would be 2nd Division (which also had to slip southward to keep aligned with 1st Division), while 3rd Division was on its right.

The southward move required longer than Currie's staff had anticipated and was only completed at 1100 hours. Zero Hour was shoved back to 1310. The 3rd Division was unable to move even then because the 4th Division had yet to secure its start line just beyond Le Quesnel—a final objective for August 8 that the division had failed to gain and spent the following morning winning despite stiffening German resistance. All the delays forced Currie to abandon hopes the corps would gain nine miles of ground this day. Instead, he expected at best to win only four miles.[28]

From the moment 2nd Division crossed the start line it faced a hard fight while 1st Division met only marginally less opposition. Maj.-Gen. Archie Macdonnell put his 1st and 2nd Brigades forward with 3rd Brigade's battalions parcelled out and lurking in support. While 14th and 15th Battalions backed up 2nd Brigade, 16th Battalion marched to new positions behind 1st Brigade. This brigade, advancing on the division's left flank toward Beaufort and the village of Rouvroy-en-Santerre beyond, advanced while being flayed by heavy machine-gun fire from a height of ground to its right. With 3rd Division not yet on its start line, the brigade's 1st Battalion jogged over to clear this enemy position—an action that forced Brig.-Gen. W. A. Griesbach to advance his 2nd Battalion to fill the gap the battalion left in its wake. This meant that the brigade had three of its four battalions committed almost from the outset. But the quick adjustment of its lines to include some of 3rd Division's front prevented the attack from stalling. Meanwhile, 2nd Brigade set a cracking pace across flat country broken by little more than a few villages and the occasional small wood or rise of ground that typified the countryside east of Amiens. Soon Warvillers was secure.

On the right flank, 3rd Division's 4th Canadian Mounted Rifles made good progress once it was able to get moving and came up alongside 1st Division adjacent to Foilies by late afternoon. But to the right of this battalion, the 5th Canadian Mounted Rifles met intense head-on machine-gun fire from Bouchoir and flanking fire from Arvillers, a village that the adjacent French troops had failed to gain. This situation was only resolved when a combined Canadian-British force of infantry and tanks struck out from 3rd Division's line of advance and cleared Arvillers in tough fighting that centred on a large beet-sugar factory.[29]

With the Canadian Corps advance progressing rapidly, and in accordance with Currie's revised battle plan, the reserve brigades were never called forward. So the Canadian Scottish did little but walk along some distance behind the forward troops, tasting "the heady wine of victory. In the hot, August day, with everybody in high spirits, the whole countryside was alive with movement. Generals and their staffs were galloping to and fro. Command pennants, which had been laid aside since 1914, fluttered in the breeze over the escorts; divisional headquarters, a hive of bustle, with attendant motor cars, signal wagons and wireless aerials were grouped near the cover of copse and hedge; supporting troops in formed bodies were streaming forward; reserve troops lay on the ground waiting the summons to advance."

Only as dusk began to settle did 16th Battalion return to the grim realities of war as it marched along the Amiens-Roye road toward Beaufort in what was the third major move of the day. Just as it turned dark the men heard the drone of aircraft overhead and recognized them as German. They "flew low, backward and forward, over the lines of the tall elms that bordered the highway" jammed with "troops, guns, and transport."

After a few passes the planes roared down and "bombed and machine-gunned the roads, the horse lines, and villages where troops were quartered. The airmen shot out parachute flares which lit up every feature of the ground, and flung down egg bombs which, bursting on contact into a shower of ragged fragments, caused widespread injuries. Then, the terror of death, and maiming stalked the night." Confusion reigned all along the roadway as hundreds of horses "terrified by the roar of the planes' engines, stampeded, and many men were hit." Serendipitously, the Canadian Scottish were unscathed while units either side of them were struck hard. When the planes flew off, the battalion continued past "the dead and wounded lying by the roadside [that] told their own story of the losses incurred by other units." [30]

How many of the 2,574 total Canadian casualties for August 9 resulted from the air raid went unrecorded, but all the units caught in it were badly shaken. The frequency and deadly result of air raids had increased dramatically with each passing month in 1918. The raid on the night of August 9 was yet another example of how technological advances stacked the odds against a soldier's chances of survival.

The Canadian Scottish halted at Beaufort, Lt.-Col. Peck establishing his headquarters in the battered village while the troops distributed by companies in nearby fields where stooks of newly cut grain stood in orderly rows amid the black shell craters. Few could sleep, for the German shelling intensified hourly. "A shell here, a shell there, sometimes inflicting casualties and always so close as to disturb the resting troops."

By 0420 hours, when Peck ordered the battalion to advance into battle positions near Rouvroy, a thick fog draped the land. Unable to take any bearings, the troops counted on the guides to know their way. As they set up in a series of old trenches, the guides assured them that once the fog lifted the Germans beyond would have them in their sights. Company commanders needlessly instructed the wary soldiers to stay under cover and avoid moving in the open. All across the front, the sounds of men working with entrenching tools carried on the air—telling them that the Germans were close and frantically preparing their defences. [31]

Intelligence staff at Fourth Army headquarters reported German reserves being rushed to the Amiens battlefront by train, bus, and truck. The numerical advantage Fourth Army had enjoyed was so reduced by the morning of August 10 that its thirteen forward divisions faced precisely the same number of German divisions. Given the loss of impetus and the growing resistance little more ground could be won, but Haig still hoped to at least establish the line set out in the orders he had issued on the evening of August 8. This meant the Canadians must win another five miles of ground.

But they would have a fresh division, for the British 32nd Division was now committed to advance alongside 4th Division—the two passing through the front lines won the day before. This assault began at 0930 with the 32nd moving through the 1st and 3rd Division lines and 4th Division past the 2nd Division.[32] The sudden appearance of the British troops caught the Canadian Scottish by surprise when "out of the vanishing fog, large bodies of cavalry, guns and infantry in close order suddenly burst into their view. As these units came forward they gradually opened out into battle formation in spectacular fashion, as if they were on the manoeuvre field. Their men were in high spirits, the staffs were all business, everybody concerned was confident of success.

"The attacking battalions passed out of sight into the haze, and later in the morning, after the mist had cleared, further bodies of cavalry and horse artillery went through. In the distance, to the east, the smoke of burning towns or dump could be seen rising in the sky, but whether it had reference to the advance of the earlier hours 16th Battalion did not know. No news of the operation was received until the late afternoon, when rumour began to whisper dark tales of its failure, which found some confirmation in the gloomy looks and depressed men of the personnel of the brigade headquarters established in the field near at hand," the battalion's historian noted.

By midday, the advance had been checked. The 32nd Division gained virtually no ground this day and the 4th did only somewhat better. That night, the Canadian Scottish advanced a mile into a series of old French trenches east of Rouvroy. They moved past "derelict tanks, demolished by direct hits—'the inside of them like charnel houses'—the dead men and dead horses scattered everywhere around, told very surely of its location and fate. The 32nd British Division had met with disaster in the old system of trench defences, in use from the beginning of trench warfare until the Germans broke through in March–April 1918."[33]

Despite Fourth Army's and that of the French on its flank the day before, plans were hatched for a renewed offensive on August 11. But the

Amiens offensive was spent and there were few gains. The 4th Canadian Division moved not at all, instead forced to parry three separate German counterattacks. Because of this, Currie decided "that it was inadvisable to try to progress mainly by Infantry fighting, and recommended that the operations should be slackened to give time to organize a set piece attack on a broad front."[34] Only limited objectives were set for an attack scheduled to begin either on August 15 or 16 wherein Canadian Corps would cover the French army's left flank during a drive on Goyencourt, which lay two miles short of Roye.

After several cancellations, this attack materialized on August 16. As part of Fourth Army's limited participation Currie instructed 1st Division to secure Fresnoy-les-Roye and La Chavette with 2nd Division advancing immediately to the left.[35] Having learned only early that morning that the offensive was proceeding, Currie's orders did not reach 1st Division headquarters until mid-morning. Maj.-Gen. Archie Macdonnell quickly assigned seizing Fresnoy-les-Roye to 1st Brigade and La Chavette to 3rd Brigade. At 1130 hours Brig. George Tuxford urgently phoned the commanders of the 13th and 16th Battalions with orders that the former was to attack La Chavette with the latter covering its left flank.

None of the battalion commanders had expected a battle; Lt.-Col. Peck had instructed his company commanders they were to merely maintain a holding pattern. It was a clear, hot morning that promised a scorching afternoon. Everyone was looking forward to happily sitting the day out in relative peace. The battalion was currently disposed with Nos. 2 and 3 Companies holding the line respectively from right to left. No. 4 Company was in close support and No. 1 was farther back in reserve. As seizing La Chavette was assigned to 13th Battalion, Peck considered the Canadian Scottish role relatively limited.

Peck summoned the officers from No. 4 Company to his headquarters and said only that unit would go forward. Brigade intelligence indicated the German strength across the Amiens front was weakening, which was why the offensive was being undertaken. Because the ground was dead level with little natural cover, the platoons would advance by means of a series of old communication trenches running from the battalion's current front lines in fairly straight lines to beyond La Chavette. These trenches passed on either flank of the only tactically important ground. This was Schwetz Wood, a small copse of scrubby trees and

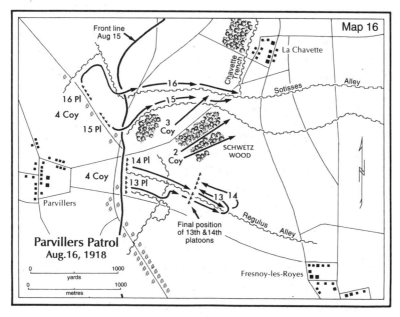

Map 16

Front line
Aug 15

La Chavette

Chavette Trench

Sotisses

Alley

16

15

16 Pl

4 Coy

15 Pl

3
Coy

SCHWETZ
WOOD

2
Coy

N

14 Pl

13 Pl

4 Coy

13 14

Parvillers

13 14

Regulus Alley

Final position
of 13th & 14th
platoons

Parvillers Patrol
Aug.16, 1918

0   1000
yards

0   1000
metres

Fresnoy-les-Royes

dense gorse about 700 yards east of the Canadian Scottish front. Peck
wanted the company to surround the wood and pin any Germans there
in place so they were unable to interfere with the Royal Highlanders
of Canada's capture of La Chavette. To this purpose No. 13 and No. 14
Platoons would pass through No. 2 Company's lines and outflank the
wood to the south via two parallelling trenches while No. 15 and No. 16
Platoons shoved out from No. 3 Company's lines and followed two parallelling trenches that passed to the north of the wood.

Less than an hour after the briefing, the four platoons moved warily up
the communication trenches. No. 13 Platoon, under Sgt. Alexander Reid,
was in the most southerly trench while Lt. William Douglas Macpherson's
platoon followed one, codenamed Regulus Alley, which lay 250 yards
south of the wood. Reid's men surprised a small German position, captured one soldier, and sent the others scampering just a few minutes after they entered the trench. Not long afterward, the platoon came to an
intersection and Reid realized their intelligence had been wrong and the
trench had trended north rather than running in a straight line past the
wood. The platoon was now in Regulus Alley. Reid saw the back of No.
14 Platoon out ahead and sent a runner to find out what Macpherson
wanted him to do. Macpherson replied that Reid's platoon should follow his in line.

The two platoons snaked along the trench until they were well past Schwetz Wood and Macpherson could see Fresnoy-les-Roye to his right. West of the village, a series of trenches were crowded with German infantry who looked to be forming up for an advance right toward his position. Realizing his force was badly outnumbered, but would likely be detected if they tried to withdraw, Macpherson ordered Reid to deploy his men in the trench while he slipped No. 14 Platoon out to the left into a string of shell holes. This established the men in an L-shaped formation that enabled them to cover their flanks and also be positioned to try blocking the Germans if they advanced toward Schwetz Wood. Macpherson had no intention of provoking the Germans into action. He ordered the men to stay hidden.

North of the wood, No. 15 and No. 16 platoons, respectively under Lt. William Houston and Lt. Edward Payson Thompson, had snuck along parallel trenches to where they intersected the southern terminus of Chavette Trench and the westward terminus of Sottises Alley. Chavette Trench was the main defensive work running in front of the village of La Chavette, while Sottises Alley provided a protected route for the Germans to bring supplies and reinforcements up to the front from their rear areas well to the east of Schwetz Wood. According to the brigade plan, the Royal Highlanders should have, by this time, launched their attack on La Chavette. So the two Can Scot lieutenants expected Chavette Trench to have been cleared of Germans. But as they led their men past the junction and into the entrance to Sottises Alley, a large German force burst out of Chavette Tunnel and attacked their rear. At the same time more Germans charged toward them from Sottises Alley. A desperate close-quarters fight ensued as the forty-five Canadian Scottish tried to open an escape route back through the Germans behind them. Both Thompson and Houston were killed in the fight's opening seconds.

Back on the battalion's front lines, No. 3 Company commander Captain Ernest Otto Rietchel heard the sharp gunfight, gathered a rescue party, and headed toward the action. The thirty-two-year-old Rietchel had come to the battalion in April 1915, been wounded a month later, and returned the following October with a lieutenant's rank. In March 1918 he had been awarded the Military Cross for bravery. Deeply religious, Rietchel made it plain that he loathed war. But his sense of duty and "abhorrence of what was wrong … overruled his private dislike of going to war to kill." Rietchel acted with his normal decisiveness, running out into No Man's Land at the head of the rescue party. Moments later a machine-gun burst killed the officer. His men faltered, pulling back to the safety of their trenches. After a while the remains of the two No. 4 Company platoons escaped into the lines. They numbered just twenty-five of the original forty-five and reported having to abandon their wounded.

Back at headquarters, Peck realized that the Germans were determined to make a stand at Schwetz Wood and ordered a two-company attack to clear them out. No. 2 Company was directed at the wood while No. 3 Company advanced to the trench junction north of it where the two platoons had been ambushed. When Peck phoned No. 2 Company commander Major James Scroggie, he simply said: "Get Schwetz Wood." "Yes, sir" was all Scroggie replied. "Good man," Peck added and hung up.

Scroggie was gathering his men when a runner from Lieutenant Macpherson reported that the No. 4 Company officer had surreptitiously withdrawn his two platoons back down Regulus Trench from where they had been originally hiding in sight of the Germans in the trenches near Fresnoy and established another L-shaped position that extended toward the wood's southwestern corner. Scroggie was heartened by this news, as it meant Macpherson would be covering No. 2 Company's right flank as it attacked the wood. With no time to tee up covering artillery or mortar fire, Scroggie simply formed two platoons into a line and led a 700-yard charge straight across open ground. Not a shot opposed them and the men crashed into Schwetz Wood to find it undefended. After struggling through the tangled undergrowth, Scroggie and several men stepped out of the other side of the wood and immediately came under heavy machine-gun fire. Ducking back into cover, Scroggie sent word that he would need artillery support before any advance beyond the wood could be made. When the shells started falling, 2nd and 3rd Companies went forward together about 300 yards beyond the wood and took control of the Chavette Trench-Sottises Alley junction. North of this position, the Canadian Scottish could hear the Royal Highlanders heavily engaged in front of La Chavette. The 13th Battalion made three attempts to gain a toehold inside the village, but was repulsed each time. Not until the following day would the Royal Highlanders take La Chavette.

At the trench junction the Canadian Scottish discovered some of the wounded No. 4 Company had been forced to abandon. The Germans had bandaged the men's wounds and, when they withdrew, left them to be recovered. This reduced the 16th Battalion losses, which still totalled sixty with three officers and fifteen other ranks killed, thirty-three other ranks wounded, and nine of the men from the two overrun No. 4 Company platoons lost as prisoners.[36]

This action marked the end of 16th Battalion's role in the Amiens offensive, which sputtered to conclusion on August 22. By then, Canadian Corps was once again on the move, this time to join British First Army in the Arras sector. The Canadians left the Amiens area proudly, knowing that although the offensive had cost a total of 11,822 casualties they had given better than they received. Currie wrote that his corps had "fought against 15 German Divisions: of these 10 were directly engaged and thoroughly defeated, prisoners being captured from almost every one of their battalions; the five other Divisions, fighting astride our flanks, were only partially engaged by us.

"In the same period the Canadian Corps captured 9,131 prisoners, 190 guns of all calibres, and more than 1,000 machine guns and trench mortars.

"The greatest depth penetrated approximated to 14 miles and an area of over 67 square miles containing 27 towns had been liberated.... Considering the number of German Divisions engaged, and the results achieved, the [Canadian] casualties were very light."[37]

Unlike so often in the past the Germans were to be allowed no opportunity to regroup or regain the ground lost. "If we allow the enemy a period of quiet," Haig warned the General Staff in London, "he will recover, and the 'wearing out' process must be recommenced." The Germans were on the ropes and his gut "feeling [was] that this is the beginning of the end." Amiens had proved that boldly executed offensives could bring victory. Haig cautioned his subordinates that they would never again "advance step by step in regular lines as in the 1916–17 battles. All Units must go straight for their objectives, while Reserves should be pushed in where we are gaining ground."[38]

chapter eleven

The Finest Performance

- AUGUST 20–SEPTEMBER 3, 1918 -

During the last days of August, the Allies struck hard across an ever-enlarging front. On August 20, with the Amiens offensive still smouldering, the French Tenth Army had thrown twelve divisions northward from Aisne and gained five miles between Noyon and Chauny in two days. The Third French and British Third armies weighed in on August 23 and General Sir Julian Byng's divisions advanced two miles toward Bapaume, sweeping up 5,000 prisoners. Field Marshal Douglas Haig next committed Fourth Army on the Somme River and then directed First Army to be ready for an operation on August 26 with the Canadian Corps leading.

Having only completed relocating from Fourth Army, the Canadians had anticipated a short respite for rest and refitting. But, as the official Canadian historian later put it, such a period after "extensive operations ... was denied the Canadians for in these last hundred days of the war each major offensive so rapidly succeeded its predecessor that unprecedented demands had to be made on the stamina of the forces employed."[1]

By the end of August, almost all the losses of the spring and early summer had been reversed, but the Allied plan was less about winning ground than destroying the German army before it could take refuge inside the heavily fortified Hindenburg Line. Constructed in the winter of 1916–1917, this line stretched from the North Sea to Verdun and consisted of a network of deep trenches tying together hundreds of steel-reinforced concrete pillboxes protected by a 60-foot-wide wall of barbed wire. To ensure that any Allied attack became disorganized well short of this main defensive line, the Germans had constructed an outpost zone about two miles to its front that was 1,100 yards deep. The mile-and-a-half stretch of ground between the outpost line and

Hindenburg proper was designated a "Battle Zone" meticulously pre-sighted and range-marked to be swept by masses of machine guns and artillery. Any Allied attackers would first have to fight through the outpost line, then cross the gauntlet of the "Battle Zone," before facing the deadly wall of the Hindenburg fortifications.[2]

If the Germans were allowed to conduct an orderly withdraw-al into the Hindenburg Line, a return to stalemate was certain. But the Hindenburg Line was not without an Achilles' heel. If the Allies could advance east along the Arras-Cambrai road immediately to the south of the Scarpe River and gain the rolling country beyond Cambrai, the Hindenburg Line would be outflanked and rendered indefensible. Realizing this, the Germans had been frantically preparing to meet such an offensive here and the hilly, wooded country between Arras and Cambrai was ideal for defence.

By late summer, the Germans had created five distinct defensive zones. The first consisted of ground they had won in the spring of 1918 covered with a maze of old British and German trenches and their wire entanglements. Behind this ad hoc defensive line were four that were carefully engineered. The first lay east of Monchy le Preux, and two miles behind this was the double-barrelled Fresnes-Rouvroy Line and Vis-en-Artois Switch. Taken together, these three initial lines constitut-ed a forward defence intended to serve the same disorganizing function of the Hindenburg Line's outpost line. Behind these the Germans had constructed two lines, fortified as close to Hindenburg Line standards as possible. The first was the Drocourt-Quéant Line with the Canal du Nord Line behind. Breaking through these two lines would require an advance of eight miles across heavily defended ground that descended gradually toward the uncompleted Canal du Nord and was exposed to fire from a height of wooded ground to the east called Bois de Bourlon.[3] Although a couple of weaker lines had been constructed behind Canal du Nord to block the way to Cambrai, once the canal fell the Germans would be hard-pressed to hold the city and the Allies would have reached the Hindenburg Line. Carrying Cambrai was the task given to First Army, and Gen. Henry Horne had specifically asked for the Canadians to lead the offensive.[4]

Lt.-Gen. Arthur Currie established his headquarters at Hautecloque, a village twenty miles west of Arras, on August 23. Although 2nd and

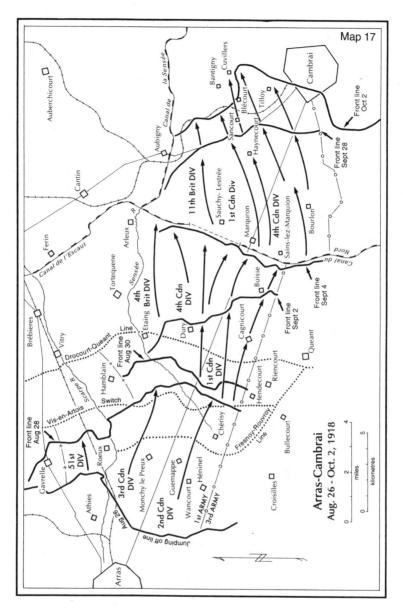

Map 17

Arras-Cambrai
Aug. 26 - Oct. 2, 1918

3rd divisions were already in place, 1st and 4th divisions would not arrive until August 25 and 28 respectively. Consequently Currie was giv-
en the Scottish 51st Highland Division to participate in the first phase of
his offensive. General Horne's instructions told Currie he was to "attack
eastwards astride the Arras-Cambrai Road, and by forcing ... through
the Drocourt-Quéant line south of the Scarpe to break the hinge of the

Hindenburg System and prevent the possibility of the enemy rallying behind this powerfully defended area." Canadian Corps's operation would
begin in conjunction with an attack by Third Army on Sunday, August
25. Currie protested that "this gave barely 48 hours to concentrate the
necessary Artillery, part of which was still in the Fourth Army area, and
that, furthermore, the Canadian Corps had sentimental objections to
attacking on the Sabbath Day. It was then agreed that the attack should
take place on Monday the 26th."[5]

Currie considered the German defences his corps must breach
"among the strongest on the Western Front. The ground was pocked
with the scars of 1917 and early 1918, and in the litter of old trenches
and fortifications German engineers had found ready-made positions
which they had considerably strengthened. Furthermore, topography was
on the side of the Germans. The battle area spread over the northeastern
slopes of the Artois Hills, whose summits about Monchy were over 300
feet above the valley-bottoms of the Scarpe and Sensée. The latter river,
flowing generally eastward, together with its tributaries had dissected
the hills into numerous deep valleys. The intervening ridges and high
points, often mutually supporting, the enemy had fortified with a skill
that demonstrated his mastery in military engineering."[6] The Germans
had concentrated eight infantry divisions directly in the path of the
Canadian line of advance.[7]

Currie decided to advance two divisions in line, each rotating its
brigades to the front one at a time so that they could "carry on the battle for three successive days" and then be replaced by his other two divisions, which should have arrived by then. The 51st Highland Division
would cover the Canadian left flank with an advance along the Scarpe's
north bank.[8]

At 0300 hours on August 26, the Canadian 2nd and 3rd divisions
struck with fifty tanks in support. The village of Monchy-le-Preux fell
quickly before the Germans recovered from their surprise to bitterly
contest the loss of every subsequent height of ground. Two thousand
prisoners were taken, but the advance slowed as the day wore on. With
heavy rain turning the battleground into a muddy morass the following day, the Canadians and Highlanders slogged grimly onward. Such
was the ferocity of enemy resistance that Currie's original plan to have
only one brigade at a time on the sharp end had to be abandoned and

The first of four Canadian Scottish Victoria Cross winners, Piper James Cleland Richardson.

Lance Corporal William Metcalf's courage at the Drocourt-Quéant Line garnered him a posthumous Victoria Cross.

Pozières Ridge.

By 1916, it was hard for wounded soldiers like these ones not to grin if their "blighty" meant a long, or even permanent, escape from the battle lines.

In the lead up to the Canadian Corps assault on Vimy Ridge, powerful naval guns were used to batter the German defences.

April 9, 1917. Canadian troops advance under fire toward Vimy Ridge.

PRIVATE W. J. MILNE,
(Vimy Ridge, April 9, 1917)

William Johnstone
Milne's bravery at Vimy
Ridge resulted in a
posthumous Victoria
Cross.

Machine-gun posts in the muddy quagmire of
Passchendaele.

Major James Scroggie was also one of the most indomitable Canadian Scottish officers.

The Canadian Scottish Pipe Band, February 1918.

Officers of the Canadian Scottish, February 1918.

The portly Lieutenant Colonel Cyrus Peck proved a brave and agile battalion commander, who led the Canadian Scottish through many of its hardest battles. His fearless actions at the Drocourt-Quéant Line were recognized by a Victoria Cross in 1919.

Minister of Militia Major General S. C. Mewburn shakes Pipe Major James Groat's hand during an inspection in July 1918.

On October 1, 1918, Major Roderick Ogle Bell-Irving went missing while serving as acting commander of the 16th Battalion during the advance on Cuvillers.

Some days after the battle, Bell-Irving's body was discovered in No Man's Land, and he was buried by the regiment with full honours on October 17 at Eterpigny cemetery.

Heavy artillery laid down a heavy barrage at the Drocourt-Quéant Line on October 2, 1918, which helped shatter the German defences.

Highlanders stand amid the ruins of Arras.

Canadian Scottish advance on Cambrai.

The end of a long march, 1st Canadian Division crosses the Rhine at Cologne on December 13, 1918.

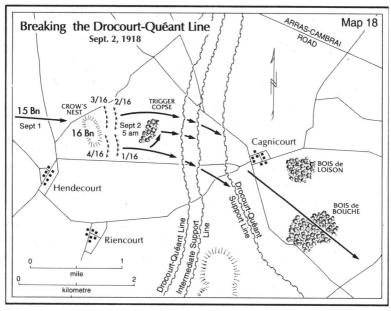

Map 18. Breaking the Drocourt-Quéant Line, Sept. 2, 1918

each division put two brigades forward. Consequently, by the night of August 28, both divisions had, at a cost of 5,801 casualties, shot their bolt well short of the Drocourt-Quéant Line.[9]

As the Germans were pouring reinforcements into the D-Q Line, as it was nicknamed, First Army headquarters agreed to delay the next advance to September 1. Then the Canadians would attempt to not only carry the D-Q Line but also Canal du Nord in one jump. Before this offensive could be undertaken, however, the ground between the Canadian current position and the ideal jumping-off line roughly parallelling the D-Q Line from a distance of 600 yards needed to be secured. That task was assigned to 1st Canadian Division on the right and the 4th British Division, placed under Currie's command, to the left with Brig. Raymond Brutinel's independent mobile brigade's Canadian Cyclist Battalion guarding the British left flank immediately south of the Scarpe. Heavy fighting ensued and not until the evening of August 31 was the jumping-off line secured. Currie placed one of 4th Canadian Division's brigades between 1st Division and the British 4th Division with plans to hit the D-Q Line the next morning.

The previous fighting, however, had so worn the British division that its commander told Currie he could not advance across the breadth of frontage assigned, so Currie widened 4th Canadian Division's frontage by another thousand yards by committing another brigade. This caused a postponement to September 2, which had the benefit of giving 1st Division's 3rd Brigade time to capture a strongpoint known as the Crow's Nest. This 60-foot-high bald bluff overlooked the D-Q Line from about a thousand yards. With one Canadian Scottish company in support, the 48th Highlanders of Canada stormed the Crow's Nest and its seizure ensured that 1st Division could form for the coming assault free of German observation.[10] Several Canadian Scottish officers climbed the knoll to study the D-Q Line. "We got out our glasses and commenced to scan the country," one officer wrote. "The first thing I saw was a line of figures emerging from a trench and advancing on the battalion [the 48th Highlanders] holding the front—no mistaking them, they were Huns." A forward observing artillery officer on the Crow's Nest phoned in co-ordinates for a barrage which soon "dropped and scattered the Huns."[11]

* * *

In 1st Division's sector, 3rd Brigade would be on the right, 2nd Brigade the left. The Royal Highlanders and Canadian Scottish would lead 3rd Brigade's advance with the latter battalion on the extreme right flank of the corps and maintaining contact with 1st Royal Munster Fusiliers of 57th (West Lancashire) Division. Beyond this broad plan many details were still hanging on the evening of September 1 when Lt.-Col. Cyrus Peck established his battalion headquarters in a large dugout alongside No. 2 Company. The other companies lacked any accommodation, their men lying in the open ground designated as forming-up positions. It was a cloudy, moonless night, but the rain had lifted so they were relatively dry.

Peck had still to receive the brigade operational order when he called the company commanders to the dugout at 2030 hours, so they ended up waiting impatiently until after midnight. Leaning close to a candle set on a table, Peck read the order out loud—the others crowding close around because German shells exploding nearby made it difficult to hear. Their instructions were straightforward—the two lead battalions would drive straight through the D-Q Line and then the Royal Montreal Regiment and 48th Highlanders would pass through to capture Cagnicourt and two woods east of this village—Bois de Bouche and Bois de Loison.

Peck designated No. 1 and No. 2 companies to the first wave with the other two companies following at an interval of 30 yards.[12] Three tanks would accompany the Canadian Scottish and it also would be followed by a mobile artillery piece from the 25th Battery of the 6th Brigade, Canadian Field Artillery to provide close support as directed by the battalion commander.[13] Zero Hour was 0500 hours.

Several shells had fallen near the dugout while Peck had been reading the orders, shaking dirt down from the ceiling onto the maps spread across the table. As Peck finished up, a closer explosion rocked the dugout and then someone shouted, "The M.O.'s killed!" Peck rushed out and discovered the battalion's medical officer, Captain John Cathcart, had been hit. "He's done," Peck mournfully reported to the other officers, after examining the man's severe wounds (which, in the end, proved not to be fatal). Word flew through the ranks that the popular medical officer, who had never hesitated to go into No Man's Land to treat wounded, had been killed. The prospect of entering battle without a doctor to treat their wounds put many of the men on edge.[14]

After this calamity the company officers returned to their units while Peck and his staff remained in the dugout. With them was No. 2 Company's sergeant pipe major, Jimmy Groat, who had garnered the Military Medal in 1917. Peck noticed that Groat "was standing not far away from me, puffing a long black pipe and straining his eyes to read a paper in the flickering light from the candle on my table. I was leaning forward on the table close by, gazing at the map of the coming battle. Word is passed down the stairs, 'Move on Number 2 Company.' Groat quietly lays down the paper, nods to me and turns to go. Then, in a moment another order comes: 'Stand fast Number 2 for ten minutes.' He turns and lays down his Pipes on the wire bed, pulls out his old pipe and lights it, picks up the paper and reads. I don't think I ever saw a finer picture of mental control."[15]

Beyond the dugout, things were anything but calm as Zero Hour approached and the forward companies scrambled to get into position amid "a turmoil of shellfire and bombing."[16] The redoubtable Captain Gus Lyons, who had led No. 1 Company into battle many times, was unable to reconcile the surrounding terrain to the map. A sunken road was to establish the boundary between the British troops and his company, but he found only a muddy track running directly eastward. Lyons decided this would serve and told his men to extend in line north from this point until they met up with No. 2 Company's right-flank platoon. No. 4 Company stood 30 yards to the rear.

No. 2 Company, meanwhile, had left the dugout and wandered through inky blackness with the clock ticking down to Zero Hour, its newly appointed commander increasingly anxious that he would fail to be in position left of No. 1 Company on time. Lt. Max Reid had taken over the company from Major James Scroggie on August 25 when he moved up to battalion second-in-command. Reid had served in the ranks until being wounded during the Battle of Festubert, returned to Canada for commissioning, and risen to the rank of Captain before voluntarily reverting to a lieutenancy in order to be posted back overseas. While not new to combat, Reid knew his debut as a company commander was off to a shaky start.

Reid was not the only one lost. Behind, No. 3 Company had also strayed off in the wrong direction only to be gathered in by a headquarters staffer and guided to its start point. The same officer then realized No. 2 Company was missing and Peck cast out a net of men to search for it.

No. 2 Company's whereabouts were still unknown when No. 1 Company's second-in-command, Captain Sydney Douglas Johnston, passed word from the right flank that there was no trace of the Royal Munsters. It was 0430 hours. Fifteen minutes later, "when every second was precious," Johnston ran up to where Lyons was standing with a couple of other officers to report he had chanced upon a Munster outpost only to have the non-commissioned officer there claim he "knew nothing whatever of the attack about to take place, and ... was positive his unit was not taking any part in it."

Lyons greeted this news with dumbfounded silence. Just then Peck and his piper approached and Lyons gave him the news. "Well, it doesn't make any difference, we've got to go forward whether they do or not," Peck said calmly.

The lieutenant-colonel was putting on a show, for the British absence worried him almost as much as the presence of increasing numbers of German soldiers mysteriously popping up in small holes running along the length of the battalion start line. Peck had dismissed the first ones to appear as men stationed in advanced listening posts—all eager to surrender when approached—but soon there were just too many for that explanation to hold. Finally, one prisoner confessed that his battalion had been forming precisely on the start line for a counterattack scheduled for 0600 hours. More battalions, he said, were deployed between 800 and 1,000 yards to the front of the German wire in preparation for this attack. Peck realized the Canadian Scottish would have to drive through these forward forces to gain the D-Q Line. If his leading companies got tangled in a point-blank shootout short of the wire, the attack would be stalled. But there was no option but to proceed as planned.

Right on schedule, the supporting barrage slammed down on the great drapes of wire and German trenches behind. The Canadians advanced toward the rising sun and the shells exploding in great gouts of flame and smoke. Lt. Reid had got his lost company into position at the last moment, so Nos. 1 and 2 Companies walked forward in a broad line. The artillery had dropped a covering smokescreen through which the Canadian Scottish glimpsed hundreds of German infantry approaching with hands raised in surrender. There was little resistance and the Canadians were soon closing on the wire, their only casualties being caused by friendly fire from one artillery battery whose rounds persistently fell short. Shrapnel from one exploding round cut down Captain Lyons with a wound that would cost him a leg.[17]

At headquarters, Peck was feeling like a helpless bystander as the attack unfolded. His angry calls did nothing to get the friendly fire lifted off his men. Nor could he establish contact with the promised tanks or single artillery piece that were supposed to be advancing behind the troops.[18]

As Reid's men closed on the wire, they came under machine-gun fire from a wood identified as "Trigger Copse." The company's Lewis gunners immediately returned fire, while Reid sent one platoon from his company and another from No. 4 Company round to take the enemy from behind. As these troops pushed into the wood, the Germans surrendered.

From the heights to the right of the Canadian Scottish a hellish rate of fire was cutting right across their front and many a man cursed the Royal Munsters for their absence that day. Lt. Reid's No. 2 Company pushed through this hail of lead to the first band of wire only to find the artillery had failed to open any holes. Unable to find a way through, the two companies on this flank were rapidly shredded by the German machine gunners. All eight officers were wounded, five of them mortally.

One survivor wrote: "I saw John Elliott dead.… [Alex] Campbell-Johnston and [Eric] Drummond-Hay gone west. Drummond-Hay was playing his [kazoo] during the advance, and when I saw him dead he had the [kazoo] in his hand.

"We came up against the 'darndest' mess of barbed wire I ever saw; the Hun in front and on the right, doing a lot of damage. The wire is perfect and there we stick. I got a machine-gun bullet in the shoulder, and it entirely dispelled any preconceived notions I had as to the burning pains or sting of a bullet; it was more like the village blacksmith swinging on one with a thirty-pound hammer. It whirled me around and I heard someone laugh. Looking down I saw it was [Captain] Joe Mason in a shell-hole with one of our fellows and a scared-looking Hun."[19]

Sgt. Frank Earwaker of No. 1 Company's No. 4 Platoon had taken cover in a shell hole until Lt. Campbell-Johnston ordered another advance. About twenty men accompanied the officer, who was only eighteen and had enlisted as a private when not yet sixteen. "We all got up together," Earwaker wrote, "and didn't get more than five yards before we met with the heaviest fire from the trench in front of us that I have ever faced. Down I went into a shell-hole; Lieutenant Campbell-Johnston flopped on his stomach right in the wire about twelve feet to my right.… [He] raised himself on his hands, looking to the front, evidently trying to see how much chance he would have to go forward, when they got him in the head." Earwaker and the survivors from the two companies were trapped in the shell-holes, unable to go further or to retreat. They could hear a tank grinding around behind them and, on spotting it, a number of men waved their helmets to draw its attention to their plight. But the tank stayed back.[20]

Peck had also spotted a couple of tanks. Running out in front of them, he pointed to the high ground where the German machine gunners were stationed and gestured that they should advance against that position. Instead, to Peck's consternation, the tanks "turned about and left the vicinity." Accompanied by Lt. John Dunlop, Peck decided to go back to headquarters and use the phone to direct artillery fire on the heights. En route he came upon a large number of Royal Munsters and encouraged them to attack the German positions, but his remonstrations "had no effect upon them." Finding a number of Canadian heavy machine gunners in a trench near the start line, Peck pointed out the ridge and soon had them firing on it. Deciding this was as good as the artillery, he and Dunlop started back toward the front only to be driven into a shell hole by heavy enemy fire.[21]

The Canadian Scottish, who were having difficulty penetrating the wire, were, meanwhile, being subjected to intensifying rates of fire from their right. Sgt. Earwaker risked a glance out of his hole to investigate the cause and spotted a lone tank advancing toward them with Can Scot signaller L/Cpl. William Metcalf "walking beside it, a little to the right in front of it, pointing with his signal flags in our direction. It was still pretty early and you could hardly recognize him [in the poor light] except by the flags. The tank was coming on at an angle from the left flank. I saw Metcalf walking about thirty yards and then we decided it was our turn to help. We made a dash for the trench and made it before the Germans got their guns on us. When we captured the trench, we found a nest of machine guns on not more than a fifty-foot frontage."

Metcalf stayed alongside the tank, using his signal flags to direct it across the trench and toward the German positions behind. Heavy fire continuously hammered against the tank's armour, and, as it spanned the trench, German infantrymen attempted to knock it out with grenades. Pte. J. H. Riehl later recalled the thirty-seven-year-old signaller—an American from Maine—strolling calmly alongside the tank and wondered how "Metcalf escaped being shot to pieces." Metcalf's courage this day would be recognized with the Victoria Cross.[22]

The soldier's bravery got the advance going and within minutes the battalion broke through the main D-Q Line. Making use of the opportunity the distraction Metcalf and the tank presented to escape their shell-hole, Peck and Dunlop managed to join No. 2 Company as it moved through the centre of the D-Q Line's wire. Pushing right up to the front ranks, Peck led the men toward a wooden hut used for storing tools and wire during the defence line's construction. Upon gaining the building the men discovered a wide lane behind it that provided a clear run through the rest of the wire to the trench that formed the heart of the D-Q Line. Moments later the barrage that had been methodically working forward struck the trench and then lifted. With Peck out front, the Canadian Scottish rushed the trench only to find most of the garrison, which outnumbered them three to one—standing on the fire-step with hands raised in surrender. As Peck stepped to the edge of the parapet a non-commissioned officer suddenly pointed a rifle at him. Peck was saved from being shot by a German soldier who knocked the rifle from the man's hands.

Peck called a halt to reorganize. The remnants of Nos. 1 and 4 Companies were put under command of Major James Scroggie and formed up alongside what was left of Nos. 2 and 3 Companies. The battalion struck out for the D-Q Intermediate Support Line just 250 yards away on the summit of a gradual slope. Several gaps in the wire provided easy routes, and the Germans that the Canadians encountered generally surrendered without firing a shot. This also proved the case as the Canadian Scottish reached the defensive trench.[23] Peck later commented that he had "never seen the enemy so cowardly; prisoners surrendered in shoals. They outnumbered us vastly and had they made a determined stand could have hindered our advance to a considerable degree."

* * *

From the Intermediate Support Line, the Canadian Scottish could see the Support Line—their final objective and the D-Q Line's last strongpoint. It lay down a "bare slope and across a hollow." To the right, another height of ground dominated the line of advance. It was a little after 0800. The sky was clear and the sun bright. There was not a scrap of protective cover. The moment Peck led the men into the open, the heights to the right erupted with heavy machine-gun fire. Finally, the men could stand this storm no longer and took refuge in a series of shell holes. Peck shouted for them to throw smoke bombs ahead to create a protective screen and was about to order a renewed advance when a tank (probably the one that had worked earlier with Metcalf) rolled down the slope. The machine gunners immediately shifted their attention to it.

Deciding he could better direct the fight from the relative safety of the Intermediate Line, Peck was readying to make a dash back up the slope when another tank growled directly down toward his position. Thirty yards from the infantry, the tank halted and then turned around.

Peck had just fifteen men close by, mostly from No. 2 Company. Peering out of his hole, Sgt. William Reith later wrote, he watched as

Peck left "the shell hole where he was taking cover and, under heavy machine-gun fire, ran back to the tank. He stood directly in front of it. He forced it to turn around. But directly he returned to the shelter, the tank instead of continuing toward the Drucourt Support, turned about and proceeded to move back.... I do not know how the Colonel escaped being riddled by bullets."

The situation was critical. Escaping up the hill was impossible, but so was going forward. Determined to break the impasse, Peck and Lt. Dunlop dashed up the hill through intense enemy fire. Gaining the Intermediate Line, Peck found the men there thoroughly disorganized. All jumbled together were a remnant of Canadian Scottish, the leading edge of the 48th Highlanders waiting to pass through once the D-Q Line was carried, and, inexplicably, a large number of Royal Munsters seeming to have no idea where they should be. Peck separated the British troops from the rest and sent them away. He then directed the Canadian machine-gun officers from each battalion to concentrate their guns on the high ground to the right and had the artillery forward observation officer target the same area. This quelled much of the enemy fire. Gathering the rest of his battalion, Peck led the men down the slope to rescue the leading wave and carry the attack into the Support Line, where the enemy again promptly surrendered. It was now about 0930 hours and the Canadian Scottish had obtained their final objective. Peck's gallantry would be recognized with the Victoria Cross. This gave 16th Battalion the rare distinction of having two of its own awarded the V.C. in a single day.[24]

Soon after, the 48th Highlanders passed through the Canadian Scottish lines. Although now in reserve, the battalion spent the next five hours clearing small pockets of resistance bypassed earlier. The Canadian Scottish paid a heavy price for the ground won this day. Five officers were dead, another ten wounded, thirty-three other ranks had been killed, and 155 suffered wounds. Peck noted ruefully that "this Battalion has lost 27 officers in the last two actions or in less than 27 days."

He also felt an opportunity had been lost. "I never saw the enemy in a more demoralized condition, and although this was one of the most successful actions in which the Battalion or Brigade have ever been engaged, I certainly think, that, had our flank been kept up, we would have driven the enemy beyond the Canal du Nord in a short time."

But Peck could find no fault with the performance of the Canadian Scottish. "I again find that I cannot speak too highly of the valour and discipline of the Troops under my command. It is impossible for me to describe in words the numberless acts of personal bravery that came under my observation. The Old Battalion kept up its great reputation, advancing with unfaltering courage and steadiness and sweeping away the powerful and heavily manned defences of the Drocourt-Quéant Line with the greatest ease. I may safely say of all ranks, that they without exception, did their duty."[25]

As had the rest of Canadian Corps, for by day's end the leading battalions were two miles beyond the D-Q Line. Total casualties for the day, however, were 5,622 killed or wounded. The advance continued the following day with the enemy virtually on the run before the advancing 1st British and Canadian 2nd and 3rd Divisions. By nightfall, Canadian Corps controlled all the ground west of Canal du Nord—a total advance in the offensive of five miles.

Currie wondered "whether our victory of yesterday or of August 8 is the greatest, but I am inclined to think yesterday's was." He singled out 1st Canadian Division's as "one of the finest performances in all the war."[26] Indeed, such was the level of gallantry that Canadian Corps collected seven Victoria Crosses—the most Canada garnered on any single day in history.

The Canadian achievements were barely recognized at First Army headquarters, some of its staff officers snidely suggesting that better leadership and more determination on the part of the soldiers would have carried Canal du Nord and gained the eastern bank. But a "thorough reconnaissance of our front," Currie responded, "had shown that the frontal attack of the Canal du Nord line was impossible, the eastern bank of the Canal was strongly wired and was generally much higher than the western bank.

"The whole of our forward area was under direct observation ... and any movement by day was quickly engaged by hostile artillery." Time was needed to bring up supporting artillery. The canal, which was not dug, but created by constructing thick earth and brick walls, itself posed "a serious obstacle. It was under construction at the outbreak of the war and had not been completed.... The average width was about 100 feet and it was flooded as far south as the lock, 800 yards southwest of Sains-lez-Marquion, just north of the Corps southern boundary. South of this and to the right of the Corps front the Canal was dry, and its bottom was at the natural ground level, the sides of the Canal consisting of high earth and brick banks.

"The attack of the Canal du Nord could not, therefore, be undertaken singly by the Canadian Corps, but had to be part of a larger scheme." Until that scheme was in place, the corps would stay put, regrouping while holding the line, and then it would carry the canal.[27]

* * *

While Currie began planning this offensive, to the south, the British Third Army slowly fought its way through the Hindenburg Line's outworks. This advance was possible only because, in breaching the D-Q Line, Canadian Corps had outflanked the Germans there and caused a withdrawal to the Hindenburg's main line. North of First Army, the reversal prompted abandonment of the Lys Salient for a line running between Ypres and Lens. "Disagreeable decisions," the German high command called the surrendering of ground on both fronts and worried that the situation would deteriorate entirely if the Canadians crossed Canal du Nord.

The Germans were determined to hold and, while Currie and his staff worked on their plan, there were constant small clashes on the front lines. The daily Canadian casualty rate averaged one hundred. On September 16, Currie decided to stem the alarming losses by pulling the front line back to where it was out of range of the machine guns stationed on the higher ground on the opposite bank.

The day before, Field Marshal Haig had held a conference of his army commanders and outlined an Allied plan that would involve "four great hammer-strokes delivered at crucial points" between the Meuse and the English Channel. In France, the British would strike at Cambrai and St. Quentin, the French would force the Aisne River, and the newly deployed American Expeditionary Force would eliminate the St. Mihiel Salient and then join the French Fourth Army's advance on Mézières. Meanwhile, in Belgium, a combined force under King Albert would push toward Ghent and Bruges.

Regarding the capture of Cambrai, Haig instructed General Horne to have Canadian Corps seize the Bourlon Wood, so the left flank of

Third Army was covered as it moved on the city. Bourlon Wood was a dark, high mound that, on a clear day, the Canadians could see silhouetted against the sky directly east of their position. To reach it, they must cross the canal. Every bridge had been destroyed and the Germans had flooded the surrounding countryside. Intelligence officers in 2nd Canadian Division were so discouraged they told Currie the canal was "practically impassable by any force larger than a platoon without considerable preparation." Currie agreed this was true for the northern part of the canal that the corps faced, so he sidestepped 2,600 yards southward to cross the canal at a point where it had not been flooded.

Here he would cross with a rapier thrust by 1st Canadian Division on a two-brigade front with the 4th Canadian Division on its right with one brigade forward. In this formation, the two divisions would claim the canal and then capture Bourlon Wood. After that, Currie would widen the front fanwise in a northeasterly direction by as much as 9,700 yards with 11th British Division, placed under his command, coming up on 1st Division's left while 3rd Canadian Division advanced on 4th Division's right flank. The four divisions would advance as one, protecting Third Army's left during its move on Cambrai.

The First and Third armies were scheduled to begin their offensive on September 27 with Fourth Army's drive on St. Quentin following two days later. Days before the offensive began Third Army's commander, General Sir Julian Byng, visited Currie's headquarters. Byng scrutinized Currie's battle plan thoroughly and then turned to him. "Old man, do you think you can do it?" he asked. Currie assured Byng the corps would succeed.[28]

By 1918, the Canadian Corps was one of the most professional forces in the Allied army. Its staff officers were masters of the methodical offensive and plans for the Canal du Nord attack evidenced this. The initial assault would be supported by a rolling barrage as normal, but instead of precisely defined lifts set to a repetitive distance, they would range between 500 and 1,500 yards, depending on the estimated speed at which infantry should cross specific stretches of ground. A dense smokescreen projected by firing smoke shells and bombs ahead of the troops and wind-borne smoke issuing from drums filled with burning oil would screen the advance. Teams of engineers equipped to quickly bridge the canal would follow right behind the leading wave of infantry and tanks. By the night of September 26–27, all was in readiness and at 0520 hours, with a miserable, cold rain falling, the barrage signalling the advance began.[29]

The Canadian Scottish were in reserve and took no part initially beyond holding a front facing Saint-les-Marquion while the Royal Montreal Regiment forced a crossing to the right and took the village from the rear. All along the line, the Canadian attack was perfectly executed, the engineers installing bridges or ladders across the canal for the infantry crossings and ramps that enabled the tanks and vehicles to negotiate their way over. With 14th Battalion in possession of Saint-les-Marquion, after a fierce fight, the Royal Highlanders of Canada leapfrogged through to continue widening 1st Division's front. On schedule, 3rd Brigade reached its final objective of the outskirts of Sauchy-Lestrée and the 56th British Division came up to widen the front further. Although 4th Canadian Division was exposed to brutal enfilade fire from the right flank, it managed to take Bourlon Wood.

Cambrai lay only two miles away at day's end, seemingly within easy grasp. But September 28 proved a day of frustration. The Germans had poured in reinforcements during the night and the Canadians encountered many delays getting sufficient artillery across the canal and within range of the city. A grim slog ensued with gains being measured in yards and a rapidly rising butcher's bill. On September 29, 2,089 men were killed or wounded for barely any ground won. Among the fallen was 1st Division's much loved senior chaplain, Canon Frederick Scott, who was evacuated with a severe wound. Currie tried again, on the last day of September, to loosen the German front, but was forced to cancel the operation's second phase due to heavy casualties. Canadian Corps was in possession of Tilloy, a village immediately north of Cambrai, but still lacked a toehold in the city. Prisoners reported that their commanders were stressing "the supreme importance" of Cambrai, and that it must "be held at all costs."

Currie pondered quitting, but he knew "the enemy had suffered severely, and it was quite possible that matters had reached a stage where he no longer considered the retention of this position worth the severe losses both in men and morale consequent upon a continuation of the defence." One more push, he decided, with four divisions in line "attacking simultaneously under a heavy barrage."[30]

On 1st Division's front, 1st and 3rd brigades would lead with 1st on the left and 3rd to the right. Flanking 1st Brigade would be the 11th British Division, while 4th Canadian Division would be to the right. On the corps' extreme right flank, 3rd Canadian Division would hit Cambrai with a frontal assault.

The advance by 1st Division would be 5,000 yards north of Cambrai and 3rd Brigade's first task would be completed by the Royal Highlanders advancing 1,000 yards to capture the villages of Sancourt and Blécourt. As soon as Sancourt fell, the Royal Montreal Regiment and Canadian Scottish would pass to its south and advance on a two-battalion-wide front. The target for the Montrealers was Bantigny while the Canadian Scottish had sights on Cuvilliers. Once past these villages, the two battalions were to go hell-for-leather to a sunken road well east of Cuvilliers and dig in until reinforced.[31]

To the Canadian Scottish's dismay, they would attack without the leadership of Lt.-Col. Peck, for Brig. George Tuxford had barred him from active participation in another attack due to his being physically and mentally exhausted. The brigadier "told me I must not go into action," Peck scribbled in his diary that evening. "Very disappointed." After briefing Major Roderick Bell-Irving, who was to command in his absence, Peck had gone to Boulogne for a rest. But he had no intention of staying there long. He would return on the evening of September 30 to monitor the fighting from Canadian Scottish headquarters. Arriving there as planned, Peck was surprised to see that the detailed plan worked out by Canadian Corps headquarters had not been disseminated down to battalion level. He considered the orders Tuxford gave Bell-Irving "ambiguous" and "sudden."[32]

* * *

To position itself for the attack, the Canadian Scottish moved immediately to Haynecourt and took over the lines held by 2nd Brigade's 10th Battalion shortly before midnight. The Canadian Corps offensive kicked off at 0500 hours and the Royal Highlanders advanced behind a creeping barrage toward Sancourt. As soon as the sounds of a fierce gunfight were audible from the village, Major Bell-Irving ordered the Canadian Scottish forward. No. 4 Company under Major Arnott Grier Mordy led

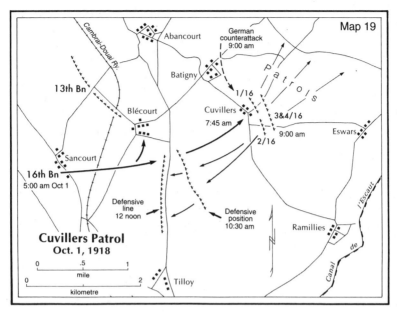

Map 19

German counterattack 9:00 am

Abancourt

Batigny

13th Bn

1/16

Cuvillers 7:45 am

Blécourt

3&4/16 9:00 am

Eswars

2/16

Sancourt

16th Bn 5:00 am Oct 1

Defensive line 12 noon

Defensive position 10:30 am

Ramillies

Cuvillers Patrol
Oct. 1, 1918

0   .5   1
mile

0   2
kilometre

Tilloy

with Captain George Mason's No. 3, Captain George McCreary's No. 2, and finally Captain Robert McIntyre's No. 1 companies following in line. Bell-Irving's headquarters section advanced in company with No. 1 Company. Leading from the rear was not the twenty-seven-year-old Bell-Irving's natural inclination. His close friend, Major Hugh Urquhart, often commented that Bell-Irving "had the faults of his virtues." One of those virtues was a fearless courage that made him seek the sharp end. But the major knew that personally breathing down Mordy's neck would do little to instill confidence, so he hung back to give the officer room to breathe.[33]

It was a miserably cold day with heavy rain that drenched the men. The rain and thick overcast cut visibility so badly that the Canadian Scottish could see neither the Royal Highlanders at Sancourt nor any sign of the Royal Montreal Regiment supposedly advancing on their immediate left. Nor was 4th Division's 102nd Battalion visible to the right. The persistently heavy gunfire from the direction of Sancourt told Bell-Irving that the Royal Highlanders were still engaged there and not moving on schedule toward Blécourt. That meant the battalion's left flank was unprotected as it passed Sancourt and crossed the Cambrai-Douai rail line. Routine tactical doctrine would have held that Bell-Irving should hold the Canadian Scottish in place until the Royal Highlanders completed the execution of the original plan by capturing Blécourt. But one message emanating down from First Army headquarters had been crystal clear—every battalion was expected to press "forward irrespective of flanks." These were instructions that appealed to Bell-Irving's impetuous nature. And, as the battalion had yet to suffer a casualty, he was encouraged to believe little resistance would be met. Consequently, after only a few seconds' hesitation, the major sent word to Mordy to continue advancing to the east of the railway.

A moment later No. 4 Company surged over the raised railway bed and was immediately raked by machine-gun fire. Mordy fell, badly wounded. Lt. Frank Hill was also hit but—the wound being less serious—insisted on remaining with the company until wounded more seriously a few minutes later. Bell-Irving responded immediately by ordering No. 3 Company to slip sideways and come up alongside the staggered No. 4 Company while the other two companies adopted a two-company formation a little to the rear with the battalion headquarters between them.

The two leading companies ran straight at the gunners to their front and overran a string of machine-gun positions that were mostly still in the process of being established along the verge of a sunken road south of Blécourt. Twelve machine guns and a hundred prisoners were captured. Ahead lay the village of Cuvillers, and Bell-Irving ordered the men to charge it. As the Can Scots emerged from the sunken road German artillerymen inside the village began firing at them over open sights while more guns and machine guns on an overlooking ridge poured fire in from the left. Had all this fire not been wildly inaccurate, the battalion would have been shredded. Instead, the advance continued with the Lewis gun crews scattering into firing positions and striking the German gunners in Cuvillers with such accurate fire that they fled. At 0745 hours Cuvillers was overrun, but as the Can Scots began consolidating to defend it they started taking heavy fire from Blécourt to their rear.

Captain George McCreary's No. 2 Company was most exposed to the fire coming from Blécourt, so he ordered Lt. James Rodgers to take his platoon back to the village and take out the Germans there. Working their way into the village, Rodgers closed on a church with an attached convent that the Germans had fortified. Men were firing out of every window and doorway and also from the steeple. The platoon busted into the church and cleared it, but stalled trying to get inside the convent until a Lewis gun crew arrived. Once they opened fire, the remaining Germans abandoned the convent.

With Blécourt cleared and Cuvillers taken, the Canadian Scottish set up a defensive front to fend off any counterattacks. No. 1 Company, acting as the reserve, dug in along Cuvillers' eastern outskirts. About 100 yards farther out, No. 2 Company established a support line from where they could quickly move to reinforce the other two companies dug in on a ridge about 200 yards ahead. Both Nos. 3 and 4 Companies had sent patrols almost a thousand yards beyond the ridge to the sunken road that marked their final objective. Bell-Irving confidently expected to complete the battalion advance to the road once the battalions on either of his flanks appeared. It was only 0900 hours, the day was young, and there was much daylight yet for finishing the assignment. The only German resistance in the battalion's area consisted of sporadic artillery fire from the ridge that was concentrated on Blécourt, which the Canadian Scottish had withdrawn from once the church and convent had been taken. Such calm reigned that the battalion's cooks rolled their kitchen wagons into Cuvillers and prepared a hot meal.

As the morning wore on, however, and there remained no sign of friendly troops on either of their flanks Bell-Irving began to worry. With Assistant Adjutant Lt. Robert Kerans for company, he went forward to the ridge where No. 3 and No. 4 companies were deployed. Kerans was increasingly anxious. Gesturing to their flanks, he said, the battalion was "in the air." Not looking up from the map he was studying, Bell-Irving replied, "I know that, but I'm going to push on to the men in the road." Kerans was to go back and have the two companies back of the ridge change positions so that the Canadian Scottish was covering its own flanks. The two men parted, Bell-Irving walking down the slope and out into the countryside between the ridge and the sunken road. Major Roderick Ogle Bell-Irving would not again be seen alive.[34]

Kerans was still on his way to the rear when the quiet was shattered by intense fire from the overlooking ridge on the left flank that ripped the battalion lines all the way from where Nos. 3 and 4 Companies were positioned back to Cuvillers. As Kerans sprinted into the village he saw Germans slipping into it from the direction of Bantigny to the north. The Royal Montreal Regiment was supposed to be over there, but clearly they weren't. From the overlooking ridge the German machine gunners were able to cover every inch of ground the Canadian Scottish held and prevent them organizing a measured counterattack to meet the enemy infantry vying for control of the village.

When the Germans first appeared, RSM James Kay had immediately ordered all the men in the village to fall back to a position on the northern outskirts. By the time Kerans joined him, Kay had broken the headquarters section into fighting details—strengthened by the cooks and other troops who normally provided support functions. Each detail was strategically placed in a house from which they could provide mutual fire support to the others while also maintaining control of the road that ran to Blécourt. The road was the battalion's escape route, Kay told Kerans. He added that the situation they were in was untenable. Kerans agreed, but escaping it seemed equally untenable because there was now German fire coming from Blécourt. The four rifle companies, all to the front of Cuvillers, would be surrounded if the small force in Cuvillers was unable to turn the advancing Germans back. Kerans and Kay agreed that their current positions were no good. The only viable defensive ground for such a small unit was a sunken road that ran southwestward from the village. Once they were in place on that road, the rifle companies could fall back on them.

Out to the front of Cuvillers, Captain Robert McIntyre of No. 1 Company had taken No. 2 Company's lieutenant, James Rodgers, and his platoon out to the left in hopes of making contact with the Royal Montreal Regiment. He had just decided the Montreal regiment was obviously nowhere near where they were supposed to be when a wave of Germans suddenly appeared and began moving to cut the platoon off. The Canadians sprinted back to the company lines, which were being saturated with heavy fire. McIntyre learned that No. 3 Company's captain, George Mason, had been killed and No. 2 Company's captain, McCreary, seriously wounded. That left McIntyre the senior officer in the front area. He told Rodgers to go to battalion headquarters in Cuvillers and ask for reinforcements. As Rodgers ran off, McIntyre reorganized Nos. 1 and 2 Companies into a composite unit. There was nothing he could do for the two companies out on the ridge. All contact with them had been lost.

As Rodgers entered the village he came face-to-face with a group of Germans. He sprinted back the way he had come until finally outdistancing the pursuing Germans, who gave up the chase. During his return to McIntyre's position, Rodgers met four lost Royal Montreal Lewis gunners and took them under his wing. Rodgers reported that the Germans were in control of Cuvillers and McIntyre decided the only course of action open to him was to withdraw to positions west of the village. That meant leaving the two forward companies to their own devices, but there seemed no choice. As McIntyre's men moved back they came upon the group led by Kerans. The two officers decided to send patrols toward Blécourt and Bantigny, for surely the Royal Highlanders would be in the former while Bantigny was an objective for the Royal Montreal Regiments. Once they located either battalion, the Canadian Scottish could withdraw to their position.

In the minutes it took to organize the patrols, the Germans appeared in strength south of Bantigny. Cut off from that village, McIntyre sent both patrols toward Blécourt. One happened on a Montrealer corporal with six men who were dug into the side of a sunken road southeast of the village. The patrol hurried back to McIntyre, who then moved his force there. Here he hoped to stand until the two forward companies caught up.

It was a forlorn hope, for German machine guns positioned inside Blécourt opened up with fierce fire directed straight along the length of the sunken road. Staying in the funnel of the road meant dying there, so McIntyre and his men retreated cross-country to another road farther south. This one had a southwest-trending dogleg that prevented the Germans firing directly along it from Blécourt. It was now noon. McIntyre had no idea what was happening with the other 3rd Brigade battalions.

Everywhere the brigade's situation was dire. At 1030 hours, Lt.-Col. Peck acted with disregard for Brig. Tuxford's orders to stay well back. With the battalion's acting adjutant Captain Robert Robertson, Peck had ridden forward to Sancourt only to be forced to dismount on the outskirts by German machine-gun fire. "This amazed us, as we thought ourselves well behind the battle line. We turned hastily about and galloped back on to the road in Sancourt, where we were sheltered by some buildings. We turned our horses over to the grooms, and proceeded forward on foot, being careful to seek such shelter as we could find."

At the railroad in front of Sancourt the two men took shelter in a siding. From here they quickly determined "the whole position was one of uncertainty and that a serious situation had developed." When a machine gun opened up on them, Peck and Robertson ran to a small brick tower where they found a company of 48th Highlanders forming. Peck could see Canadian troops advancing to the left in a disorderly formation and surmised these must be part of 1st Brigade. He suggested the 48th Highlanders use the railway embankment's cover to join the other Canadians going forward.

A few minutes after the 48th Highlanders headed out, Lt.-Col. Dick Worral appeared with a runner at his side. Worral told Peck he had lost all contact with his Royal Montreal Regiment. Peck said they could do nothing where they were and must go forward. Dodging heavy machine-gun fire, the four men dashed one at a time over patches of open ground until they finally encountered a platoon of Royal Highlanders in Blécourt. The platoon commander said he knew nothing of any units beyond his small group. Pressing on alone, the four men were finally driven to ground in an abandoned enemy dugout. Here they hunkered down until just how confused the situation had become was proven by the arrival of a party of signallers who, unreeling telephone line in their wake, walked into the dugout. Suddenly Peck was talking directly over a phone with Brig. Tuxford. After briefly describing what he had seen so far, Peck had the signallers pack up the line and ordered everyone to withdraw to the relative safety of a sunken road farther back. Here, he ordered Captain Robertson to locate the Canadian Scottish or any other battalion he could find on the brigade front.

Robertson took three of the signallers with him as runners and made his way to a chapel on the Blécourt road. This six-sided shrine had windows on every side and provided "a splendid view of the whole country." Through his binoculars, Robertson could see "enemy movement … in the outskirts of Blécourt, on my extreme left, and at Cuvillers in front." In the road running from the chapel to Cuvillers, Robertson could see McIntyre's Canadian Scottish while, off in the other direction, the road was packed with a lot of men from 4th Division. Given the presence of so many Canadian troops, Robertson decided the road would serve as a rallying point. He sent word to the Canadian Scottish survivors to fall back on the chapel and dig in to the left of it while the 4th Division men were ordered to do the same on the right. Once this line was established, Robertson put several patrols out to the east to bring any Canadians they found back to the road.

The road served fairly well as a trench and the Canadians were able to keep the ever-growing numbers of German infantry at bay with rifle fire. RSM Kay steadied the men by walking along the length of their line to offer encouragement and caution them against wasting their dwindling ammunition supply by firing when the Germans were not actually counterattacking.

Peck, meanwhile, had phoned Tuxford again and been ordered to take command of the front line. With a semblance of a defensive line established, he was able to direct artillery against targets threatening it. Cuvillers was quickly reduced to ruins. He also arranged an ammunition re-supply. A stalemate set in. The Germans held Blécourt, the Canadians the road position. Each attempted to drive the other out of their position with artillery and machine-gun fire, but neither budged. When night fell, Tuxford ordered further offensive action abandoned.[35]

The determined resistance that 3rd Brigade had met had been matched all along the Canadian Corps front and convinced Lt.-Gen. Currie that to "continue to throw tired troops against such opposition, without giving them an opportunity to refit and recuperate, was obviously inviting a serious failure, and I accordingly decided to break off the engagement. The five days' fighting had yielded practical gains of a very valuable nature, as well as 7,059 prisoners and 205 guns.

"We had gone through the last organized system of defences on our front, and our advance constituted a direct threat on the rear of the troops immediately to the north of our left flank, and their withdrawal had now begun.

"Although the ground gained on the 1st was not extensive, the effects of the battle and of the previous four days' fighting were far-reaching and made possible the subsequent advances of October and November, in so far as the Divisions engaged against the Canadian Corps drew heavily on the enemy's reserves, which had now been greatly reduced." Intelligence reports indicated the Germans had been forced to commit ten divisions to block the Canadian advance while only requiring three divisions to reinforce the front running from Honnecourt to Cambrai, which was 18,000 yards in length. He was proud of his troops and their commanders, believing they had effectively seized the initiative for the Allies and it now rested with others to ensure the Germans had no time to regroup.[36]

But the cost in blood had been terrific. When relieved from the road position on October 2, the Canadian Scottish had only three officers and seventy-five men fit for combat. Five officers and nineteen men were dead, eight officers and two hundred men wounded. A further 103 men were missing, presumed captured.[37] Major Bell-Irving was originally considered to have been captured, but on October 15 his body was discovered about a hundred yards from where he and Kerans had last exchanged words.

The Canadian Scottish casualties were not unique. The RMR had been reduced to just ninety-two men. In his account of the action, Lt.-Col. Worral said the battalion had gone into the battle with only thirteen officers, even fewer non-commissioned officers, and seriously under-strength. He was not surprised that, under such circumstances, the offensive failed in the face of determined resistance.[38] Since August 8—what would later be called the beginning of the Hundred Days that ended the war—Canadian Corps had lost 30,000 men killed, wounded, or missing. By October 1, the Canadian Corps was simply too weak to carry the brunt of the Allied offensive. Currie had committed his troops with the understanding that 11th British Division would bolster his strength with three full battalions. But this division had been so badly beaten up, it provided just three companies that proved of no value. Currie angrily decried the lack of support from First Army headquarters as an "absolute betrayal."[39]

chapter twelve

Drive to Victory

- OCTOBER 2–NOVEMBER 11, 1918 -

The question at the beginning of October was which army would collapse first: the German or the Allies? The French Army endured only because the American Expeditionary Force assumed some of its front. But, on September 26, the inexperienced Americans ventured into the Argonne Forest near Verdun and narrowly avoided decimation as their generals adopted tactics that mirrored the Allied blunders of 1914 and 1915 rather than those now practised. A bloody seesaw battle ensued in the Argonne that dragged interminably into October. The B.E.F., meanwhile, was so reduced by casualties it slashed divisional strengths from twelve battalions to nine, a decision that rendered each division less capable of prolonged combat. Australia's rejection of conscription left its corps so under-strength that the troops were in a mutinous mood. Despite conscription, Canadian morale was equally poor with many a bunkhouse orator telling anyone within earshot that Lt.-Gen. Arthur Currie was "a glory-seeker, demanding the bloodiest tasks for his corps."[1] The reality was that Field Marshal Douglas Haig and his army commanders realized at this juncture in the war that the Canadians and ANZACs were indisputably the B.E.F.'s best fighting soldiers and that realization put them repeatedly on the sharp end.

However, the Germans had even more problems than the Allies. By September's end, all the gains of the spring offensive had been erased with the massive casualties the German troops had suffered. Bulgaria and Turkey were lost as allies. At home, influenza and famine raged. On October 2, the German army high command advised the Reichstag's party leaders that "we cannot win the war." A negotiated peace was attempted for the first time by tentatively extending feelers to U.S. president Woodrow Wilson, whose Fourteen Points proposal offered a possible face-saving resolution. But the Allies sought unconditional surrender, which the Germans would not agree to. So the war would continue until one side or the other was crushed.[2]

The day the Reichstag finally determined that Germany could not win, the 1st Canadian Division had left the rest of Canadian Corps facing Cambrai and withdrawn to a rest position west of the Canal du Nord. The Canadian Scottish knew nothing of the larger picture around them. They saw only their battalion's dire condition. "The future is anything but certain, and the days of yore belong to another world;" one soldier wrote, "a world we feel we will never see again. All is dead but hope, so who should worry? I think we shall end our days here, from what we have gone through. I can't see any daylight as to when this damn war will end." But he did not regret marching to war in the summer of 1914. "I did the right thing … whether the war was wrong or not does not alter that fact."[3]

Death seemed inescapable. The fate in past weeks of so many veterans proved that. There was the case of twenty-nine-year-old Sgt. Mathew Barrett. An Irishman who had enlisted in Winnipeg and joined the battalion in December 1914, he had been wounded on May 10, 1915, and again in the Ypres Salient on April 4, 1916. This tough, courageous survivor died on August 8 during the opening phase of the Amiens Battle.[4]

The same day Barrett was cut down, Pte. Robert Murdoch had been blessed with a "Blighty." Entering the ranks on March 20, 1917, he had been wounded that September and again in November. At Amiens he scored passage home with a wound so severe he was invalided to England and then to Canada.[5]

Physically debilitating wounds were seen as the only road to survival. And many a man envied Murdoch and also Pte. George Nairn this escape. Nairn had been taken on strength March 2, 1916, wounded twice within months, and again on April 28, 1917. Each time the wound was too minor to earn more than a brief hospitalization, but on September 2, 1918, when the Canadian Scottish carried the Drocourt-Quéant Line, Nairn was hit hard and was now convalescing in England with a homeward ticket assured once his health was sufficiently improved.[6]

RSM James Kay, the tough veteran who had come to the battalion as the Cameron Highlander company sergeant major, was considered one of the rocks upon which the foundation of the Canadian Scottish was built. The twenty-eight-year-old had distinguished himself as "a splendid battle leader, cool and clear-headed." At 2nd Battle of Ypres he had gathered in 150 men from a hodgepodge of battalions, kept them in the fight, and been awarded the Distinguished Conduct Medal. The Military Medal followed. Only in February 1918 had Kay reluctantly left the battalion for a three-month leave that was part of a program ensuring all married men who had deployed with 1st Division in 1914 a brief return to Canada. Everyone was happy to see Kay, who had been showing clear signs of extreme exhaustion, sent home and the general sentiment was that he should remain with his family in Winnipeg. But on August 21, just five days before the great Battle of Arras, Kay had reported for duty—having shrugged off offers from the staff at the regimental headquarters in Winnipeg of postings that would keep him at home. His worth in combat was quickly proven on October 1 in the fight for Cuvillers that resulted in a Military Cross recommendation. But Kay's colour was visibly poor, his face an ashen grey. It looked as if the respite had done him little good.[7]

Then there was Lt.-Col. Cyrus Peck. The battalion commander had been ordered to his bed by the medical officer on the evening of October 3. There he remained for six days before insisting on returning to duty only to be evacuated to hospital the following day. Major James Scroggie became the Canadian Scottish acting commander.[8] It was feared that Peck would not return. Scroggie was popular, but he could not fill Peck's shoes. The rotund battalion commander might never look the part of a soldier, but his fearlessness in action and his obvious concern for the well-being of the old originals in particular was recognized by everyone. "The poor skipper," one soldier wrote, "he hates like hell to see the old fellows go." While the men knew that Peck would put them in harm's way as needed, they trusted him to know when it was *needed.*[9]

Consequently the Canadian Scottish were in an uneasy state of mind and spirit when they returned to the battle lines in early October and manned a front close to Douai that extended from the south bank of the Scarpe River at Biache St. Vaast to the south of the Sensée River at Etaing. 1st Division was the first unit in Canadian Corps to deploy here as part of a relief of XXII Corps completed on the evening of October 11.

* * *

For the few days it took for the rest of Canadian Corps to arrive, the 1st Division faced Trinquis Brook—which meandered across the breadth of the valley between the Scarpe and Sensée rivers to join the latter watercourse—and attempted to gain the village of Sailly-en-Ostrevent. On October 8, 3rd Canadian Infantry Brigade's Royal Highlanders carried out a "Chinese Attack." This consisted of undertaking conspicuous pre-attack preparations that ended with a rolling barrage from the Canadian outpost line toward the German positions. Such demonstrations were intended to deceive the Germans into reacting as they would to a full assault in the targeted sector, so valuable intelligence could be gained.[10] Such was the lack of response, divisional command ordered strong patrols to test rumours that the enemy was withdrawing from the Drocourt-Quéant Switch Line, a major defensive work behind Trinquis Brook that was an offshoot to the north of the main Drocourt-Quéant Line broken by Canadian Corps in early September.[11]

In the darkest hours of morning on October 10, the Royal Highlanders aggressively probed Sailly-en-Ostrevent and easily secured the village. Encouraged, the troops advanced into D-Q Switch and captured one officer and forty-seven men before hastily withdrawing to their start line to escape a strong counterattack. The Canadian Scottish took over from the Royal Highlanders that evening with orders to mount a full-scale assault intended to gain not only the D-Q Switch but the high ground just beyond—a total advance of 4,000 yards. The 48th Highlanders would advance on the left toward Virty-en-Artois, while the Canadian Scottish seized Sailly-en-Ostrevent and then swung through the Q-L Switch in a northwesterly push to gain the village of Noyelle. At the same time 2nd Brigade would cross the Sensée River right of the Canadian Scottish, extending the entire attack's frontage to 12,000 yards.

After Cuvillers, Scroggie was worried about getting too far ahead of the units on his flanks, so ordered the advance carried out in phased steps. Phase one sent No. 4 Company—now commanded by Lt. Robert Kerans—to secure Sailly. The only resistance being light machine-gun fire from the Q-L Switch, Kerans completed the task without a single casualty.

Scroggie kicked off phase two by having Major John Hope's No. 3 Company break into the Q-L Switch fortifications. Worried that passing through the village would slow his men down, Hope passed two

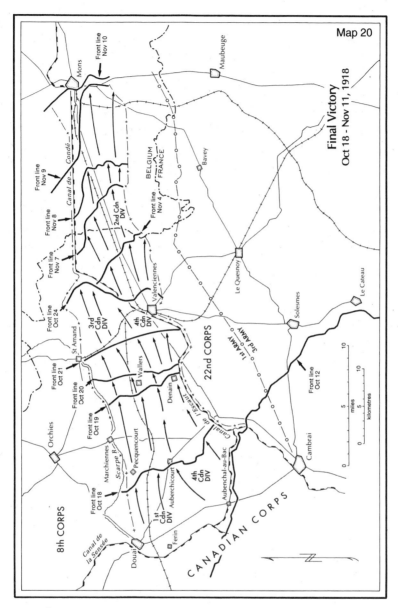

platoons on either side of it. Then the company "regained touch … and advanced in two lines of sections with scouts ahead. They entered the [Q-L Switch] with no resistance other than light M.G. fire from the high ground beyond," Scroggie wrote afterward.

Assuming these gunners to be the same who had fired earlier from the Q-L Switch, Scroggie decided they were on the run and rushed Captain

James Wallis's No. 2 Company forward to widen the battalion hold. As the company took up inside the Q-L Switch on Hope's left, about a dozen Germans in an outpost position began sniping at it from the rear. A Lewis gunner spun about and raked their position, scattering the Germans into several shell-holes. A section of men sent against them by Wallis soon brought the Germans back with their hands raised.

Q-L Switch firmly in hand, Scroggie headed for Noyelle with Nos. 2 and 3 Companies leading. The 48th Highlanders matched their pace to the left, and the right flank was protected by ground the Germans had earlier flooded. On the other side of the boggy ground, 2nd Brigade battalions could be seen moving alongside the Sensée River and closing on its intersection with the Trinquis Brook. Scattered shots from a few Germans was the only opposition the Canadian Scottish met and these enemies were quickly convinced to surrender when a section of the 3rd Trench Mortar Battery dropped a few bombs in their vicinity. At 1800 hours, the battalion stopped for the night under the open sky about 600 yards beyond their original objective of Noyelle. The casualty toll for a day in which the battalion had advanced almost 5,000 yards amounted to just one man killed and two wounded. The fact that only eighteen prisoners had been taken and no German dead discovered told intelligence officers that the enemy might be in full flight.[12]

A major corps advance was teed up for dawn that put three divisions on the move. 1st Division was on the left, the 56th British Division (placed temporarily under Currie's command) in the centre, and 2nd Division to the right.[13] The goal for 1st Division was to force the Germans off all the ground north of the Sensée River and west of Canal de la Sensée. There was no resistance at all until the Canadian Scottish were but 300 yards from the canal and drew heavy and accurate machine-gun fire from the other side. The leading companies took cover, reporting back that the fire came from Ferin. This little hamlet stood on high ground dominating the canal's opposite bank. Major Scroggie told his men to lay low while he worked Ferin over with artillery. A few well-placed shells slackened the German rate of fire but, lacking bridging material, the Can Scots found the canal impossible to cross. At nightfall, 3rd Brigade was relieved by 1st Canadian Infantry Brigade and went into divisional reserve at the village of Eterpigny. In the day's fighting the entire brigade had incurred only twelve casualties, with no fatalities.[14]

The troops were elated. They had driven the Germans back more than five miles in two days with hardly any fighting required. Rumours swirled that the enemy was on the run all over. The rumour mill had sworn this to be the case many times before, of course, but this time there seemed a grain of truth to it because of the badly demoralized state of those prisoners the battalion had taken. The Germans also reported that, far behind the front, stores were being removed or destroyed and bridges, railways, and roads readied for demolition.[15]

* * *

As the 3rd Brigade went into reserve, the 56th British Division erected a floating bridge over the Sensée Canal during the night and established a toehold on the north bank only to abandon it later in the day when a German counterattack appeared to be mustering. On October 14, the 1st Division manned the bridge with patrols, but these pulled back when counterattacked. Lt.-Gen. Arthur Currie ordered a pause to organize a proper attack. Each day, as the preparations were underway, the canal's north bank was subjected to test barrages and aggressive patrols to test enemy strength. Meanwhile, 4th Division replaced the British 56th Division in the corps centre. The front, anchored by the three forward divisions, was unusually wide—about 20 miles. At dawn on October 17, Major General Archie Macdonell advised Currie that the canal opposite his front seemed suspiciously quiet. Several patrols crossed and encountered only light resistance. Macdonell dispatched larger fighting patrols and these soon reported good progress. But 4th Division's attempts to force a crossing were all repelled by heavy machine-gun fire. Wanting to get this division on line for any advance beyond the canal, Currie had its 87th Battalion use the crossings gained by 1st Division and then fight its way along the canal to clear the Germans off their division's frontage. By late afternoon, 4th Division began advancing troops beyond the canal while to the right 2nd Division was also over and on the move. Resistance consisted of only "enemy rearguards ... and the opposition was nowhere heavy," Currie reported.[16]

With the enemy in full retreat Currie requested reinforcement by mobile units in the form of a squadron of the Canadian Light Horse, a company of the Canadian Cyclist Battalion, two medium machine-gun batteries, and two armoured cars for attachment to each of the 1st and

4th Divisions. At 0600 hours the morning of October 18, a pursuit began in earnest.

The advance carried the Canadians into the heart of a large industrial area choked with towns that had to be secured. In Pecquencourt, the troops were met by about 2,000 civilians, who said the Germans had left them behind rather than forcing them to precede their retreat. But not a scrap of food or other supplies had been provided. With only one bridge across the canal capable of carrying horse transport, Currie was challenged with not only keeping his advancing troops supplied but also seeing to the needs of a desperate civilian population.[17]

That night 3rd Brigade was billeted around the village of Ecaillon, but on the move early and by 0700 hours had passed through 2nd Brigade and was advancing with orders to go as far as possible. A low, dense fog affected visibility as the Canadian Scottish's No. 1 Company on the right and No. 4 Company to the left started off. The Royal Montreal Regiment was to their left and a 1st Brigade battalion the right. By mid-day the fog lifted and the Canadian Scottish were amazed to see no signs of fighting anywhere around them.[18]

Across the entire corps front the Germans were in full flight. Cryus Peck, who had returned to the battalion from hospital on October 15, scrawled in his diary: "Remarkable day."[19] Truly it was, for the battalion advanced seven miles, finally pausing for the night a mile-and-a-half beyond the town of Hornaing. Peck wrote:

> When we reached a town, we deployed and swept through and around it. I gave Major Scroggie immediate charge of the Battalion and reserved a roving commission for myself.
>
> The country was nearly level.... I rode into the town we occupied—sometimes alone, sometimes with my groom. The people seemed stunned. For four years they had been under the heel of the enemy who had left that morning, and the spell still seemed to be upon them. I rode across our fronts ahead of the scouts to the road that leads to Bruille les Marchiennes. A man had come down the road and was shouting loudly at somebody. I don't remember seeing any of the inhabitants except this man. The Germans had left them with terrible threats, and they seemed cowed and uncertain until we were actually among them...

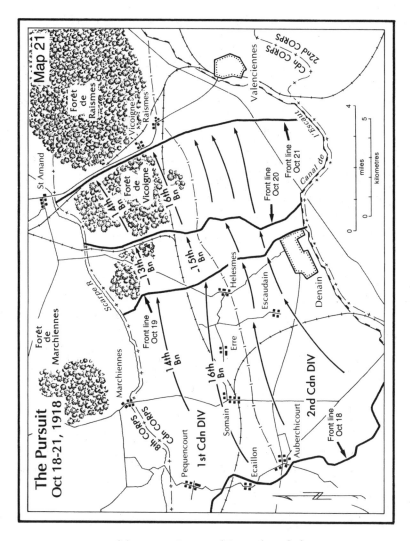

In one of the towns I entered I saw the inhabitants coming out of a house bringing with them six or seven German military police who had overslept themselves. The police were being savagely menaced by the population, and I had to take them under my protection and hand them over to the leading troops of my Battalion when they arrived. These were the only prisoners we captured that day.

The German engineers carried out the work of demolition with consummate skill. Huge craters were to be seen at cross roads and railway crossings. The entire railway had been rendered useless [the Douai-Valenciennes railway]—a stick of dynamite had been placed under each alternate rail end, which on being blown up had rendered the rails useless.

I don't know whether the presentations of flowers started here or farther on, but by the time we got to Erre my groom and myself had to discharge our floral load of huge bouquets, only to be loaded up again at a later stage. Wines and liqueurs were hastily dug up from gardens at short notice and insistently pressed upon us.

The first large town we came to was Somain. I believe it normally has a population of about four thousand. I rode in [with a guard of six men] and halted before a huge crowd. One man seized the hem of my dirty trench coat and kissed it passionately. I shouted 'Vive la France!' The people shouted back and went wild with enthusiasm…. I felt quite imposing as the liberator of Somain.

Peck's triumphal liberation ride continued for the duration of the day. Only once were any German forces seen—five Uhlan cavalry armed with lances outside Escaudain—"retiring over the ridge in front. As they reached the summit, they turned around and I could see their lances against the sky-line. I rode rapidly toward them for a space, a bouquet of flowers in one hand and holding the reins and my revolver in the other."

Entering Hornaing, he was greeted by another large crowd. Seeing the uncertain looks on their faces, Peck shouted, "Vive la France!" Nearby a street sign nailed to a wall read: Kaiser Wilhelm Strasse. Peck "rode up to it, tore it off, spat on it and hurled it to the ground, exclaiming, in what I thought to be French, 'To hell with the Germans!' This produced the desired result and the crowd went wild with enthusiasm.

"The Battalion arrived shortly afterwards and I took up my headquarters with the transport on the road north of Helesmes, near the railway. Thus passed my most enjoyable day in the War; bloodless withal, but most moving, witnessing the unbounding joy of a delivered people."[20]

Fog and drizzling rain greeted the marching troops on October 20. At 0900 the 48th Highlanders passed through the Canadian Scottish and the two battalions advanced in column toward the St. Amand-Raismes road. Whereas the day before the Germans had been on the run, now they began to offer ever-stiffening resistance that slowed the rate of advance. In the distance, explosions could be heard, indicating engineers were busy with their demolitions and that the German infantry was buying them time to complete their work. Despite the resistance, the Canadians still gained over a mile of ground and the Canadian Scottish suffered no casualties.

The following morning, the Royal Highlanders and 48th Highlanders led the way onto the St. Amand-Raismes road where they met the Royal Montreal Regiment and Canadian Scottish and leapfrogged to the front. The new objective was the Valenciennes-St. Amand road, which cut through the Forêt de Vicoigne. Entering the woods on several narrow tracks at 1100 hours, the Canadian Scottish became entangled in a running fight with withdrawing Germans that dragged into the afternoon. About 1600 hours the leading troops reached a large clearing and saw behind it the village of Vicoigne, which consisted of two straggling rows of houses. The road that was their objective ran between the buildings. From the forest to the road, the ground was wide open for 500 yards. Nos. 3 and 4 Companies slipped out of the trees into the cover of a deep ditch. From inside the village, machine guns opened fire. Peck considered the rate of fire light and decided the Germans were not holding in strength. Night was falling. Peck saw no need to hurry men into an open field still washed by sun.

When it was almost dark, the German fire intensified—a sure sign of a feint intended to cover their retirement. Peck ordered two patrols forward to contact the enemy. After a long wait with no sign of activity in the village, Lt. William Stark returned at 2200 hours to report the Germans gone. Major Scroggie led the two companies out of the ditch into the village. As the company commanded by Captain Alec MacLennan started forward, Peck impulsively joined him. It was midnight, and the soldiers warily walked across the open ground, careful not to make much noise. Once they entered the village, Peck "knocked at the door of a small house standing a little bit away from the other houses and heard female voices pleading in great terror not to harm them. We finally persuaded them to open the door and found two old women so frightened out of their wits that they could give us no information on the enemy.

"We entered the village.... It was a bright, moonlight night, and the street was deserted; not even our patrols were to be seen. Knocking loudly at a street door, a woman came out—a middle-aged lady—cool and courageous. When we asked for the 'Allemand,' she pointed to a house in a little square, or rather a triangle, with a light showing over the transom. Alec MacLennan and the others went over to this house and entered it, returning afterwards with the news that the enemy had evidently just left, for all the place was in a medley, things scattered about and a candle … still burning on the table. We went over to the billet and as we were crossing the street heard the steady march of Number 3 Company coming up towards us. We then felt secure so sent back for the two remaining companies, placed our outposts on the double-track railway which runs east of the village and such of us as could, were soon comfortably sleeping in billets."[21]

At his headquarters Currie noted that 1st Division "had now been in the line for two weeks without having an opportunity to rest and re-fit since the hard-fought battle of the Canal du Nord" and ordered it relieved by 3rd Division on October 22.[22] The 43rd Battalion (Cameron Highlanders of Canada) passed through the Canadian Scottish outposts ahead of Vicoigne at noon and shortly thereafter the battalion joined went into reserve positions at Somain. The troops settled into comfortable billets after a "rousing reception" by the civilians Peck had liberated four days earlier.[23] Although they didn't know it, the Canadian Scottish had fired their last shots of the war.

* * *

Some fighting remained for Canadian Corps. October 23 brought it to the Canal de l'Escaut and the fortified city of Valenciennes. South of the city stood 150-foot-high Mont Houy. Five German divisions waited to defend the city and the low mountain to the south. First Army paused to prepare an attack and allow the 51st British Division time to catch up with the Canadians on the left flank. So confident was this division's commander that he assaulted Mont Houy with just a single battalion on October 28. Although initially winning the hill, the battalion was soon driven off with heavy casualties.

Gen. Henry Horne ordered Canadian Corps to immediately launch another attack, but Currie refused unless allowed to conduct the kind of methodical operation he preferred. Throwing away Canadian lives because everyone was in a rush would not do, Currie warned. A heavy barrage on November 1 deluged the hill with steel and explosives. The hill soon fell and, after some heavy fighting for its outskirts, Valenciennes was taken the following day. Eighty Canadians died and three hundred were wounded.

Once again the pursuit was on, but slowed by terrain and weather. Heavy rain dogged the troops as they moved through a mélange of hills, fast-running brooks, fields bound by hedges, and dense woods. The transport trucks and wagons could not keep pace, so the men carried their daily needs in heavy packs. A stiff fight on November 5 won a crossing over the Aunelle River on the French-Belgian frontier. November 9 brought the Canadians to Jemappes, outside Mons. This was a country of coalfields, dominated by huge slag heaps that provided ideal positions for German machine gunners. Against stiffening resistance, the Canadians pressed on. On November 10, 3rd Division gained Mons at a cost of 116 men killed or wounded. The following morning, at 10:58 a.m., Pte. George Price was shot dead by a sniper inside Mons. Two minutes later the war officially ended.

Earlier that morning a telegram had been received by 1st Division headquarters and disseminated. "Hostilities will cease at 1100 hours on November 11th," it read. "Troops will stand fast on the line reached at that hour, which will be reported to Corps H.Q. Defensive precautions will be maintained. There will be no intercourse of any description with the enemy. Further instructions follow—From Canadian Corps 0645."[24]

The Canadian Scottish war diarist recorded: "Arrangements were made for a celebration at 2000 hours in conjunction with 15th Battalion. A great bonfire was made, all of the people of the village attending. During the night there were scenes of great enthusiasm."[25]

* * *

The November 11 armistice ended the war, but there was still soldiering to be done. On November 13, 1st Division learned it would participate in an Allied occupation of the west bank of the Rhine and a series of bridgeheads east of it. Canadian Corps and II British Corps would lead a British Second Army march to one of these sectors.[26] In preparation, 1st Division was to concentrate near Mons and begin the march four days later. The troops were still savouring the taste of victory. Neither they nor their officers were inclined to make haste to the concentration area. Instead the pace of march was leisurely, the Canadian Scottish repeatedly stepping to the side of the road to let hordes of returning refugees—who had fled their homes in 1914—pass. "The scenes en route are indescribable," noted the Canadian Scottish war diarist. "Every description of means of conveyance was met with, the road being packed with civilians returning to their homes."[27] It was two days before the battalion reached Wasmuel, the town southwest of Mons where it was to concentrate.

That Sunday, November 17, the pipe—responding to a request by Wasmuel's mayor—attended a celebration in the parish church where the *Te Deum* and Belgian National Anthem were both sung. In the afternoon word spread that Lt.-Col. Peck had been officially awarded the Victoria Cross for heroism during the Amiens battle for the D-Q Line. Peck was away from headquarters and preparations were quickly made in his absence for a full-scale battalion surprise celebration. When Peck returned that evening the band with the entire battalion in its finest Highland finery formed outside the headquarters and let out a loud cheer. The men shouted for Peck to come out and make a speech, which he did. "Afterwards they took him and carried him round the town with the band playing."[28] When the men finally released Peck and returned to their billets, he wryly noted in his diary: "[Battalion] celebrated elaborately in evening. A great day for the Irish."[29]

The next morning the march to the Rhine began with 1st Division's three brigades setting off from Wasmuel, past Mons, and toward Soignies. This village lay on the German side of the Armistice Line. Also on the move was 2nd Division, but each division followed a different route to reduce road congestion. The weather was good, the division covering the assigned 19 miles quickly and everyone was in billets by 1530 hours.[30]

Despite the armistice, the Canadians were wary of attacks by German army diehards. Each division was preceded by a cavalry screen travelling a day's march ahead. The infantry also provided its own flank protection with patrols scouting on either side of the secondary roads they used to free the main road for use by divisional transport and heavy guns. Defensive outposts were established on overlooking heights and other tactically threatening terrain. Also working the flanks were sections of cavalry and cyclists drawn from the Corps Troops.

1st Division's final destination was Cologne with 2nd Division moving toward Bonn—both about 250 miles from Mons. The Rhineland area of occupation had been divided into zones wherein the Germans were instructed to leave all their war materiel before withdrawing precisely the day before the Allied forces arrived.

Originally, 3rd and 4th Divisions were to have followed the leading two divisions to the Cologne occupation zone, but the German destruction of railways and road damage created a logistical nightmare that made it impossible to supply such large numbers of troops. The decision was soon made that only the two divisions already on the march, along with Corps Headquarters and some inherent troops, would participate in the occupation. All the rest of Canadian Corps—the 3rd and 4th Divisions, 8th Army Brigade Canadian Field Artillery, 1st and 3rd Brigade's Canadian Garrison Artillery—transferred to IV Corps of the British Fourth Army and billeted initially in Belgium until the end of the year before moving to England to begin demobilization.[31]

The divisions bound for occupation duty, meanwhile, enjoyed a near triumphal march through Belgium en route to Germany. In every town where the Canadian Scottish billeted they were feted as liberators. Their reception at Soignies was typical—the mayor renaming the village's main square "Place Canadian Scottish." On November 21, the battalion entered Nivelles and was greeted by throngs of cheering civilians. "Nothing was too good for us at Nivelles," wrote one soldier, "soft feather beds and warm billets. Eight thousand bottles of wine were dug up from the château grounds."[32]

Until November 25, the weather remained favourable, but from then on it rained almost daily. With the side roads reduced to muddy quagmires each division abandoned them, and infantry, trucks, and horses moved in one great column stretching along the main road. To avoid overtaxing the small towns in the Ardennes and Eifel districts, each division broke into brigade formations separated by a day's march, so as one moved forward the town in which it had stayed the night before became available for use by the next in line. "The long hours of marching over cobblestones or through heavy mud," noted the army's official historian, "were taking a toll in blistered feet, and the continual drizzling rain had an added depressing effect."[33]

Despite these problems the Canadian Scottish completed its longest march to date on November 27—23 miles—with only a few men falling out en route, arriving at its billet in Stant d'Avril at 1730 hours. But there was grumbling aplenty when no rations arrived that evening for the following day and the men had to set off without breakfast.³⁴ Each division had advanced about 100 miles at this point from the single supply railhead west of Valenciennes, and the deteriorating road conditions made it increasingly difficult for the Army Service Corps to get supplies up to the troops. After what was a thankfully short march, the Canadian Scottish solved the immediate problem by breaking open the canteen stock and buying whatever they could acquire from the local citizenry.

November 29 brought no respite as the Canadian Scottish headed for Andenne, a town in the Meuse valley on the edge of the Ardennes mountains. This was "a barren country, the hunting ground of the wealthy in times of peace and fit for little else," the battalion's historian recorded. "The home of a peasantry, who toiled from morning to night, summer and winter, raising miserable crops and cutting faggots and peat to earn a living. Up the slopes and over the rough roads of those pine-clad hills rising bleak and forbidding in front through the driving sleet of a November storm, lay the next stage of the journey."

At Andenne the battalion was dismayed to find no billets. The preceding brigade had not advanced as scheduled, but word of this change reached 3ʳᵈ Brigade headquarters only after the Canadian Scottish—who led that day—had long departed. "Everybody's [up] in the air," the war diarist wrote, but the officers scrounged up sufficient barns and other buildings to provide the men with some shelter. And to the relief of all, rations arrived after nightfall.

The next morning the battalion climbed the "steep, torturous roads that led into the mountains." With the ration supply continuing to be problematic and the marching conditions continuing to be difficult, the grousing in the ranks worsened. Two days later, three platoons from one company refused to move, their spokesmen claiming that they "had been told … the brigade in front had not moved when rations were short, and why should they be asked to march." The company commander bullied the "insubordinate platoons" into forming up and the march proceeded on schedule.

Learning of the problem with these platoons, Lt.-Col. Peck had the men pulled aside and "in one of those 'straight from the shoulder' rebukes which he could deliver when the occasion demanded, let the trouble makers know exactly how any repetition of such conduct would be dealt with."³⁵

Next morning the battalion recovered its usual good spirits despite marching through "a thick, damp mist which later in the day turned to a steady rain." Marching over a rough road that was little more than a muddy horse track, the men logged a remarkable 24 miles. "The troops," one officer noted, "were in fine form. The last two laps of the journey they perked right up, and came into billets—which were not reached until after dusk—singing, merry and bright."

They were closing on the frontier and passing through Belgian territory where the civilians were pro-German. No longer did the crowds cheer the soldiers tramping through their villages and towns. Instead they showed only a "forced politeness." Provost marshals preceded the marching troops, posting notices bearing Field Marshal Douglas Haig's signature that warned any "acts of hostility against His Majesty's Forces or any wanton destruction of roads, railways or telegraph lines would be punishable by death."

On December 6, while marching across "a stretch of scrubby bogland high up in the Ardennes, the Battalion reached the German frontier. The pipe band drew to one side, struck up 'The Blue Bonnets' and the 16th passed into the enemy's homeland. The Battalion had travelled 140 miles from the starting point; three weeks had elapsed since the march to the Rhine had begun. Thereafter the marches daily grew easier, roads gradually improved, and billets became more comfortable."[36]

Hereafter the only spectators who watched the passing troops were "children with close-cropped heads who stared, curiously from the roadside. Their elders remained discreetly out of sight, peering through half closed doors or shuttered windows at the marching columns." Lt.-Gen. Currie was anxious about a potential German threat and issued a warning for them to remain "a close-knitted army in grim, deadly earnest" that afforded lurking German agents no "evidence of disintegration in your fighting power." Discipline would remain strict. "In short, you must continue to be, and appear to be, that powerful hitting force which has won the fear and respect of your foes and the admiration of the world."[37]

Finally, on December 12, the long march ended when the Canadian Scottish reached Bayenthal, a western suburb town of Cologne. Here they billeted preparatory to crossing Hohenzollern Bridge the next morning. "We have a large flat in an apartment house," one soldier wrote of his billet. "The Hun gent occupying the house resents us very much; we had quite a row with him. The flat we have was occupied by a Guard's officer and his wife. They apparently fled in haste, for clothing, jewelry and money are lying about. I called the janitor but he refused to have anything to do with it."

Friday, December 13, was dark with heavy rain. The men formed up at 0745 hours. As the Germans might oppose the crossing, the men were in battledress. By the time the order to advance came at 0830 everyone was drenched and shivering in the icy cold. Despite the discomfort, as the troops tromped along the cobbled streets of Cologne toward the bridge they sang lustily, deriving some pleasure from the fact their marching songs appeared to unsettle the small groups of Germans watching bleakly.

3rd Brigade was to lead the division over Hohenzollern Bridge and the battalion commanders had drawn lots earlier to see which unit would be first. Peck had been unlucky, so the Canadian Scottish were third in line. He ordered bayonets fixed and the men "stepped on to the bridge which was the end of the road to victory."[38] On the other side Maj.-Gen. Archie Macdonell and his staff took the salute, as the battalion passed through the city to its assigned destination—the suburb of Heumar.

No resistance was offered and it became clear that occupation of the Cologne Bridgehead garrison was to be an exercise in tedium. The biggest worry came from persistent rumours that Canadian Corps and all the units therein were to be broken up and the men returned home on the basis of a priority system dictated by length of overseas service and marital status. General feeling in the battalion was that they should go home as they had served, together. Finally it was announced that, at a November 23 meeting of all divisional and brigade senior command- ers, a unanimous decision had been agreed "that from every point of view it was most desirable to demobilize the Corps by Units and not by Categories." Initially the Canadian federal cabinet maintained the op- posing view, but when Currie dug in his heels the politicians had grudg- ingly agreed to the wishes of the Canadian Corps officers.[39]

On Christmas Eve, half the battalion attended midnight mass in a Cologne cathedral. The troops awoke on Christmas morning to find snow blanketing the ground. In the windows of houses, Christmas trees adorned with lit candles provided a festive setting. The real celebration came, however, on New Year's Day when, by companies, the battalion held sumptuous dinners.

The new year proved a time of ever-quickening numbers of fare-wells. On January 3, 1919, Peck departed for Canada after emotionally reviewing the battalion. *In absentia* he had stood as the Unionist candidate for the British Columbia riding of Skeena in the December 1917 federal election and won. But he had refused any suggestion of taking his seat in the House of Commons until his army duties were done. Now he was free to go. Peck would hold the seat until 1921 and then turn to provincial politics—sitting in the British Columbia legislature from 1924 to 1933.

The battalion passed to James Scroggie, but it would be under the temporary command of Major John Hope that the Canadian Scottish turned their backs toward the Rhine on January 6 and left the army of occupation. Along with the 13th and 14th Battalions of 3rd Brigade, they were the first units of 1st Division embarked by train to new billets in Belgium. By January 18, the entire division was gone with 2nd Division and the rest of the Canadian Corps units engaged in the occupation completing the move on February 6.

1st Division set up at the city of Huy, midway between Namur and Liège. The Canadian Scottish cared little for their new billet in the near-by village of Antheit, which most agreed was "a 'ell of a 'ole, everything mud, Belgium at its worse." But the inhabitants took the soldiers into their hearts and would do almost anything to ensure their comfort. The truth of this was realized on February 19 when RSM James Kay staggered off the parade ground "dazed with fever, and died the same night." It soon became evident that the RSM had been suffering influenza throughout the German occupation period, but refused all entreaties that he report to the medical officer for examination and treatment. His death was a serious blow, but the men were touched when Antheit's burgomaster appeared with a delegation of citizens and requested that Kay be buried in the village cemetery where they planned to erect a memorial to the men of their Commune who had fallen in the war. Permission for Kay to be interred there was quickly granted. Years later it would be report-ed to members of the battalion in Winnipeg that the villagers had de-cided from the outset that Kay's grave would "ever be cared for and kept in repair. It is always covered with flowers," they were told.[40]

Despite the generosity of the villagers, Antheit remained a gloomy waypoint on what the Canadians considered a drawn-out journey home. The demobilization process seemed needlessly protracted. There was resentment, too, over a decision by Currie that 3rd Division would be the first returned. Logically, the 1st Division should have been first to go, for it had the longest record of service, and then 2nd Division. But these had ended up in the vanguard of the Rhine occupation force and so the order of return ended up jumbled. It helped little that many men in 3rd Division were conscripts with comparatively little overseas service.

Finally, on March 19, 1st Division began embarking at Le Havre for passage to England. The Canadian Scottish boarded a train on March 22 for the port city. Everyone was happy to be one step further along. For the officers the task "of killing time and keeping the men interested in the awful period of waiting to go home" was becoming an unwelcome burden.[41] The British transport *King Edward* carried the battalion across the Channel on March 26 and arrived late the next day at the ill-named Bramshott Concentration Camp. Here they lingered another month, enduring medical board examinations to determine whether men qualified for various disabilities and taking what periods of leave were granted. At long last, at 0300 hours on April 26, the battalion travelled by train to Liverpool. By 1845, the men were aboard the *Empress of Britain* and the ship sailed that night for Canada. On Sunday, May 4, *Empress of Britain* entered harbour at Quebec. Cyrus Peck stood on the wharf, greeted his men ashore, and assumed their command for the journey westward.

Although the Canadian Scottish had been a mongrel composed of men from regiments that hailed from Hamilton, Winnipeg, Vancouver, and Victoria, the army had decided in 1917 to designate the 16th Battalion as a Manitoba-based unit. So it was in Winnipeg that the Canadian Scottish mustered at 0951 hours on May 7, 1919, for its final march and disbandment. Few of the local citizenry turned out. Several battalions that had been entirely raised by local militia regiments had already returned and been disbanded here. A great deal of tension also prevailed, with talk of a general strike in the air. The arrival of more soldiers only increased the anxiety that restive labour and local government authorities might be headed for a showdown.

Accordingly, noted the battalion's official historian, the reception was "only lukewarm. After detraining [the Battalion] marched out of the

Canadian National station on to Main Street and along the wide thoroughfare to Portage Avenue. It turned up Portage, passed and gave the salute to the District Officer commanding; and afterwards, at a point clear of the city's traffic, without being given the opportunity of saying one word of final goodbye, Col. Peck was ordered by a staff officer to halt his battalion on the street, and give it orders to right turn, and dismiss."

Most of the men simply trailed off at that point down the Winnipeg streets while just sixty officers and men remained in formation. These were men from British Columbia, who boarded a train the next day and headed "via Prince George, Prince Rupert and Vancouver to Victoria, men dropping off as they reached their homes. This group was hailed with honour as returning conquerors at all of the points mentioned.

"Reaching Victoria, the few still left of the group dispersed to their homes. The career of the 16th Battalion (The Canadian Scottish), Canadian Expeditionary Force, in the flesh, was at an end."[42]

*   *   *

There is a postscript to this story. Within weeks of its disbandment, various officers and men began quietly corresponding and occasionally meeting. They had a single objective. "The Battalion must not die" was their watchword. Several of the most outspoken and influential lived in Victoria, which had two regiments—the 50th Gordon Highlanders and the 88th Battalion. By 1920 these two regiments had been convinced that the Canadian Scottish legacy—the 50th Gordons having furnished many of the battalion's originals and several reinforcement drafts thereafter—could be preserved as a single Victoria regiment. On March 15 of that year, General Order No. 30 reorganized the two militia regiments into the Canadian Scottish Regiment. Precisely seven years later the regiment became allied, per Canadian militia tradition, with a British regiment—the Royal Scots (The Royal Regiment). Then on April 24, 1930, Princess Mary was appointed her Colonel-in-Chief and it was formally designated the Canadian Scottish Regiment (Princess Mary's).

And so it remains today, one of only a small number of World War I battalions whose identities were preserved. During World War II, the Canadian Scottish was in the leading wave of troops to storm ashore on June 6, 1944, at Juno Beach. It served with distinction through the remainder of the war, gathering up one battle honour after another. As a reserve regiment, the Canadian Scottish has since provided personnel for service on most army overseas deployments. The young men and women who serve in its ranks today are acutely aware of the regiment's historical roots and remain faithful to its motto: *Deas Gu Cath* (Ready for the Fray).

Endnotes

Prologue: Make Every Sacrifice
August 1914

1 H. M. Urquhart, *The History of the 16ᵗʰ Battalion (The Canadian Scottish) Canadian Expeditionary Force in the Great War, 1914–1919* (Toronto: The MacMillan Company of Canada, 1932), 367–68.

2 G. W. L. Nicholson, *Canadian Expeditionary Force, 1914–1919* (Queen's Printer: Ottawa, 1964), 5.

3 Ibid, 6.

4 Urquhart, *16th Battalion,* 369.

Chapter One: "Ready, Aye, Ready!"
August 1914—February 1915

1 H. M. Urquhart, *The History of the 16ᵗʰ Battalion (The Canadian Scottish) Canadian Expeditionary Force in the Great War, 1914–1919* (Toronto: The MacMillan Company of Canada, 1932), 370.

2 G. W. L. Nicholson, *Canadian Expeditionary Force, 1914–1919* (Queen's Printer: Ottawa, 1964), 18.

3 Urquhart, *16ᵗʰ Battalion,* 6.

4 Nicholson, 21.

5 Urquhart, *16ᵗʰ Battalion,* 9.

6 Ibid, 84.

7 Ibid, 14.

8 Kenneth Radley, *We Lead Others Follow: First Canadian Division, 1914–1918* (St. Catharines, ON: Vanwell Publishing Limited, 2006), 46.

9 J. L. Granatstein, *Canada's Army: Waging War and Keeping the Peace* (Toronto: University of Toronto Press, 2002), 57.

10 Urquhart, *16ᵗʰ Battalion,* 14.

11 Ibid, 15.

12 Nicholson, 25.

13 Ibid, 24.

14 Urquhart, *16ᵗʰ Battalion,* 17–18.

15 Ibid, 24–25.

16 Ibid, 25–26.

17 Ibid, 25.

18 Ibid, 32.

19 Nicholson, 35–36.

20 16ᵗʰ Infantry Battalion War Diary, December 1914, Library and Archives Canada, 1.

21 16th Infantry Battalion War Diary, January 1914, Library and Archives Canada, 2.

22 Ibid

23 Urquhart, *16ᵗʰ Battalion,* 30.

24 Ibid

25 16ᵗʰ Infantry Battalion War Diary, December 1914, 2.

26 Nicholson, 38–39.

27 Ibid, 27–28.

28 Tim Cook, *At the Sharp End: Canadians Fighting The Great War, 1914–1918* (Toronto, Viking Canada, 2007), 78.

29 Nicholson, 27–28.

30 Urquhart, *16ᵗʰ Battalion,* 40.

Chapter Two: Learning War—
February–April 1915

1 16ᵗʰ Infantry Battalion War Diary, February 1914, Library and Archives Canada, 2–3.

2 H. M. Urquhart, *The History of the 16ᵗʰ Battalion (The Canadian Scottish) Canadian Expeditionary Force in the Great War, 1914–1919* (Toronto: The MacMillan Company of Canada, 1932), 41.

3 Ibid, 41.

4 16ᵗʰ Infantry Battalion War

Diary, February 1914, 3.

5   H. M. Urquhart personal diary, University of Victoria Special Collections, 60.

6   16th Infantry Battalion War Diary, February 1914, 4.

7   Urquhart, diary, 60.

8   G. W. L. Nicholson, *Canadian Expeditionary Force, 1914–1919* (Queen's Printer: Ottawa, 1964), 45–46.

9   16th Infantry Battalion War Diary, February 1914, 4.

10 Ibid, 5.

11 Urquhart, diary, 56.

12 Urquhart, *16th Battalion*, 96.

13 Urquhart, diary, 62.

14 Urquhart, *16th Battalion*, 44.

15 Nicholson, 49.

16 Urquhart, *16th Battalion*, 45.

17 Urquhart, diary, 64–65.

18 Urquhart, *16th Battalion*, 45.

19 16th Infantry Battalion War Diary, February 1915, 7.

20 Urquhart, *16th Battalion*, 46–47.

21 16th Infantry Battalion War Diary, March 1915, n.p.

22 Urquhart, *16th Battalion*, 48.

23 Urquhart, diary, 70.

24 Nicholson, 51.

25 Urquhart, *16th Battalion*, 49.

26 Nicholson, 51.

27 Urquhart, *16th Battalion*, 47.

28 Nicholson, 53.

29 Urquhart, *16th Battalion*, 49.

30 Urquhart, diary, 72.

31 Urquhart, *16th Battalion*, 50.

32 Ibid, 405.

33 Urquhart, diary, 77.

34 Urquhart, *16th Battalion*, 50.

35 Nicholson, 54–55.

36 Urquhart, diary, 80.

37 Ibid, 83–84.

38 Ibid, 83–85.

39 Urquhart, diary, 85.

40 Nicholson, 56–57.

41 Urquhart, *16th Battalion*, 55.

Chapter Three: Baptism—April 22– May 4, 1915

1   G. W. L. Nicholson, *Canadian Expeditionary Force, 1914–1919* (Queen's Printer: Ottawa, 1964), 58.

2   Daniel G. Dancocks, *Welcome to Flanders Fields: The First Canadian Battle of the Great War: Ypres, 1915* (Toronto: McClelland and Stewart, 1988), 107.

3   Nicholson, 60–61.

4   Ibid, 56.

5   3rd Canadian Infantry Brigade War Diary, April-May 1915, Appendix A, Library and Archives Canada, 8.

6   H. M. Urquhart, *The History of the 16th Battalion (The Canadian Scottish) Canadian Expeditionary Force in the Great War, 1914– 1919* (Toronto: The MacMillan Company of Canada, 1932), 55.

7   H. M. Urquhart personal diary, University of Victoria Special Collections, 86.

8   Urquhart, *16th Battalion*, 55.

9   16th Battalion War Diary, April 1915, Library and Archives Canada, n.p.

10 3rd Brigade War Diary, April-May 1915, 8.

11 Lyn Macdonald, *1915: The Death of Innocence* (London: Penguin Books, 1997), 193.

12 Nicholson, 61–62.

13 Macdonald, 195.

14 Urquhart, diary, 86.

15 Urquhart, *16th Battalion*, 56.

16 Urquhart, diary, 86–87.
17 16th Infantry War Diary, April 1915, n.p.
18 Nicholson, 64.
19 Ibid, 63.
20 Dancocks, 122.
21 16th Battalion War Diary, April 1915, n.p.
22 Dancocks, 125.
23 Urquhart, 16th Battalion, 57–58.
24 Urquhart, diary, 87.
25 William Rae, "Letter to Mother, April 28, 1915," Col. H. M. Urquhart Fonds, Correspondence–1915–1980, Box 22, File 18, University of Victoria, Special Collections, 3.
26 Urquhart, diary, 87.
27 Rae, 3.
28 Urquhart, *16th Battalion*, 58–59.
29 Rae, 3–4.
30 Urquhart, *16th Battalion*, 59.
31 Urquhart, diary, 86–87.
32 Urquhart, *16th Battalion*, 60.
33 Urquhart, diary, 87.
34 Dancocks, 130.
35 Urquhart, diary, 88.
36 16th Battalion War Diary, April 1915, n.p.
37 Urquhart, *16th Battalion*, 61.
38 Ibid, 61.
39 Ibid, 62–63.
40 Urquhart, diary, 88.
41 Urquhart, *16th Battalion*, 64–65.
42 Nicholson, 92.
43 Rae, 1.
44 Urquhart, diary, 89–90.
45 Ibid, 92.
46 Urquhart, *16th Battalion*, 84.
47 Ibid, 405.

Chapter Four: Blown To Hell—May 14–June 13, 1915
1 H. M. Urquhart, *The History of the 16th Battalion (The Canadian Scottish) Canadian Expeditionary Force in the Great War, 1914–1919* (Toronto: The MacMillan Company of Canada, 1932), 73.
2 G. W. L. Nicholson, *Canadian Expeditionary Force, 1914–1919* (Queen's Printer: Ottawa, 1964), 93–96.
3 Ibid, 97.
4 Ibid, 97–98.
5 H. M. Urquhart personal diary, University of Victoria Special Collections, [as of May 6, 1915, Urquhart started numbering his pages from one forward again without explanation of the reason], 5.
6 Urquhart, *16th Battalion*, 75.
7 Ibid, 76.
8 Urquhart, diary, 5.
9 Ibid, 5–6.
10 Ibid.
11 Urquhart, *16th Battalion*, 78.
12 Ibid.
13 Urquhart, diary, 5–6.
14 16th Battalion War Diary, May 1915, Library and Archives Canada, n.p.
15 Urquhart, *16th Battalion*, 79.
16 Urquhart, diary, 7.
17 Urquhart, *16th Battalion*, 79–80.
18 Urquhart, diary, 7–8.
19 Urquhart, *16th Battalion*, 405.
20 Nicholson, 103–04
21 Urquhart, *16th Battalion*, 81.
22 Ibid, 81–82.
23 16th Battalion War Diary, June 1915, n.p.

**Chapter Five: Trench Warfare
Drudgery—June 1915–March 1916**

1 H. M. Urquhart, *The History of
the 16ᵗʰ Battalion (The Canadian
Scottish) Canadian Expeditionary
Force in the Great War, 1914–
1919* (Toronto: The MacMillan
Company of Canada, 1932),
88–89.

2 Ibid, 95.

3 Ibid, 97–98.

4 H. M. Urquhart personal diary, University of Victoria Special
Collections, 36–37.

5 Urquhart, *16ᵗʰ Battalion*, 99–100.

6 G. W. L. Nicholson, *Canadian
Expeditionary Force, 1914–1919*
(Queen's Printer: Ottawa, 1964),
109–15.

7 Urquhart, diary, 34.

8 Urquhart, *16ᵗʰ Battalion*, 101–02.

9 Ibid, 103–04.

10 Urquhart, diary, 35.

11 Urquhart, *16ᵗʰ Battalion*, 105.

12 Nicholson, 115.

13 Ibid, 120–21.

14 Urquhart, *16ᵗʰ Battalion*, 111–14.

15 Urquhart, diary, [as of November
24, 1915, Urquhart started numbering his pages from one forward once again without explanation of the reason], 3.

16 Ibid, 2.

17 15ᵗʰ Battalion War Diary,
December 1916, Library and
Archives Canada, n.p.

18 Kenneth Radley, *We Lead, Others
Follow: First Canadian Division,
1914–1918* (St. Catherines, ON:
Vanwell Publishing Limited,
2006), 65–66.

19 Urquhart, diary, 8.

20 Urquhart, *16ᵗʰ Battalion*, 114.

21 Radley, 81–82.

22 14ᵗʰ Battalion War Diary,
December 1915, Library and
Archives Canada, n.p.

23 Urquhart, diary, 8.

24 Urquhart, *16ᵗʰ Battalion*, 115.

25 Ibid, 122.

26 Andrew Godefroy, "Portrait
of a Battalion Commander:
Lieutenant-Colonel George
Stuart Tuxford at the Second
Battle of Ypres, April 1915,"
Canadian Military Journal,
Summer 2004, 55–56.

27 Urquhart, *16ᵗʰ Battalion*, 123.

**Chapter Six: Return to the
Salient—March 28–August 9, 1916**

1 Winston Groom, *A Storm in
Flanders: The Ypres Salient,
1914–1918: Tragedy and Triumph
on the Western Front* (New York:
Grove Press, 2002), 67.

2 H. M. Urquhart, *The History of
the 16ᵗʰ Battalion (The Canadian
Scottish) Canadian Expeditionary
Force in the Great War, 1914–
1919* (Toronto: The MacMillan
Company of Canada, 1932),
123–24.

3 Groom, 138–39.

4 G. W. L. Nicholson, *Canadian
Expeditionary Force, 1914–1919*
(Queen's Printer: Ottawa, 1964),
133–13.

5 Ibid, 138.

6 Groom, 144.

7 Nicholson, 139.

8 Ibid, 140–41.

9 Urquhart, *16ᵗʰ Battalion*, 125.

10 http://www.greatwardifferent.
com/Great_War/British_Front/
Hills_01.htm, accessed August
16, 2007, reproduction of text
from *The War Illustrated*, 11

May, 1918, Lovat Fraser, "The Epic Battles for the Hills," 3.

11 Urquhart, *16ᵗʰ Battalion*, 125.

12 Ibid, 127–28.

13 Ibid, 126–27.

14 Nicholson, 142–44.

15 Ibid, 145–47.

16 Roland H. Hill, "Holding the Salient, 1916," *Canada in the Great War*, Vol. 3 (Toronto: United Publishers of Canada Limited, 1919), 257.

17 Jack Granatstein, *Canada's Army: Waging War and Keeping the Peace* (Toronto: University of Toronto Press, 2002), 88.

18 Nicholson, 148.

19 Ibid, 147–151.

20 3rd Canadian Infantry Brigade War Diary, June 1916, Appendix 35: First Operation, 2 to 7 June, 1916, Library and Archives Canada, 1.

21 Urquhart, *16ᵗʰ Battalion*, 135.

22 3rd Canadian Infantry Brigade, Appendix 35, 1.

23 Urquhart, *16ᵗʰ Battalion*, 136–37.

24 Ibid, 137–38.

25 3rd Canadian Infantry Brigade, Appendix 35, 2.

26 Nicholson, 150–51.

27 Urquhart, *16ᵗʰ Battalion*, 138.

28 Nicholson, 151.

29 3rd Canadian Infantry Brigade, Appendix 35, 2.

30 H. M. Urquhart, personal diary, University of Victoria Special Collections, n.p.

31 14ᵗʰ Canadian Infantry Brigade War Diary, June 1916, Appendix: "Counterattack on Maple Copse and Observatory Ridge Positions," Library and Archives Canada, 2.

32 Urquhart, diary, n.p.

33 3rd Canadian Infantry Brigade, Appendix 35, 4.

34 Ibid, 4.

35 Nicholson, 152.

36 Urquhart, *16ᵗʰ Battalion*, 141.

37 Ibid, 142.

38 Ibid, 142–44.

39 Nicholson, 153.

40 Urquhart, *16ᵗʰ Battalion*, 385.

41 Ibid, 144.

42 Ibid, 148–49.

43 Ian V. Hogg and John Weeks, *Military Small Arms of the 20ᵗʰ Century* (Northbrook, IL: DBI Books, n.d.), 285.

44 Urquhart, *16ᵗʰ Battalion*, 144–50.

45 3rd Canadian Infantry Brigade, June 1916, Appendix 52, 6.

46 Nicholson, 153–54.

47 Urquhart, *16ᵗʰ Battalion*, 154.

Chapter Seven: Crisis in the Somme—August 9–October 11, 1916

1 G. W. L. Nicholson, *Canadian Expeditionary Force, 1914–1919* (Queen's Printer: Ottawa, 1964), 160.

2 Jay Winter and Blaine Baggett, *The Great War: And the Shaping of the 20ᵗʰ Century* (New York: Penguin Studio, 1996), 157.

3 Nicholson, 161–62.

4 Ibid, 163.

5 H. M. Urquhart, *The History of the 16ᵗʰ Battalion (The Canadian Scottish) Canadian Expeditionary Force in the Great War, 1914–1919* (Toronto: The MacMillan Company of Canada, 1932), 163–68.

6 Ibid, 168.

7 Ibid, 169.

8   Ibid, 169–70.

9   Ibid, 169–70.

10 3rd Canadian Infantry Brigade
    War Diary, September 1916,
    Appendix 8, Library and
    Archives Canada, n.p.

11 Urquhart, *16th Battalion*, 172–74.

12 Nicholson, 166.

13 Urquhart, *16th Battalion*, 406.

14 Ibid, 173–74.

15 Nicholson, 168.

16 David Campbell, "A Forgotten
    Victory: Courcelette, 15
    September 1916," *Canadian
    Military History*, Spring 2007, 31.

17 Nicholson, 168–69.

18 Campbell, 31.

19 Nicholson, 169.

20 Campbell, 34–40.

21 Nicholson, 173.

22 Ibid, 172–75.

23 Urquhart, *16th Battalion*, 176–77.

24 Ibid, 177.

25 Ibid, 177–78.

26 Nicholson, 175–76.

27 Urquhart, *16th Battalion*, 178.

28 3rd Canadian Infantry Brigade,
    Appendix 52, 2–3.

29 16th Infantry Battalion War
    Diary, September 1916, Library
    and Archives Canada, n.p.

30 Urquhart, *16th Battalion*, 178–79.

31 14th Canadian Infantry Battalion
    War Diary, September 1916,
    Appendix 4, Library and
    Archives Canada, 2.

32 Urquhart, *16th Battalion*, 179.

33 14th Canadian Infantry Battalion
    War Diary, Appendix 4, 2.

34 Nicholson, 178–79.

35 14th Canadian Infantry Battalion
    War Diary, Appendix 4, 3.

36 Urquhart, *16th Battalion*, 179.

37 Ibid, 406.

38 Nicholson, 183.

39 3rd Canadian Infantry Brigade
    War Diary, n.p.

40 Urquhart, *16th Battalion*,

41 Ibid, 385.

42 Ibid, 181–82.

43 Ibid, 182.

44 http://www.vac-acc.gc.ca/cvw-
    muploads/published/183893_
    4.jpg, accessed July 17, 2007.

45 Urquhart, *16th Battalion*, 185–87.

46 Ibid, 184.

47 Ibid, 187.

Chapter Eight: Vimy—October 12, 1916–May 4, 1917

1   H. M. Urquhart, *The History of
    the 16th Battalion (The Canadian
    Scottish) Canadian Expeditionary
    Force in the Great War, 1914–
    1919* (Toronto: The MacMillan
    Company of Canada, 1932), 406.

2   *G. W. L. Nicholson, Canadian
    Expeditionary Force, 1914–1919*
    (Queen's Printer: Ottawa, 1964), 199.

3   Desmond Morton and J. L.
    Granatstein, *Marching to
    Armageddon: Canadians and the
    Great War, 1914–1919* (Toronto:
    Lester & Orpen Dennys, 1989).

4   Urquhart, *16th Battalion*, 188–89.

5   Tim Cook, *At the Sharp End:
    Canadians Fighting the Great
    War, 1914–1916* (Toronto:
    Viking Canada, 2007), 263.

6   Morton and Granatstein,
    137–38.

7   Urquhart, *16th Battalion*, 191.

8   Morton and Granatstein, 140.

9   Urquhart, *16th Battalion*, 192.

10 Ibid, 192.

11 Ibid, 195.

12 Ibid, 198–99.

13 Jack Granatstein, *Canada's Army:*

Waging War and Keeping the Peace (Toronto: University of Toronto Press, 2002), 110–11.

14 Urquhart, *16ᵗʰ Battalion*, 192–93.
15 Ibid, 193.
16 Nicholson, 236–37.
17 Urquhart, *16ᵗʰ Battalion*, 202–03.
18 Ibid, 202–03.
19 Nicholson, 249–50.
20 Ibid, 249.
21 Ibid, 248.
22 Ibid, 250–51.
23 Ibid, 247.
24 Urquhart, *16ᵗʰ Battalion*, 212–13.
25 Cyrus Wesley Peck Fonds, MG30–E134, Library and Archives Canada, n.p.
26 Urquhart, *16ᵗʰ Battalion*, 218.
27 Ibid, 218–19.
28 Percy Twidale, Interview by Elizabeth Hazlitte, June and August 1983, Victoria BC, University of Victoria Special Collections.
29 16ᵗʰ Battalion War Diary, April 1917, Library and Archives Canada, n.p.
30 Twidale Interview.
31 Urquhart, *16ᵗʰ Battalion*, 213–14.
32 Milne Award Citation, http://www.vac-acc.gc.ca/content/collections/virtualmem/photoview.cfm?casualty=157921, accessed 9/3/2007.
33 Twidale interview.
34 Milne Award Citation.
35 Urquhart, *16ᵗʰ Battalion*, 214–15.
36 Peck Fonds.
37 Urquhart, *16ᵗʰ Battalion*, 406.
38 Ibid, 216.
39 Nicholson, 258–65.
40 Winston Groom, *A Storm in Flanders: The Ypres Salient, 1914–1918, Tragedy and Triumph*

on the Western Front* (New York: Grove Press, 2002), 155–59.

Chapter Nine: It Isn't Worth a Drop of Blood—June 7, 1917–August 4, 1918

1 G. W. L. Nicholson, *Canadian Expeditionary Force, 1914–1919* (Queen's Printer: Ottawa, 1964), 269–85.
2 Daniel G. Dancocks, *Legacy of Valour: The Canadians at Passchendaele* (Edmonton: Hurtig Publishers, 1986), 95.
3 Nicholson, 286–87.
4 H. M. Urquhart, *The History of the 16ᵗʰ Battalion (The Canadian Scottish) Canadian Expeditionary Force in the Great War, 1914–1919* (Toronto: The MacMillan Company of Canada, 1932), 231.
5 Ibid, 233–34.
6 Ibid, 233.
7 Ibid, 232.
8 Ibid, 232–34.
9 Nicholson, 289–91.
10 Urquhart, *16ᵗʰ Battalion*, 233.
11 Ibid, 234–35.
12 Ibid, 406.
13 Dancocks, *Legacy of Valour*, 94.
14 Nicholson, 297.
15 Urquhart, *16ᵗʰ Battalion*, 406.
16 Daniel G. Dancocks, *Sir Arthur Currie* (Toronto: Methuen, 1985), 110.
17 Winston Groom, *A Storm in Flanders: The Ypres Salient, 1914–1918, Tragedy and Triumph on the Western Front* (New York: Grove Press, 2002), 207–08.
18 Ibid, 213–17.
19 Dancocks, *Legacy of Valour*, 97–98.
20 Nicholson, 312.

21 Ibid, 314.

22 Urquhart, *16ᵗʰ Battalion*, 236.

23 Nicholson, 312.

24 Ibid, 318–27.

25 Urquhart, *16ᵗʰ Battalion*, 236.

26 Nicholson, 333.

27 Ibid, 335–36.

28 Urquhart, *16ᵗʰ Battalion*, 243.

29 Ibid, 238–40.

30 Ibid, 248–50.

31 Nicholson, 382.

32 Urquhart, *16ᵗʰ Battalion*, 262.

Chapter Ten: Decision at Amiens—August 8–20, 1918

1 G. W. L. Nicholson, *Canadian Expeditionary Force, 1914–1919* (Queen's Printer: Ottawa, 1964), 372–78.

2 Daniel G. Dancocks, *Spearhead to Victory: Canada and the Great War* (Edmonton: Hurtig Publishers, 1987), 2.

3 Nicholson, 386.

4 Ibid, 388–90.

5 Ibid, 395–97.

6 H. M. Urquhart, *The History of the 16ᵗʰ Battalion (The Canadian Scottish) Canadian Expeditionary Force in the Great War, 1914–1919* (Toronto: The MacMillan Company of Canada, 1932), 269–70.

7 Ibid, 267.

8 16ᵗʰ Battalion War Diary, August 1918, Appendix: Lt.-Col. Cyrus Peck Account, "Narrative of Action in Front of Amiens, August 8, 1918," Library and Archives Canada, 1.

9 Urquhart, *16ᵗʰ Battalion*, 398.

10 Ibid, 398–99.

11 J. L. Granatstein, *Hell's Corner: An Illustrated History of Canada's Great War, 1914–1918* (Vancouver: Douglas & McIntyre, 2004), 160.

12 Urquhart, *16ᵗʰ Battalion*, 270.

13 Ibid, 268.

14 Cyrus Wesley Peck Fonds, MG30–E134, Library and Archives Canada, n.p.

15 16ᵗʰ Battalion War Diary, Appendix, Account by Peck, 1.

16 Urquhart, *16ᵗʰ Battalion*, 271–72.

17 16ᵗʰ Battalion War Diary, Appendix, Account by Peck, 2.

18 Ibid, 1.

19 Urquhart, *16ᵗʰ Battalion*, 260–61.

20 Ibid, 273–78.

21 Peck Fonds, n.p.

22 Nicholson, 407.

23 Ibid, 407–08.

24 Lt.-Gen. Sir A. W. Currie, *Canadian Corps Operations During the Year 1918* (Ottawa: Department of Militia and Defence, 1919), 38.

25 Nicholson, 408.

26 James McWilliams and R. James Steel, *Amiens: Dawn of Victory* (Toronto: Dundurn Press, 2001), 187–88.

27 Nicholson, 410.

28 J. D. Craig, *The 1st Canadian Division in the Battles of 1918* (London: Barrs & Co., 1919), 14–15.

29 Nicholson, 413.

30 Urquhart, *16ᵗʰ Battalion*, 279.

31 Ibid, 279–80.

32 Nicholson, 414–15.

33 Urquhart, *16ᵗʰ Battalion*, 280.

34 Currie, 40.

35 Nicholson, 419.

36 Urquhart, *16th Battalion*, 280–84.

37 Currie, 41.

38 Nicholson, 425.

Chapter Eleven: The Finest Performance: August 20– September 3, 1918

1 G. W. L. Nicholson, *Canadian Expeditionary Force, 1914–1919* (Queen's Printer: Ottawa, 1964), 426.

2 Ibid, 426–27.

3 H. M. Urquhart, *The History of the 16th Battalion (The Canadian Scottish) Canadian Expeditionary Force in the Great War, 1914– 1919* (Toronto: The MacMillan Company of Canada, 1932), 285.

4 Nicholson, 426–27.

5 Lt.-Gen. Sir A. W. Currie, *Canadian Corps Operations During the Year 1918* (Ottawa: Department of Militia and Defence, 1919), 44.

6 Nicholson, 426.

7 Currie, 53.

8 Ibid, 45–46.

9 Nicholson, 427–32.

10 Currie, 47–52.

11 Urquhart, *16th Battalion*, 288.

12 Ibid, 290–91.

13 3rd Canadian Infantry Brigade War Diary, September 1918, Appendix 3a, Library and Archives Canada, 5–7.

14 Urquhart, *16th Battalion*, 289.

15 Ibid, 290.

16 J. D. Craig, *The 1st Canadian Division in the Battles of 1918* (London: Barrs & Co., 1919), 27.

17 Urquhart, *16th Battalion*, 292–93.

18 16th Battalion War Diary, September 1918, Appendix: "Narrative of Second Battle of Arras, 2nd September, 1918," Library and Archives Canada, 1–3.

19 Urquhart, *16th Battalion*, 293–94.

20 Ibid, 294.

21 16th Battalion War Diary, September 1918, Appendix: "Narrative of Second Battle of Arras," 1.

22 Urquhart, *16th Battalion*, 295–96.

23 Ibid, 296–97.

24 Ibid, 297–300.

25 16th Battalion War Diary, September 1918, "Narrative of Second Battle of Arras," 3.

26 Nicholson, 440.

27 Currie, 54–55.

28 Nicholson, 442–44.

29 Ibid, 445.

30 Currie, 60–61.

31 Urquhart, *16th Battalion*, 303.

32 Cyrus Wesley Peck Fonds, MG30–E134, Library and Archives Canada, n.p.

33 Urquhart, *16th Battalion*, 314.

34 Ibid, 303–05.

35 Ibid, 305–11.

36 Currie, 62–63.

37 16th Battalion War Diary, October 1918, Appendix: "Narrative of Action at Cuvillers, October 1st 1918," Library and Archives Canada, 1–2.

38 14th Battalion War Diary, October 1918, Appendix No. 1, 1–3.

39 Desmond Morton and J. L. Granatstein, *Marching to Armageddon: Canadians and the Great War, 1914–1918* (Toronto: Lester and Orpen Dennys, 1989), 228.

Chapter Twelve: Drive to Victory: October 2–November 11, 1918

1 Desmond Morton and J. L. Granatstein, *Marching to Armageddon: Canadians and the Great War, 1914–1918* (Toronto: Lester and Orpen Dennys, 1989), 228.

2 G. W. L. Nicholson, *Canadian Expeditionary Force, 1914–1919* (Queen's Printer: Ottawa, 1964), 461.

3 H. M. Urquhart, *The History of the 16th Battalion (The Canadian Scottish) Canadian Expeditionary Force in the Great War, 1914–1919* (Toronto: The MacMillan Company of Canada, 1932), 344–46.

4 Ibid, 492.

5 Ibid, 689.

6 Ibid, 723.

7 Ibid, 330.

8 Cyrus Wesley Peck Fonds, MG30–E134, Library and Archives Canada, n.p.

9 Urquhart, *16th Battalion*, 336.

10 Nicholson, 467.

11 16th Battalion War Diary, October 1918, Appendix: "Narrative of Actions of 11th and 12th October 1918," Library and Archives Canada, 1.

12 Ibid.

13 Nicholson, 467.

14 *16th Battalion*, October 1918, Appendix: "Narrative of Action of 11th and 12th October 1918," 1–2.

15 Urquhart, *16th Battalion*, 317–18.

16 Lt.-Gen. Sir A. W. Currie, *Canadian Corps Operations During the Year 1918* (Ottawa: Department of Militia and Defence, 1919), 72.

17 Ibid, 74.

18 Urquhart, *16th Battalion*, 318.

19 Peck fonds, n.p.

20 Urquhart, *16th Battalion*, 319–20.

21 Ibid, 321–22.

22 Currie, 75.

23 16th Battalion War Diary, October 1918, Library and Archives Canada, n.p.

24 J. D. Craig, *The 1st Canadian Division in the Battles of 1918* (London: Barrs & Co., 1919), 50.

25 16th Battalion War Diary, November 1918, Library and Archives Canada, n.p.

26 Nicholson, 524.

27 16th Battalion War Diary, November 1918, n.p.

28 Ibid.

29 Peck Fonds, n.p.

30 16th Battalion War Diary, November 1918, n.p.

31 Nicholson, 525.

32 Urquhart, *16th Battalion*, 325.

33 Nicholson, 526.

34 16th Battalion War Diary, November 1918, n.p.

35 Urquhart, *16th Battalion*, 326.

36 Ibid, 327.

37 Nicholson, 525–26.

38 Urquhart, *16th Battalion*, 328.

39 Nicholson, 528–29.

40 Urquhart, *16th Battalion*, 329–30.

41 Ibid, 330–31.

42 Ibid, 331.

Bibliography

This is not intended as a full bibliography of books consulted during research or of books published on Canada's participation in World War I. Only books cited in the Notes to the text are cited here. For simplification I have not listed the operational orders, reports, and war diaries cited, as these are housed and accessible at Library and Archives Canada, Ottawa. The war diaries can be consulted on-line through a searchable database at: http://www.collectionscanada.gc.ca/archivianet/020152_ e.html. Where private fonds were consulted at Library and Archives Canada, full citations are provided in the bibliography.

Books

Anonymous. *The Canadian Scottish Regiment.* (Ottawa: n.p., 1935.)

Cook, Tim. *At The Sharp End: Canadians Fighting the Great War, 1914–1916* (Toronto: Viking Canada, 2007).

Craig, J. D. *The 1st Canadian Division in the Battles of 1918* (London: Barrs & Co., 1919).

Lt.-Gen. Sir A. W. Currie, *Canadian Corps Operations During the Year 1918* (Ottawa: Department of Militia and Defence, 1919).

Dancocks, Daniel G. *Legacy of Valour: The Canadians at Passchendaele* (Edmonton: Hurtig Publishers, 1986).

———, *Spearhead to Victory: Canada and the Great War* (Edmonton: Hurtig Publishers, 1987).

———, *Welcome to Flanders Fields: The First Canadian Battle of the Great War: Ypres, 1915* (Toronto: McClelland and Stewart, 1988).

Granatstein, J. L. *Canada's Army: Waging War and Keeping the Peace* (Toronto: University of Toronto Press, 2002).

———, *Hell's Corner: An Illustrated History of Canada's Great War, 1914–1918* (Vancouver: Douglas & McIntyre, 2004).

Groom, Winston. *A Storm in Flanders: The Ypres Salient, 1914–1918: Tragedy and Triumph on the Western Front* (New York: Grove Press, 2002).

Hogg, Ian V., and John Weeks, *Military Small Arms of the 20th Century* (Northbrook, IL: DBI Books, n.d.).

Macdonald, Lyn. *1915: The Death of Innocence* (London: Penguin Books, 1997).

McWilliams, James, and R. James Steel, *Amiens: Dawn of Victory* (Toronto: Dundurn Press, 2001).

Morton, Desmond, and J. L. Granatstein, *Marching to Armageddon: Canadians and the Great War, 1914–1919* (Toronto: Lester & Orpen Dennys, 1989).

Nicholson, G. W. L. *Canadian Expeditionary Force, 1914–1919* (Queen's Printer: Ottawa, 1964).

Radley, Kenneth. *We Lead, Others Follow: First Canadian Division, 1914–1918* (St. Catharines, ON: Vanwell Publishing Limited, 2006).

Urquhart, H. M. *The History of the 16th Battalion (The Canadian Scottish) Canadian Expeditionary Force in the Great War, 1914–1919* (Toronto: The MacMillan Company of Canada, 1932).

Winter, Jay, and Blaine Baggett, *The Great War: And the Shaping of the 20th Century* (New York: Penguin Studio, 1996).

Magazines, Newspapers, Articles

Campbell, David. "A Forgotten Victory: Courcelette, 15 September 1916," *Canadian Military History*, Spring 2007.

Godefroy, Andrew. "Portrait of a Battalion Commander: Lieutenant-Colonel George Stuart Tuxford at the Second Battle of Ypres, April 1915," *Canadian Military Journal*, Summer 2004.

Hill, Roland H. "Holding the Salient, 1916," *Canada in the Great War*, Vol. 3 (Toronto: United Publishers of Canada Limited, 1919).

Websites

http://www.greatwardifferent.com/Great_War/British_Front/Hills_01.htm, accessed August 16, 2007, reproduction of text from *The War Illustrated*, 11 May, 1918, Lovat Fraser, "The Epic Battles for the Hills."

http://www.vac-acc.gc.ca/cvwmuploads/published/183893_4.jpg, accessed July 17, 2007.

Milne Award Citation, http://www.vac-acc.gc.ca/content/collections/virtualmem/photoview.cfm?casualty=157921, accessed September 3, 2007.

Bibliography

Unpublished Materials

Peck, Cyrus Wesley. Cyrus Wesley Peck Fonds, MG30–E134, Library and Archives Canada.

William Rae, William, "Letter to Mother, April 28, 1915," Col. H. M. Urquhart Fonds, Correspondence–1915–1980, Box 22, File 18, University of Victoria, Special Collections.

Twidale, Percy. Interview by Elizabeth Hazlitte, June and August 1983, Victoria BC, University of Victoria Special Collections.

Urquhart, H. M., personal diary, University of Victoria Special Collections.

Index of Formations, Units, and Corps

CANADIAN

Canadian Expeditionary Force, 5, 17, 146, 257

CORPS

Army Service Corps and Ordinance, 10, 252

Canadian Corps, 85, 90, 91, 95, 96, 98, 103, 111, 117, 123, 129, 130–33, 136, 138, 143, 146, 147, 152–55, 163, 165, 167, 170, 174–77, 180, 182, 187, 188, 191, 192, 201, 203, 206, 210, 211, 214, 224–28, 235, 236, 238–40, 248, 249, 251, 254, 255

Newfoundland Medical Corps, 88

DIVISIONS

1st Canadian Infantry Division, 5, 12–14, 16, 17, 24, 30, 32, 33, 35, 38, 40–41, 44–45, 52, 62, 63, 78, 81, 84–86, 90, 94, 96, 98, 100, 104, 106, 111–12, 123, 127, 130, 133–37, 146, 157, 161, 163, 178–79, 184, 188, 192, 202, 203, 206, 215, 216, 226–28, 239, 240, 243, 248–50, 255–56

2nd Canadian Infantry Division, 24, 82, 85, 86, 90, 98, 100, 102, 104, 111, 123, 127, 128, 130, 133, 135–36, 146, 163–65, 169, 173, 179, 187, 192, 201–02, 205–06, 242, 243, 250, 255–56

3rd Canadian Infantry Division, 98, 104, 105, 106, 107, 108, 111, 123, 128, 130, 136, 146, 157, 174, 201–03, 205, 213, 214, 224, 248–49, 256

4th Canadian Infantry Division, 98, 141, 143, 146, 157, 164, 168, 174, 179, 201, 202, 205, 213, 215, 226, 229, 234, 243–44, 251

BRIGADES

1st Canadian Infantry Brigade, 48, 53, 98, 110, 112, 124, 137, 139, 163–65, 179, 192, 202, 206, 228, 234, 242, 244

2nd Canadian Infantry Brigade, 24, 45, 48, 51, 53, 62–63, 73, 86, 93, 96, 106, 108, 109, 111, 127, 130, 133, 135, 157, 163, 165, 169, 170, 192, 202–3, 216, 228, 240, 242, 244, 148

INFANTRY BATTALIONS/REGIMENTS

FRENCH

French Second Army, 91
French Fourth Army, 91
French Sixth Army, 120
French Eighth Army, 30
French Tenth Army, 30, 66, 91

11th Division, 42
58th Division, 67

79th Régiment, 42

GERMAN

German Sixth Army, 66, 175
German Eighth Army, 143

XXIII Reserve Corps, 46
XXVI Reserve Corps, 46, 52
52nd Reserve Corps, 52

26th Infantry Division, 111
51st Reserve Division, 52

120th Regiment, 111

OTHER UNITS

II Bavarian Corps, 90
45th Division (Algeria), 48, 53, 54
Italian, 190
Portuguese, 190

General Index

Ranks given for individuals are highest attained as of November 1918.

About the Author

Mark Zuehlke has been hailed by Jack Granatstein as Canada's most popular military historian. Of his twenty books, nine have been works of military history. *For Honour's Sake: The War of 1812 and the Brokering of an Uneasy Peace* won the Canadian Authors Association 2007 Lela Common Award for Canadian History. In 2006, *Holding Juno: Canada's Heroic Defence of the D–Day Beaches, June 7–12, 1944* was awarded the City of Victoria Butler Book Prize. Also a novelist, Zuehlke is known for the acclaimed Elias McCann mystery series, which chronicles the misadventures of a coroner in British Columbia's Tofino. *Hands Like Clouds* garnered a Crime Writers of Canada Arthur Ellis Best First Novel award in 2000, and *Sweep Lotus* was a finalist for the Arthur Ellis Best Novel in 2004. Zuehlke lives in Victoria, BC. He can be found on the web at www.zuehlke.ca.